State and District Administration in India

State and District Administration in India

D.D. Aggarwal

Delta Book World
New Delhi-110 002

First Published in 2015
Edition 2025

ISBN 978-81-926244-9-5

Published by **Abhishek Goel** on behalf of

Delta Book World
G-4, Prahlad House
4832/24, Ansari Road
New Delhi - 110 002 (India)

Tel.: 011-4707 2321
E-mail: deltabookworld@gmail.com

PRINTED IN INDIA

Preface

India is one of the oldest civilizations in the world with a kaleidoscopic variety and rich cultural heritage. It has achieved all-round socio-economic progress during the last 67 years of its Independence. India has become self-sufficient in agricultural production and is now one of the top industrialised countries in the world and one of the few nations to have gone into outer space to conquer nature for the benefit of the people.

The Administrative divisions of India are Indian subnational administrative units; they compose a nested hierarchy of country subdivisions. Indian states and territories frequently use different local titles for the same level of subdivision (e.g., the mandals of Andhra Pradesh correspond to tehsils of Uttar Pradesh and other Hindi-speaking states and taluka of Gujarat, Maharashtra, Karnataka, Kerala and Tamil Nadu).

The smaller subdivisions (villages and blocks) exist only in rural areas. In urban areas Urban Local Bodies exist instead of these rural subdivisions.

In the context of the Indian Constitution, local government bodies are the subject of the State List and are thereby governed by State Statutes, or in the case of Union Territories, by the Union Parliament. Federal recognition of local government was substantively expressed in the 74th Constitution Amendment Act of 1992.

The Administration at the State level is the cutting edge of the public administration system in the country. Be it the issue of ration or electoral identity cards, procurement of foodgrains, implementation of employment guarantee schemes, supply of drinking water, mutation of land records, functioning of primary schools and healthcare centres or control of epidemics in the countryside, it is the instrumentalities of the State and District administration with which citizens have to interact.

The book has structured in the following manner:

1. Introduction
2. Reorganisation of the State Secretariat and Departments:
3. District Administration, the role and composition of line departments and parastatals in the districts after empowerment of local governments.
4. Special aspects of the administration of Union Territories (Delhi, Chandigarh, Island UTs and others).
5. Issues pertaining to the administration of the North-Eastern States
6. Managing State Finances and
7. Administrative Divisions of India.
8. District Administration since Independence
9. Issues Concerning e-Governance

The book deals with issues of modernization, increased devolution of functions and powers, effective grievance handling system, people's participation, enhancing responsiveness, process simplification and delegation of power. The book has also taken note of certain innovative measures initiated by government on issues of human resource development and social service which have resulted in better implementational practices and consequently in a marked improvement in the tenor of administration. The communitisation experiment in Nagaland and the digitised registration of documents in Bihar are two such examples. It believes that with appropriate modification it is possible to replicate such practices in other parts of the country as well. The book will be useful for students, researchers, policy-makers and development workers.

D.D. Aggarwal

Contents

1 Introduction

India is one of the oldest civilizations in the world with a kaleidoscopic variety and rich cultural heritage. It has achieved all-round socio-economic progress during the last 67 years of its Independence. India has become self-sufficient in agricultural production and is now one of the top industrialised countries in the world and one of the few nations to have gone into outer space to conquer nature for the benefit of the people. It covers an area of 3,287,590 sq. km (1,269,346 sq mi), extending from the snow-covered Himalayan heights to the tropical rain forests of the south. As the 7th largest country in the world, India stands apart from the rest of Asia, marked off as it is by mountains and the sea, which give the country a distinct geographical entity. Bounded by the Great Himalayas in the north, it stretches southwards and at the Tropic of Cancer, tapers off into the Indian Ocean between the Bay of Bengal on the east and the Arabian Sea on the west.

Lying entirely in the northern hemisphere, the mainland extends between latitudes 8° 4' and 37° 6' north, longitudes 68° 7' and 97° 25' east and measures about 3,214 km from north to south between the extreme latitudes and about 2,933 km from east to west between the extreme longitudes. It has a land frontier of about 15,200 km. The total length of the coastline of the mainland, Lakshadweep Islands and Andaman & Nicobar Islands is 7,516.6 km.

The Administration at the State level is the cutting edge of the public administration system in the country. Be it the issue of ration or electoral identity cards, procurement of foodgrains, implementation of employment guarantee schemes, supply of drinking water, mutation of land records, functioning of primary schools and healthcare centres or control of epidemics in the countryside, it is the instrumentalities of the State and District administration with which citizens have to interact.

The institutions of the State and District administration exist primarily to provide these services to the citizens. There are laid down rules and procedures for every aspect of the government's functioning and its interaction with the common man but, due to weaknesses of the bureaucracy, growing complexities of administration and absence of commitment and responsiveness, a wide gap has emerged between "Government" and "Governance".

In this background, the terms of reference of the Second Administrative Reforms Commission identify the following issues on which the Commission has been asked to make specific recommendations.

The book has structured the following manner:

1. Introduction
2. Reorganisation of the State Secretariat and Departments:
   a. Role and functions of the Secretariat, Departments and Agencies (Societies, Cooperatives, Statutory Bodies and Government Corporations).
   b. Some issues of personnel administration including those relating to State Public Service Commission, enactment of Civil Services Law and appointment and tenure of senior functionaries in the State Government.
   c. The future of the office of the Divisional Commissioner and Regional Offices of line departments.

d. Vigilance set up in the States.

3. District Administration, the role and composition of line departments and parastatals in the districts after empowerment of local governments.
4. Special aspects of the administration of Union Territories (Delhi, Chandigarh, Island UTs and others).
5. Issues pertaining to the administration of the North-Eastern States
6. Managing State Finances and
7. Administrative Divisions of India.

The book deals with issues of modernization, increased devolution of functions and powers, effective grievance handling system, people's participation, enhancing responsiveness, process simplification and delegation of power. The book has also taken note of certain innovative measures initiated by government on issues of human resource development and social service which have resulted in better implementational practices and consequently in a marked improvement in the tenor of administration. The communitisation experiment in Nagaland and the digitised registration of documents in Bihar are two such examples. It believes that with appropriate modification it is possible to replicate such practices in other parts of the country as well.

The Union Territories and the North-Eastern States have special features, which call for careful study. Generally, except perhaps for Delhi, the administration of the Union Territories has not been studied in detail, as it has been considered as part of the Union Government. In the case of the North-Eastern States, it found that knowledge of their special features was rather limited in the Ministries; the approach until recently, has been to deal with the administrative challenges in more or less the same way as in the rest of the country, without taking into account the special features of each of them, as for example, extensive powers given to the Autonomous Councils in the Sixth

Schedule areas. Therefore, thought it fit to deal with the Union Territories and North- Eastern States at some length in this Report. The suggestions given here are in addition to the recommendations made in earlier Reports like the one on "Conflict Resolution".

In order to have a composite view of the issues and challenges being faced by the State and District administration across the country, the Commission visited 20 States viz. Andhra Pradesh, Tamil Nadu, Maharashtra, Karnataka, Gujarat, Rajasthan, Punjab, Haryana, Jammu & Kashmir, Assam, Meghalaya, Nagaland, Manipur, Tripura, Uttar Pradesh, Bihar, West Bengal, Orissa and Chhattisgarh. It also visited 5 Union Territories viz. Andaman & Nicobar Islands, Lakshadweep, Puducherry, Chandigarh and Delhi. During these visits, the Commission had detailed discussions with the Governors, Chief Ministers, Lt. Governors/ Administrators and senior officials of the States/UTs concerned on their programmes, schemes and innovative practices. In order to elicit suggestions and perceptions of people on administration, the Commission organised public hearings in the States' capital and State and District Administation Introduction also interacted with scholars, litterateurs, retired officials and the media on common issues of governance and administration. The Commission expresses its deep gratitude to all of them for their help, cooperation, and valuable suggestions.

GEOGRAPHY OF INDIA

Particulars	Description
Location	The Indian peninsula is separated from mainland Asia by the Himalayas. The Country is surrounded by the Bay of Bengal in the east, the Arabian Sea in the west, and the Indian Ocean to the south.
Geographic Coordinates	Lying entirely in the Northern Hemisphere, the Country extends between 8° 4' and 37° 6' latitudes north of the Equator, and 68° 7' and 97° 25'

Particulars	Description
	longitudes east of it.
Indian Standard Time	GMT + 05:30
Area	3.3 Million sq. km
Telephone Country Code	+91
Border Countries	Afghanistan and Pakistan to the north-west; China, Bhutan and Nepal to the north; Myanmar to the east; and Bangladesh to the east of West Bengal. Sri Lanka is separated from India by a narrow channel of sea, formed by Palk Strait and the Gulf of Mannar.
Coastline	7,517 km encompassing the mainland, Lakshadweep Islands, and the Andaman & Nicobar Islands.
Climate	The climate of India can broadly be classified as a tropical monsoon one. But, in spite of much of the northern part of India lying beyond the tropical zone, the entire country has a tropical climate marked by relatively high temperatures and dry winters. There are four seasons: winter (December-February)summer (March-June)south-west monsoon season (June-September)post monsoon season (October-November)
Terrain	The mainland comprises of four regions, namely the great mountain zone, plains of the Ganga and the Indus, the desert region, and the southern peninsula.
Natural Resources	Coal, iron ore, manganese ore, mica, bauxite, petroleum, titanium ore, chromite, natural gas, magnesite, limestone, arable land, dolomite, barytes, kaolin, gypsum, apatite, phosphorite, steatite, fluorite, etc.
Natural Hazards	Monsoon floods, flash floods, earthquakes, droughts, and landslides.
Environment	**Current Issues:** Air pollution control, energy conservation, solid waste manage-ment, oil and gas conservation, forest conservation, etc. **International Agreements:** Rio Decla-ration on environment and development, Cartagena Protocol on biosafety, Kyoto Protocol to the United Nations Framework Convention on climatic change, World

Particulars	Description
	Trade Agreement, Helsinki Protocol to LRTAP on the reduction of sulphur emissions of nitrogen oxides or their transboundary fluxes (Nox Protocol), and Geneva Protocol to LRTAP concerning the control of emissions of volatile organic compounds or their transboundary fluxes (VOCs Protocol).
Geography - Note	India occupies a major portion of the south Asian subcontinent.

GOVERNMENT

Particulars	Description
Country Name	Republic of India; Bharat Ganrajya
Government Type	Sovereign Socialist Secular Democratic Republic with a Parliamentary system of Government.
Capital	New Delhi
Administrative Divisions	28 States and 7 Union Territories.
Independence	15th August 1947 (From the British Colonial Rule)
Constitution	The Constitution of India came into force on 26th January 1950.
Legal System	The Constitution of India is the fountain source of the legal system in the Country.
Executive Branch	The President of India is the Head of the State, while the Prime Minister is the Head of the Government, and runs office with the support of the Council of Ministers who form the Cabinet Ministry.
Legislative Branch	The Indian Legislature comprises of the Lok Sabha (House of the People) and the Rajya Sabha (Council of States) forming both the Houses of the Parliament.
Judicial Branch	The Supreme Court of India is the apex body of the Indian legal system, followed by other High Courts and subordinate Courts.

Particulars	Description
Flag Description	The National Flag is a horizontal tricolour of deep saffron (kesaria) at the top, white in the middle, and dark green at the bottom in equal proportion. At the centre of the white band is a navy blue wheel, which is a representation of the Ashoka Chakra at Sarnath.
National Days	26th January (Republic Day) 15th August (Independence Day) 2nd October (Gandhi Jayanti; Mahatma Gandhi's Birthday)

2

State Administration

INTRODUCTION

Constitutional guarantees and provisions, Union and State laws as well as policies and programmes for economic and social development are relevant to the daily lives of the people only to the extent they are implemented honestly and efficiently. The Constitution of India gives a special role and responsibility to the State Governments for preserving public order and ensuring the welfare of citizens. The Seventh Schedule which clearly demarcates the legislative and functional domain of the Union and the States, highlights the critical role envisaged for State Governments in fulfilling the aspirations set out in the Directive Principles of State Policy.

So far the Commission has submitted fourteen Reports, each of them containing recommendations to be acted upon by the Union, State, District and Local Governments - by one or all of them - as well as by institutions of civil society. The Reports dealt with:-

(i) Right to Information;

(ii) Implementation of NREGA;

(iii) Crisis Management;

(iv) Ethics in Governance;

(v) Public Order;

(vi) Local Governance;

(vii) Capacity Building for Conflict Resolution;

(viii) Combatting Terrorism;

(ix) Social Capital;

(x) Refurbishing of Personnel Administration;

(xi) Promoting e-Governance;

(xii) Citizen Centric Administration

(xiii) Organisational Structure of Government of India

(xiv) Strengthening of Financial Management Systems

RELEVANT RECOMMENDATIONS OF THE COMMISSION IN ITS EARLIER REPORTS

While contemplating reforms in the State and District Administration, all the above Reports of the Commission need to be considered together. For ease of reference, the relevant recommendations of the earlier Reports have been recapitulated below. There are some areas in which action needs to be taken primarily by the Union Government; in such cases, the States' role would be to provide support and cooperation to the latter in the measures taken to implement the recommendations. Whereas, the measures suggested in the Reports on "Public Order", "Local Governance", "NREGA", "Crisis Management" and "Conflict Resolution" have a direct bearing on the State and District administration; hence appropriate reform actions have to be initiated by the State governments themselves. In addition, the principles enunciated in other Reports such as those dealing with "Right to Information", "Citizen Centric Administration", "e-Governance" and "Social Capital" have overarching relevance to the State and District administration.

Local Governance – Empowerment and Strengthening of Local Governments

In its Report on "Local Governance", the Commission notes that in India, the most important institutional reform brought about in governance, since the reorganization of States, has been the inclusion of local governments - Panchayats and Municipalities - as Constitutional entities, through the Constitutional 73rd and 74th amendments in 1992. But, there has been a marked reluctance on the part of most States to adequately transfer powers and functions, finances and functionaries to put local governments on the path envisaged by these Constitutional amendments. As of now, most local governments are overstructured and weakly empowered. The Commission believes that India needs a fundamental transformation in governance and that empowered citizen-centric and accountable local governments are the core around which this transformation will take place. There will be no real 'loss of power' to the State Governments as feared. With the abolition of permits and licensing needed for setting-up new projects in many sectors, the States have now got greater freedom to take major investment decisions and many of them have utilised these powers to accelerate the pace of their development. The Union Government too, has found new roles in social sectors and social security after halting major investments in public undertakings.

The major recommendations in the Sixth Report that are of particular relevance to State and District Administration in India are:

Structural Reforms

- Adopting the principle of subsidiarity in devolution of functions to local bodies.
- Creation of a District Council having representation from both rural and urban bodies, as the true third tier of government;
- Immediate transfer of functions/functionaries to the PRIs as per provisions of law;
- Autonomy of Panchayats with regard to their personnel;
- Establishing a local body Ombudsman for a group of Districts;

- Merging DRDA with the Zila Parishad;
- States not to have final powers over Panchayats/ Municipal bodies;
- Creation of a separate Ombudsman for a Metropolitan Corporation;
- Urban Local Bodies - Basic Structure
  - There should be three tiers of administration in urban local governments, except in the case of Town Panchayats, where the middle level would not be required. The tiers should be:
    - Municipal Council/Corporation (by whatever name it is called)
    - Ward Committees; and
    - Area Committees or Sabhas.
    - The Mayor of a Municipal Corporation should be its Chief Executive and should be elected directly;
    - Special powers and authorities in Metropolitan Corporations (with a population above five million).

Decentralised Planning

a. Constitution of a District Council to be empowered to exercise the powers and functions in accordance with Articles 243G and 243W of the Constitution.

b. For urban districts where town planning functions are being done by Development Authorities, these authorities should become the technical/ planning arms of the District Planning Committees (DPCs) and ultimately of the District Council.

d. Guidelines issued by the Planning Commission pertaining to the preparation of the Plan and the recommendations of the Expert Group regarding the planning process at the district level should be strictly implemented.

e. The function of planning for urban areas to be clearly demarcated among the local bodies and planning committees. The local bodies should be responsible for plans at the layout level. The District Planning Committees/District Councils - when constituted - and Metropolitan Planning Committees (MPCs) should be responsible for preparation of regional and zonal plans. The level of public consultation should be enhanced at each level.

f. For metropolitan areas, the total area likely to be urbanised (the extended metropolitan region) should be assessed by the State Government and a Metropolitan Planning Committee constituted for the same which may be deemed to be a District Planning Committee for such areas. As such an area will usually cover more than one district. District Planning Committees for those districts should not be constituted (or their jurisdictions may be limited to the rural portion of the revenue district concerned). The Metropolitan Planning Committees should be asked to draw up a Master Plan/Composite Development Plan for the entire metropolitan area including the peri-urban areas.

Accountability and Transparency

a. Audit committees may be constituted by the State Governments at the district level to exercise oversight regarding the integrity of financial information

b. There should be a separate Standing Committee of the State Legislature for the local Bodies. This Committee may function in the manner of a Public Accounts Committee.

c. A local body Ombudsman needs to be constituted

d. A suitable mechanism to evolve a system of benchmarking on the basis of identified performance indicators may be adopted by each State. Assistance of independent professional evaluators may be availed in this regard.

e. Evaluation tools for assessing the performance of local bodies should be devised wherein citizens should have a say in the evaluation. Tools such as 'Citizens' Report Cards' may be introduced to incorporate a feedback mechanism regarding performance of the local bodies.

Personnel Management in PRIs

a. Panchayats should have the power to recruit personnel and to regulate their service conditions subject to such laws and standards as laid down by the State Government.

b. In all States, a detailed review of the staffing pattern and systems, with a zerobased approach to PRI staffing, may be undertaken over the next one year in order to implement the policy of PRI ownership of staff.

PRIs and the State Government

a. The provisions in some State Acts regarding approval of the budget of a Panchayat by the higher tier or any other State authority should be abolished.

b. State Governments should not have the power to suspend or rescind any resolution passed by the PRIs or take action against the elected representatives on the ground of abuse of office, corruption etc. or to supersede/ dissolve the Panchayats. In all such cases, the powers to investigate and recommend action should lie with the local Ombudsman who will send his report through the Lokayukta to the Governor.

c. For election infringements and other election related complaints, the authority to investigate should be the State Election Commission who will send its recommendations to the Governor.

d. If, on any occasion, the State Government feels that there is need to take immediate action against the Panchayats or their elected, it should place the records before the Ombudsman for urgent investigation. In all such cases, the Ombudsman will send his report through Lokayukta to the Governor in a specified period.

e. In all cases of disagreements with the recommendations made by the local Ombudsman/Lokayukta, the reasons will need to be placed in the public domain.

Position of Parastatals

a. Parastatals should not be allowed to undermine the authority of the PRIs.

b. There is no need for continuation of the District Rural Development Agency (DRDA). Following the lead taken by Kerala, Karnataka and West Bengal, the DRDAs in other States also should be merged with the respective District Panchayats (Zila Parishad). Similar action should be taken for the District Water and Sanitation Committee (DWSC).

c. The District Health Society (DHS) and Fish Farmers Development Agency (FFDA) should be restructured to have an organic relationship with the PRIs.

d. The Union and State Governments should normally not set up special committees outside the PRIs. However, if such specialised committees are required to be set-up because of professional or technical requirements, and if their activities coincide with those listed in the Eleventh Schedule, they should, either function under the overall supervision and guidance of the Panchayats or their relationship with the PRIs should be worked out in consultation with the concerned level of Panchayat.

e. Community level bodies should not be created by decisions taken at higher levels. If considered necessary the initiative for their creation should come from below and they should be accountable to PRIs.

Local Government in the Fifth Schedule Areas

a. The Union and State legislations that impinge on provisions of PESA should be immediately modified so as to bring them in conformity with the Act.

b. If any State exhibits reluctance in implementing the provisions of PESA, Government of India may consider issuing specific directions to it in accordance with the powers given to it under Proviso 3 of Part A of the Fifth Schedule.

c. Each State should constitute a group to look into strengthening of the administrative machinery in Fifth Schedule areas. This group will need to go into the issues of (i) special administrative arrangements, (ii) provision of hardship pay, (iii) other incentives, and (iv) preferential treatment in accommodation and education. All expenditure in this regard should be treated as charged expenditure under Article 275 of the Constitution.

Ethics in Governance

The Fourth Report of the Commission deals comprehensively with the important subject of 'Ethics in Governance' and has made a number of suggestions in this regard. If implement-ed, these will increase efficiency, transparency, responsiveness and accountability in government work. A corruption-free regime would also lead to a much higher rate of growth and bring overall improvement in the economy. All this, in turn, will make the administration citizen friendly and lead to greater empowerment of the people - the core objective of a vibrant democracy - and their trust in the system.

The fourth Report has recommended a large number of measures which could enhance probity among public servants. They are - amendment of the Prevention of Corruption Act, delegating powers to grant sanction of prosecution to an empowered committee, fixing time limit for trial of anti-corruption cases, enhancing powers of the Central Vigilance Commission, repealing Article 311, creating a multi-member Lokayukta, simplifying disciplinary procedures, creating mechanism which can empower citizens to seek legal relief against fraudulent claims against the government, confiscation of property acquired by corrupt means, ensuring accessibility and responsiveness of government functionaries and adopting measures to protect honest civil servants.

Many of these recommendations will apply equally to both the Union and State Governments. But, there are some which specifically relate to the State administration. A proactive stance by the State Governments would go a long way in enhancing ethics among government functionaries.

The main recommendations applicable to States and District administration are narrated:-

Institutional Framework

i. The Constitution should be amended to incorporate a provision making it obligatory for State Governments to establish the institution of Lokayukta and stipulate the general principles about its structure, power and functions.

ii. The Lokayukta should be a multi-member body consisting of a judicial Member in the Chair, an eminent jurist or eminent administrator with impeccable credentials as Member and the head of the State Vigilance Commission as *ex officio* Member. The Chairperson of the Lokayukta should be selected from a panel of retired Supreme Court Judges or retired Chief Justices of the High Courts, by a Committee consisting of the Chief Minister, Chief Justice of the High Court and the Leader of the Opposition in the Legislative Assembly. The same Committee should select the second Member from among eminent jurists/ administrators. There is no need to have an Upa-Lokayukta.

iii. The jurisdiction of the Lokayukta would extend to only cases involving corruption against Ministers and MLAs. They should not look into general public grievances.

iv. Each State should constitute a State Vigilance Commission to look into cases of corruption against State Government officials. The Commission should have three Members and have functions similar to that of the Central Vigilance Commission.

v. The Anti-Corruption Bureaus should be brought under the control of the State Vigilance Commission.

vi. The Chairperson and Members of the Lokayukta should be appointed strictly for one term only and they should not hold any public office under government thereafter.

vii. The Lokayukta should have its own machinery for investigation. Initially, it may take officers on deputation from the State Government, but over a period of five years, it should take steps to recruit its own cadre, and train them properly. viii. All cases of corruption should be referred to Rashtriya Lokayukta or Lokayukta and these should not be referred to any Commission of Inquiry.

Ombudsman at the Local Level

i. A local bodies Ombudsman should be constituted for a group of districts to investigate cases against the functionaries of the local bodies. The State Panchayat Raj Acts and the Urban Local Bodies Acts should be amended to include this provision.

ii. The local bodies Ombudsman should be empowered to investigate cases of corruption or maladministration by the functionaries of the local selfgovernments, and submit reports to the competent authorities for taking action.

Strengthening Investigation and Prosecution

i. The State Vigilance Commissions/Lokayuktas may be empowered to supervise prosecution of corruption related cases.

ii. The investigative agencies should acquire multi-disciplinary skills and should be thoroughly conversant with the working of various offices/departments. They should draw officials from different wings of government.

iii. The prosecution of corruption cases should be conducted by a panel of lawyers prepared by the Attorney General or the Advocate General in consultation with Rashtriya Lokayukta or Lokayukta as the case may be.

iv. The anti-corruption agencies should conduct systematic surveys of departments with particular reference to highly corruption prone ones in order to gather intelligence and to target officers of questionable integrity.

v. The economic offences unit of States need to be strengthened to effectively investigate cases and there should be better coordination amongst existing agencies.

Besides, the principles mentioned in the Report on key issues such as enhancing citizen centricity, reducing discretion, promoting transparency, and enforcing accountability would be equally applicable to all levels of government.

Public Order

In its Report on Public Order, the Commission dealt with the much delayed, but essential reform of police organisation and the criminal justice system; the need for reform of prisons, the future of some special laws, and the role of political parties, civil society and the media. Since Public Order and Police are State subjects under Schedule 7 of the Constitution, the recommendations made in that Report are, to a large extent, to be acted upon by the State Governments and their law-enforcment agencies.

Some of the important recommendations of the Report relate to separation of crime investigation and police functions, insulating the police force from political interference, creation of a separate machinery for prosecution under a district attorney, setting up of police establishment committees to ensure fixed tenures for senior police functionaries, strengthening of the intelligence mechanism, setting up of a transparent complaint system by appointing independent complaint authorities both at the State as well as at the district level. In addition, the Commission has also recommended substantial reforms in the criminal justice system such as setting up local courts, citizen-friendly registration of FIRs, prescribing rules for inquest, amendment to sections 161, 162 of Cr.P.C., making confessions before the police admissible as evidence, amendments to section 311 Cr.P.C., and modernization and reforms of the prison system. One of the important suggestions is to include offences having inter-State or National ramifications into a new law. The Report also makes recommendations with regard to local policing, traffic management and metropolitan policing. It also suggests measures to enhance capacity of the local magistracy (which is actively involved with the police in maintenance of public order). All the above issues are of immediate concern to governments at the State level.

The recommendations relevant to the State and District administration in India, in brief, are:-

Streamlining the Police Functions

a. Crime investigation should be separated from other police functions. A Crime Investigation Agency should be constituted in each State. A State Police Performance and Accountability Commission should be constituted to provide the required autonomy to the police. A similar Board of Investigation should be constituted to oversee investigation and prosecution.

b. The tenure of the Chief of the Law and Order Police as well as the Chief of the Crime Investigation Agency should be at least three years.

c. Police Establishment Committees should be constituted to deal with all matters of postings and transfers.

d. A system of District Attorneys should be constituted wherein the District Attorney would supervise prosecution as well as the investigation of crimes in a district.

e. Metropolitan Police Authorities should be constituted in large cities. Theseauthorities should have powers to plan and oversee community policing and other functions.

f. Non-core police functions may be outsourced to other departments/ agencies.

g. The existing system of constabulary should be substituted with recruitment of graduates at the level of Assistant Sub Inspectors of Police (ASI), except for the Armed Police.

h. Independent City and District level Police Complaints Authorities should be constituted to look into all cases of misconduct by the police.

i. An independent Inspectorate of Police should be established to carry out performance audit of police stations and other police offices.

j. Representation of women and under represented sections of society in the police should be increased through affirmative actions. Women should constitute 33% of the police force.

Capacity Building for Conflict Resolution

The Report of the Commission on 'Capacity Building for Conflict Resolution' covers part of its TOR No.13 i.e. Public Order. In this Report, the Commission has sought to outline measures that can be taken to improve the institutional capacity of the country to resolve and manage conflicts of all types. Creating an institutional context wherein conflict management is done in a democratic manner keeping the interests of all sections of society in mind rather than resorting to short term fire fighting, is the focus of the Report. The State and District Administation State Administration Report deals with a large number of issues which cause tension in our Society such as - left extremism, land related issues, water disputes, matters related to scheduled castes/tribes and other backward classes, religious and political disturbances. The Report stresses on the need to enhance the capacity of the security forces, to speed up formation of special task forces in the effective areas, to ensure effective implementation of Forest Dwellers (Recognition of Rights) Act, 2006, to give flexibility to local agencies with regard to development schemes, to speed up implementation of land reform measures, to take steps for consolidation of land holdings, and to expand the banking system in the rural areas. The Commission has also recommended avoiding use of prime agricultural land for SEZs, diversifying risk coverage measures such as - weather insurance and price support schemes, setting up River Basin Organisations for inter-State rivers, adopting proactive measures to settle inter-State river disputes, implementing measures to end the discrimination against scheduled castes, faster disposal of such cases, sensitisation of civil and police machinery towards the special problems of SCs and STs, and involvement of local governance institutions in various programmes concerned with enforcement of various social legislations. The Report further recommends that in the Fifth Schedule Areas, various State laws and policies should be made compliant with the PESA and there should be convergence of regulatory and development programmes. With regard to religious conflicts, the suggestion is to take prompt action against spreading of hatred, to make effective use of peace committees/integration councils, provide for enhanced punishment for communal offences and set up special courts. The Report has also taken up issues arising out of regional disparities and conflicts in the North-East. The State administration has a major responsibility in preventing conflicts from escalating into violent protests and activities.

Crisis Management

In its Third Report, the Commission examined all aspects of Crisis Management and attempted to delineate a road map involving stakeholders/ agencies and organisations at every level during different phases of a crisis - from prevention to management. 'Disaster Management' as a subject is not mentioned in any of the three lists under Schedule 7 of the Constitution, but, by practice and convention the primary responsibility for managing disaster rests with the State Governments. The Union Government has enacted the Disaster Management Act, 2005 under entry 23 namely 'Social security and social insurance, employment and unemployment' in the Concurrent list. At the same time, some States too have enacted laws governing disaster management.

The following recommendations of the Report are relevant for the State Governments:-

i. Disaster/Crisis management should continue to be the primary responsibility of the State Governments and the Union Government should play a supportive role.

ii. The law should create a uniform structure at the apex level to handle all crises. Such a structure may be headed by the Prime Minister at the National level and the Chief Minister at the State level. At the administrative level, the structure is appropriately headed by the Cabinet Secretary and the Chief Secretary respectively.

iii. The role of the local governments should be brought to the forefront for crisis/ disaster management.

iv. The National Executive Committee as stipulated under the Disaster Management Act need not be constituted, and the National Crisis Management Committee (NCMC) should continue to be the apex coordination body. At the State level, the existing coordination mechanism under the Chief Secretary should continue.

v. In larger cities (say, with population exceeding 2.5 million), the Mayor, assisted by the Commissioner of the Municipal Corporation and the Police Commissioner should be directly responsible for Crisis Management.

vi. Empowering the Relief Commissioners/Disaster Management Departments to effectively discharge disaster related responsibilities.

vii. The district emergency response plan should be prepared in consultation with all concerned. The plan should be known and accepted by all the role plays. (This should be a part of the District Disaster Management Plan).

viii. Effective coordination is essential at the district and sub-district levels for rescue/ relief operations and to ensure proper receipt and provision of relief. During rescue and relief operations, unity of command should be ensured with the Collector in total command.

Organizational Structure of Government of India

In its Thirteenth Report the Commission has examined in detail the Organisational Structure of Government of India. In order to make the administration more efficient, responsive and accountable, the Commission suggests that the focus of the government should be on the following core activities.

a. i. Defence, International relations, National Security, justice and rule of law.

ii. Human development through access to good quality education and healthcare to every citizen.

iii. Infrastructure and sustainable natural resource development.

iv. Social security and Social justice

v. Macro economic management and retorted economic Planning

vi. National policies in respect of other sectors

b. The principle of subsidiarity should be followed to decentralise functions to State and Local Governments.

c. Subjects which are closely inter-related should be dealt with together.

d. Separation of Policy Making Functions from Execution: The Ministry/Department should concentrate on strategic decisions, policy making, monitoring/evaluation and budgetary processes, whereas the implementation of policies should be handed over to Executive Agencies.

e. Coordinated Implementation: Coordination is essential in implementation as in policy making. The proliferation of vertical departments makes this an impossible task except in cases where empowered commissions, statutory bodies, autonomous societies have been created.

f. Flatter Structures-reducing the number of levels and encouraging team work: The structure of an organization including those in government should be tailor-made to suit the specific objectives it is supposed to achieve. There is a need to shift to flatter organizations with emphasis on team work.

g. Well defined Accountability: The present multi-layered organizational structure with fragmented decision making leads to a culture of plausible alibis for non performance. The tendency to have large number of on - file consultations, often unnecessary, leads to diffused accountability. A clearer demarcation of organizational responsibilities would help in developing a performance management system for individual functionaries.

h. Appropriate Delegation: A typical characteristic of a government organization is the tendency to centralize power and avoid delegation of authority to subordinate functionaries or units. However, this leads to delays, inefficiency and demoralization of the subordinate staff. The principle of subsidiarity should be followed to locate authority closer to the citizens.

i. Criticality of Operational Units: Government organizations have tended to become top-heavy with a lack of authority, manpower and resources at the operational levels that have a direct bearing on citizens lives. Rationalization of Government staff pattern is necessary and commensurate with the requirements of the citizens.

Based on the above core principles, the Report has made a large number of recommendations with regard to formation and functioning of a Ministry and a Department as mentioned earlier and reframing of the Allocation of Business Rules. It has also suggested that the Ministries/Departments should concentrate on policy planning and strategic decision making and implementation work should be given over to adequately empowered Executive Agencies. Thereafter, the Report deals with issues of delegation, reduction of hierarchy, maintenance of electronic database and strengthening the coordination mechanism in the government. Finally, the Commission also dwells on issues connected with setting-up of regulatory authorities; viz. need for a Regulator, autonomy in functioning, uniformity in appointment of Chairman and Members etc.

Most of the above recommendations with minor changes are applicable to the State governments. They have been referred to at appropriate places in the subsequent Chapters of this Report.

Financial Management System

Financial Management is one of the most critical elements of Public Administration.

The Commission has carried out an elaborate study of this subject in its fourteenth Report.

The Commission is broadly of the view that the core principles for reforming the financial management system of the government in the country should consist of the following:-

i. Reforms in Financial Management System is part of overall governance reforms: Governance reforms to bring about improved transparency, greater account-ability, streamlining the structure of the Government, elimination of corruption, and fiscal and environment sustainability have to be backed up by reforms in the financial management system in order to deliver the desired results. At the same time it needs to be understood that reforms in management system are not an end in itself but a means to achieving good governance. ii. Sound financial management is the responsibility of all government departments/ agencies: Maintaining financial prudence, discipline and accountability, while at the same time, ensuring prompt and efficient utilization of resources towards achieving organizational goals is the responsibility of all government agencies/ organizations and not of the finance wing/Finance Ministry only.

ii. Medium-term plan/budget frameworks and aligning plan budgets and accounts: Medium-term plan/budget frameworks attempt to bring the gap between the short-term time horizon of annual budgets with the medium term objectives of the schemes and programmes of government. Even when there are medium term frameworks like five year development plans, there is need to aligning the annual budgets explicitly with the plans and with the accounting mechanisms so that there is a clear 'line of sight' between the medium term developmental plan and the annual budget exercise.

iii. Prudent economic assumptions: Economic assumptions that underline the budget have to be prudent and accurate in order to ensure that the budgetary estimates do not go haywire. The tendency to be overly optimistic has to be avoided.

iv. Top-down budgeting techniques: There is a need to shift from the traditional bottom up approach to budgeting to a top-down framework where the desired outcomes should point to the resources required which should be allocated thereafter at the macro level sector-wise. This in turn would lead to focus on outputs and outcomes rather than on inputs and processes.

v. Transparency and simplicity: Budget documents should be simple and easy to comprehend and be available in the public domain. Also the procedures involved in operating the budget and release of funds should be simple. Suitable financial management information systems need to be developed in order to ensure that all transactions are captured and ultimately made available for public scrutiny.

vi. Relaxing central input controls: Government agencies need to be given greater operational autonomy and flexibility by consolidating budget items and decentralization of administrative and financial powers.

vii. Focus on results: Accountability in government needs to shift from compliance with rules and procedures to achievement of results. This is all the more necessary with relaxed central input controls. There should be emphasis on 'value for money'.

viii. Adopting modern financial management practices: Modern financial management tools like accrual accounting, information technology, financial information system etc. need to be used to improve decision making and accountability. However, care needs to be exercised to ensure that congenial environment is created and adequate capacity is developed before adopting new practices.

ix. Budgeting to be realistic: Unless the projections made in the budget are reasonably accurate, the budgetary exercise lose credibility.

The above core principles which have been discussed extensively in the context of financial management in the Union Government in the 14th Report of the Administrative Reforms Commission, will apply as well to the State Governments. There are, however, some specific issues in this important area pertaining primarily to the State Governments. The Commission has analysed these in greater detail in Chapter 6 of this Report.

RESTRUCTURING STATE GOVERNMENTS

In addition to the issues on which the Commission has already made recommendations earlier, the Commission has analysed the following major aspects of State Administration in this Report:

(i) Size of the Council of Ministers

(ii) Rationalizing the number of Secretariat Departments

(iii) Executive Agencies

(iv) Internal restructuring of the State Government Departments.

(v) State Civil Services Law

(vi) Appointment and security of tenure at senior levels in the State Government

(vii) State Public Service Commission

Size of the Council of Ministers

The State executive consists of the Governor, who is the Constitutional head of the State, and the Council of Ministers with the Chief Minister as the head. Each Minister of the Council of Ministers is in charge of one or more departments and the business of the Government is carried out through Secretaries functioning at the State level.

Over a period of time, partly due to administrative needs and partly due to compulsions of coalition politics, there has been a significant proliferation of Ministers and Departments in almost all the States. This proliferation has led to administrative fragmentation. The present size of the Council of Ministers in the States, more so in the larger ones, appears to be disproportionate, particularly in view of the establishment of the third tier of Government, to whom substantive powers and functions have to be devolved as mandated by the Constitutional 73rd and 74th Amendments. An attempt was made to address this issue by way of the Ninety-first Constitutional amendment introduced with effect from 01.01.2004 by restricting the size of the Council of Ministers to a maximum of 15% of the strength of the respective State Legislative Assembly but the problem still persists. In bigger States (like U.P. where the Assembly has a strength of 404 legislators), even this restriction has not prevented formation of jumbo sized Ministries.

Article 164 of the Constitution deals with the appointment of the Chief Minister and the other Ministers. As per Article 164(1A), the total number of Ministers including the Chief Minister, in the Council of Ministers in a State shall not exceed 15% of the total number of members of the Legislative Assembly of that State provided that the number of Ministers, including the Chief Minister in a State shall not be less than twelve. In case of smaller States like Sikkim, Mizoram and Goa where the strength of the Assembly is 32, 40 and 40 respectively, a minimum strength of 7 for the Council of Ministers has been provided.

Before the 91st Constitutional amendment, there was no limit on the size of the Council of Ministers in a State. At one point, there were 76 Ministers in the Bihar Government, 69 in Maharashtra and 93 in Uttar Pradesh. The size and composition of the Council of Ministers is of basic importance to effective public administration. The Ministry and the Cabinet come into existence for the specific purpose of running the administration efficiently and impartially and not for operating a spoils system. Hence, it needs to be compact and homogenous, its size being determined by administrative needs. It would depend on factors such as the area of the State, its population, the stage of economic development and its peculiar problems.

It may be pertinent to recall that the National Commission to Review the Working of the Constitution had suggested that the size of the Council of Ministers should not be more than 10 per cent of the total strength of the lower House, the Lok Sabha at the Centre and the Legislative Assembly in the States. This recommendation was in line with the views of the First

Administrative Reforms Commission which had suggested that the size of the Council be limited to 10 per cent of the strength of the Assembly in a unicameral State and 11 percent in a bicameral State.

There is a growing realisation that there is need to further reduce the size of the Council of Ministers in the States. The number of Ministers (of all ranks taken together) should be in direct proportion to the needs of an efficient government. There should be a correlation between the number of Ministers and that of the Departments existing in the government. However, different yardsticks would be needed for different States and a distinction will have to be made on the basis of population, strength of the Assembly and specific functional needs of individual States. Table 2.1 indicates the status of various States.

The Commission feels that a compact and small sized Council of Ministers is one of the essential requirements of good governance and as indicated earlier the current ceiling of 15% which has been imposed by Article 164(1A), appears to be somewhat excessive for many of the States.

In order to arrive at some rational criteria for reducing the size of the Council of Ministers, the Commission feels that all the 28 States of the country could be conveniently placed in three groups on the basis of the strength of their Legislative Assemblies. Bigger States where the strength of the Assemblies lies between 200 and 400 could be placed in one group such as Uttar Pradesh, Bihar, West Bengal, Madhya Pradesh, Rajasthan, Gujarat, Maharashtra, Andhra Pradesh, Karnataka and Tamil Nadu. States where the strength of the Legislative Assemblies is between 80 and 200 such as Jammu & Kashmir, Punjab, Haryana, Assam, Jharkhand, Orissa, Chhattisgarh, and Kerala could be grouped together. The third Group may consist of States where the strength of their Assembly is below 80 such as Himachal Pradesh, Uttarakhand, Sikkim, Arunachal Pradesh, Nagaland, Manipur, Mizoram, Tripura, Meghalaya, and Goa.

Table 2.1 : Strength of the Legislative Assembly of Various States

Sl. No.	States	Population (in lakh)	Strength of Lagislative Assembly	Size of the Council of Ministers	No. of Depart-ments
1.	Andhra Pradesh	757.28	295	40	30
2.	Arunachal Pradesh	10.91	60	29	43
3.	Assam	266.38	126	19	31
4.	Bihar	828.78	243	35	35
5.	Chhattisgarh	207.96	90	12	43
6.	Goa	13.44	40	12	34
7.	Gujarat	505.97	182	20	26
8.	Haryana	210.83	90	10	43
9.	Himachal Pradesh	60.77	63	10	44
10.	J and K	100.70	89	10	
11.	Jharkhand	269.09	81	12	36
12.	Karnataka	527.34	224	32	28
13.	Kerala	318.39	141	19	40
14.	Madhya Pradesh	603.85	231	23	50
15.	Maharashtra	967.52	289	43	29
16.	Manipur	23.89	60	12	52
17.	Meghalaya	23.06	60	12	45
18.	Mizoram	8.91	40	12	34
19.	Nagaland	19.89	60	13	31
20.	Orissa	367.07	147	21	36
21.	Punjab	242.89	117	36	33
22.	Rajasthan	564.73	200	24	33
23.	Sikkim	5.40	32	12	35
24.	Tamil Nadu	621.11	235	29	33
25.	Tripura	31.91	60	12	26
26.	Uttar Pradesh	1660.52	404	56	77
27.	Uttarakhand	84.80	70	12	43
28.	West Bengal	802.21	295	42	54

Source: Based on the data available on State Governments' Websites.

(For The Union Territory of Delhi, Article 239AA(4) of the Constitution itself limits the size of the Council of Ministers to 7 whereas in the case of Puducherry it is limited to 6).

While suggesting reduction in the size of the Council of Ministers, the Commission is conscious of the fact that medium and smaller States should not be in a disadvantageous situation and they must have adequate number of Ministers to meet the requirements of governance. Therefore, it is of the view that a graded system could be adopted where the maximum percentage limit could be in the range of 10-15 % of the strength of the respective State Legislative Assembly. To be more specific, the larger States where membership of the Assembly is more than 200, the strength of the Council of Ministers should not exceed 10% of such strength. This maximum percentage could be 12% in case of medium States (where the strength of the Assembly is between 80 and 200) and 15% in case of smaller States (where the strength of the Assembly is below 80). This stipulation should, however, be subject to an appropriate proviso to remove the resultant anomalies. It may be ensured that the maximum number of Ministers permissible for the medium sized States should not exceed the number prescribed for a large State having 200 legislators and similarly the maximum number of Ministers permissible for the smaller States may not exceed the number prescribed for a medium sized State having 80 Legislators. At the same time there may be no prescribed minimum.

In this context, the Commission would also like to take note of the developments which have taken place in the Indian polity during the last few decades. They are (a) emergence of a large number of regional political parties based on local identities and aspiration, (these parties are now able to secure a significant number of seats in the State Legislature), (b) formation of coalition governments both at the Centre as well as in the States and (c) the third and a natural corollary has been the swearing in of large Councils of Ministers in the States.

The issue seems to be complex and there is a need to arrive at a national consensus through deliberations/discussions with the States. The Commission is of the view that the appropriate forum for these deliberations/discussions would be the Inter-State Council.

Recommendations

(a) The size of the Council of Ministers in the States needs to be reduced further considering the needs of an efficient government. For this purpose the maximum size of the Council of Ministers may be fixed in a range between 10% to 15% of the strength of their Legislative Assemblies. In the larger States (where membership of the Assembly is more than 200) such maximum percentage should be 10% where as in the medium (where the strength of the Assembly is between 80 and 200) and the smaller States (where the strength of the Assembly is below 80) it may be 12% and 15% respectively. This stipulation should however be subject to appropriate proviso to remove anomalies. It may be ensured that the maximum number of Ministers permissible for the medium sized States should not exceed the number prescribed for a large sized State having 200 legislators and similarly, the maximum number of Ministers permissible for the smaller States should not exceed the number prescribed for a medium sized State having 80 Legislators. There may not be any prescribed minimum.

(b) There is need to arrive at a national consensus on this issue through deliberations/discussions with the States at the Inter-State Council.

Rationalising the Number of Secretariat Departments

The Secretariat is the top most echelon of the State administration and its main function is to assist the political executive - the Chief Minister and other Ministers - in maintaining peace and law and order and designing policies for the socio-economic development of the State as well as in carrying out legislative responsibilities of the government. The political executive is elected for a fixed tenure, but the Secretariat consists of civil servants and others who are permanent employees of the government. Hence the Secretariat works as a memory bank providing continuity to government policies and programmes. The primary functions of the Secretariat are:

(a) Assisting the Ministers in making policies for the socio economic development of the State;

(b) Carrying out regulatory work;

(c) Drafting legislations, rules and regulations;

(d) Coordinating various policies and programmes, monitoring progress of work and analyzing results;

(e) Preparing budget and maintaining control over expenditure;

(f) Maintaining liaison with various departments of the Union Government;

(g) Monitoring the administrative system and taking steps to enhance its efficacy, competence and responsiveness.

Over the years, due to continued expansion of governmental activities in all sectors and also to some extent due to the self serving tendencies of the system and considerations of expediency, there has been a marked increase in the size of the State secretariat. There has also been accumulation of multifarious and unnecessary tasks and expansion of executive work. Though, from time to time many States have constituted their own Reforms Commissions and Committees to suggest improvements in the functioning of the secretariat, the system has remained by and large immune to change. The overall impression of the Secretariat is of an unwieldy, slow-moving organization with an in-built propensity for delays.

Creation of the departments in the State Government has not always followed administrative logic. Functions which are closely related both in terms of the scope of activities as well as staff skills have often been truncated to form separate departments. Often, an activity which is insignificant in terms of both functions as well as budgetary allocation is converted into a full-fledged department.

For example, in some States, a separate Department dealing with Administrative Reforms and Public Grievances has been carved out of the existing Department of Personnel/General Administration Department. In West Bengal, there is a separate Department for Municipal Affairs, though there is also a Department for Urban Development and Town and Country Planning. In Uttar Pradesh, Civil Aviation is a separate Department, though it has a very small functional activity - relating to operation and maintenance of just a few small aircrafts. Similarly, Dairy Development which should have been a part of the larger Animal Resources Development Depart-ment, exists as a separate entity in this State. In Madhya Pradesh, there is a separate Department of Jails, though it could have been a part of the State Home Department.

The emergence of a large number of regional parties during the last four decades has led to a situation in which coalition governments and hence large sized Council of Ministers in States have become regular features of the Indian polity. The large number of Ministers has in turn led to creation of new departments or splitting up of the existing ones. A State Government consisting of too many departments suffers from the following inherent disadvantages.

(a) There is diffusion of responsibility and accountability among the large number of functionaries working under different vertical structures.

(b) Coordination becomes a major issue and decision making becomes difficult and time consuming.

(c) It leads to needless expansion of the bureaucracy. Its own management takes a major part of the government's attention. The structure often, becomes more important than considerations of efficiency, responsiveness and service to people.

The Commission believes that there is need to emphasis that the allocation of work to different departments should be made on the basis of an empirical analysis of the functions and tasks to be performed by the government. There has to be a rational grouping of subjects among departments keeping in mind considerations of efficiency, effectiveness, homogeneity and economy.

Ideally, each of the Secretariat departments should deal with a particular segment of administrative activities which are inter-related and are more or less homogenous. It should also provide an in-built mechanism for coordination of policies and programmes. The basis for this rationalization could be as follows:-

(a) Inter-related subjects, activities and functions to be placed under one department.

(b) Need for synergy between the activities of various Departments.

(c) Devolution of a large number of functions to the PRIs/ULBs.

(d) The role of Secretaries to be redefined; to be divested of non-essential responsibilities and executive work and larger delegation of power to the executive departments/agencies.

(e) Need for streamlining the decision making process.

Based on the above principles, the State Governments need to rationalize the number of departments presently existing in the Secretariat. To give an example from the Government of Bihar, the presently separate departments of Panchayati Raj and Rural Development could be merged into one Department. Similarly, the Departments of Agriculture, Animal Resources and Dairy Development could be combined into a single entity.

The Commission is of the view that a small and compact Secretariat in which all related activities and functions are kept together in one department with more responsibilities devolved on local governments and executive work (not related to policy making and broader monitoring), hived off to executive agencies, is a *sine qua-non* for good governance at any level of public administration. Hence, there is need to rationalize the number of Secretariat Departments in the State Governments.

The Commission would recommend that all States attempt such a rationalization exercise as illustrated above keeping in view their specific requirements.

Recommendation

(a) The number of Secretariat Departments in the States should be further rationalized on the following basis:

  (i) The existing departments covering inter-related subjects, activities and functions should be merged;

  (ii) Need for synergy between the activities of various departments;

  (iii) Devolution of a large number of functions to the PRIs/ULBs;

  (iv) The role of Secretaries to be redefined; to be divested of non-essential responsibilities and executive work and larger delegation of power to the executive departments/agencies; and

  (v) Need for streamlining the decision making process.

Separate Focus on Policy Making and Implementation

There are two broad tasks of the government. The first is formulating policy in pursuance of objectives that the political leadership specifies, and the second, implementation of that policy. In a democracy, it is the political leadership-assisted by the civil servants - which sets the vision, goals and strategic directions. But sound institutional arrangements play an important role in translating the vision, goals and strategic directions into effective action.

Although precise institutional arrangements have varied, effective governments throughout the world are characterized by strong systems for strategic policy formulation. At the heart of these systems are mechanisms for preparing policy proposals after due consideration of future implications, estimating the costs of competing policy options within a disciplined framework of aggregate expenditures, ensuring horizontal coordination where policies are spread across a number of departments where delivery mechanisms are similarly divided between different parts of the government, and introduction of policy evaluation systems.

A key structural reform in various countries towards achieving good governance has been the separation of policy and operational responsibilities. There is a two-fold logic behind it:

(a) the separation of policy advice from operational functions allows those responsible for operational activities to focus on their prime objective i.e. running their operations as efficiently as possible within the policy parameters of the government, and

(b) it ensures that contestable policy options are generated and government does not get captured by provider interests.

The Commission in its Tenth Report, on Refurbishing of Personnel Administration, has recommended that policy formulation functions need to be distinguished from those relating to policy implementation, particularly in the case of senior civil servants. The Commission noted that 'the need to provide the Ministers with high quality policy advice requires that Secretaries to Government and their supporting staff in the Secretariat with policy advisory responsibilities do not get diverted by the demands of managing routine administrative and operational responsibilities. This would call for a broad separation of policy formulation and implementation responsibilities. What this would imply is that the Ministries responsible for policy advice including the monitoring and evaluation of policy implementation should be separated from the departments and other entities responsible for delivery of services, operational matters and the enforcement of regulations. What is required, therefore, is not merely a broad separation of policy operation, but also restructuring the design of the Ministries to make them less hierarchical, creating flatter structures with team based orientation and reducing the excessive degree of central control now being exercised over operational matters.

The Commission recognizes, however, that there can be no water-tight separation of the policy making and implementation functions since Ministers are ultimately accountable to Parliament for the performance of their Ministries and departments in all respects. In fact, the Government of India (Transaction of Business) Rules states that all business allocated to a Department in the Government of India, has to be disposed of under the directions of the Minister in-charge. However, Ministers can discharge their responsibilities in this regard more effectively by supervising the performance of operational agencies from time to time rather than by taking direct control of routine functions.

The Commission has considered how a degree of separation between the policy making and implementation functions of the Ministries and other government agencies can be best achieved. Under the existing scheme, it is the Minister who lays down the extent of delegation of various functions to different levels within the Ministry as well as to its attached and subordinate offices. In order to enable the Ministries to effectively fulfill their policy making role and also to ensure uniformity across Ministries, the Commission is of the view that some general principles to govern the extent of delegation may be incorporated in the Transaction of Business Rules. These principles may stipulate that the Ministries should concentrate on the following:

- Policy making and strategic decisions.
- Budgeting

- Monitoring of implementation
- Appointments of key personnel
- Coordination
- Evaluation

Attached and subordinate offices would serve as the executive agencies of the Ministries and concentrate on the implementation of government policies and programmes.

Executive Agencies

Separation of policy and implementation would also call for changes in how the policy implementing agencies are structured. Implementational bodies need to be restructured by giving them greater operational autonomy and flexibility, at the same time, making them responsible and accountable for what they do. The Executive Agency is an organization in the public sector, analogous to the self-contained, quasi-autonomous division of a corporate body. 'Agencification', that is, extensive use of executive agencies in administration has been found useful in conducting an extremely wide range of functions and has been the cornerstone of public service reforms around the world.

In the States too, a major part of implementation work is done by executive agencies of different kinds. They are structured as departments, statutory boards, commissions, departmental undertakings, societies and other parastatals. In effect, however, because of centralized controls and inadequate delegation of authority, these bodies do not function as real autonomous agencies. While the importance of delegating increased powers to the executive agencies is now getting recognized and some States have delegated more powers to the agencies, the overall approach has been one of caution and hesitancy. Delegations are also often made in a piecemeal manner and with reservations, more as a favour than as a method of organizational management. The Commission would, therefore, like to emphasise that mere creation of Executive Agencies is not an end in itself. It is necessary to ensure that they have a right balance between autonomy and accountability in their functioning. This could be achieved through well designed performance agreements, Memorandum of Understanding (MoU), contracts, etc. However, preparing and enforcing such performance contracts requires considerable upgradation of capacity in the concerned government departments.

The Commission has comprehensively examined this issue in the context of the Union Government in its Report on the 'Organizational Structure of India'. The recommendations made therein would also be applicable to the State Governments.

There may be some Executive Agencies in the States whose major functions/activities have devolved on local governments. Their role will change. Instead of spending time on personnel matters and micro-management, their role has to change to one of monitoring and supervision, ensuring of standards and quality, providing guidance to local governments on technical matters, training of personnel and giving feed back to the government on implementation and performance and advising on changes that are needed in plans and programmes. It follows that, in course of time, their number and size, as well as the skills of those manning them will have to be different.

Recommendations

(a) The State Governments should scrutinize the functions/ activities of each department to confirm whether these activities/ functions are critical to the mission of the department and can only be carried out by government agencies.

(b) Only those functions/ activities that have to be carried out by the government based on the principle should be carried out directly by the departments. Other functions/ activities should be carried out by Executive Agencies of the department.

(c) Each Executive Agency, whether a new body or an existing departmental undertaking/ agency/ board/ special purpose body, etc. that is converted into an Executive Agency, must be semi-autonomous and professionally managed under a mandate. Such executive agencies could be structured as a department, board, commission, company, society, etc.

(d) There is need for a right balance between autonomy and accountability while designing the institutional framework of executive agencies. This could be achieved through well designed performance agree-ments, Memorandum of Understanding, contracts, etc. However, preparing and enforcing such performance contracts requires considerable upgradation of capacity in the concerned governmental departments.

(e) Agencies dealing with subjects where major functions and activities have devolved on local governments would need to concentrate on monitoring and supervision, ensuring of standards and quality, providing guidance to local governments on technical matters, training of personnel, giving feedback to the government on implementation and performance and advising on changes that are needed in plans and programmes.

Internal Restructuring of the State Secretariat

Apart from the above, there are some important procedural issues related to the functioning of the Secretariat in the States which too need to be reformed. They are internal reorganization, process re-engineering, simplication of government processes and recasting the Manual of Office Procedures. The Commission has examined these issues in detail in its Report on 'Organisational Structure of Government of India' with reference to functioning of the Central Secretariat and has suggested a large number of measures to make the system efficient, responsive and citizen-friendly, such as

a. Each Department should lay down a detailed scheme of delegation at all levels so that the decision making takes place at the most appropriate level. It should be laid down in the Manual of Office Procedure that every Ministry should prescribe a detailed scheme of delegation for its officers. This delegation should be arrived at on the basis of an analysis of the activities and functions of the Ministry/Department and the type of decisions that these entail which should be dovetailed with the decision making units identified it that Department.

b. The scheme of delegation should be updated periodically and should also be 'audited' at regular intervals. The audit should ensure that the delegated authority is actually authorized by the delegate. The scheme of delegation should be placed in the public domain.

c. The number of levels through which a file should pass for a decision should not exceed three. Only in cases where the Minister's approval is required, would the file be initiated by the Deputy Secretary/Director concerned and be moved through the Joint Secretary (or Additional Secretary/Special Secretary) and the Secretary (or Special Secretary) to the Minister. Cases requiring approval of Secretary should go through just two levels (e.g. US and Director, US and JS or Director and JS). Cases requiring approval of JS/Director/DS should come through just one level. The exact combination of levels should be spelt out in the scheme of delegation for each Ministry/Department whereas the number of levels as suggested above should be prescribed in the Manual of Office Procedure. The department dealing with administrative reforms in the Union Government should be entrusted with the task of ensuring compliance with this stipulation.

d. For addressing cross cutting issues, the Secretary of the concerned Department should have the flexibility to create inter-displinary team.

e. Departments should build an electronic database of decisions that are likely to be used as precedents.

Thereafter such database should be periodically reviewed and where necessary, changes in rules introduced in order to codify them. There may also be precedents that may be the result of wrong or arbitrary decision making which the Department would prefer not to rely on for the future. In such cases the Department would have to appropriately change its policy/guidelines and if required even the rules to ensure that these precedents are not wrongly used. The above recommendations will also need to be appropriately replicated in the State Secretariats.

REFURBISHING STATE CIVIL SERVICES

Civil Services Law

In its Report on 'Refurbishing Personnel Administration' (Tenth Report), the Commission has recommended a series of measures for reforming the civil services of the Union Government. The recommendations concern:

(a) Determining a set of values for civil servants

(b) Redefining the relationship between the government and the civil servants

(c) Reforming procedures of recruitment to the civil services

(d) Reforming the procedure for placement of officers and ensuring security of their tenure - setting up an institutional mechanism

(e) Drafting fresh terms and conditions for new appointees

(f) Improving accountability mechanisms and simplifying disciplinary proceedings

(g) Creating new organisational structures in the government.

In order to provide legislative backing to these measures, the Commission has recommended enactment of a Civil Services Law which will cover all personnel holding civil posts under the Union. As recommended at paragraph 17.5 of this Report, the proposed law has the following salient features:

I. **Civil Service Values:** The Civil Services and the Civil Servants shall be guided by the following values in addition to a commitment to uphold the Constitution in discharge of their functions:

   i. Absolute integrity at all times

   ii. Impartiality and non-partisanship

   iii. Objectivity

   iv. Dedication to public service

   v. Empathy towards weaker sections

   The Heads of Departments shall be responsible for promoting these values in their organizations. The Central Civil Services Authority may from time to time review the adoption, adherence to and implementation of the Civil Service Values in the departments or organizations under the Union.

II. **Code of Ethics:** The following should be included in the Code of Ethics for civil servants:

   i. *Integrity*: Civil servants should be guided solely by public interest in their official decision making and not by any financial or other consideration either in respect of themselves, their families or their friends.

   ii. *Impartiality*: Civil servants in carrying out their official work, including functions like procurement, recruitment, delivery of services etc, should take decisions based on merit and free from any partisan consideration.

   iii. *Commitment to public service*: Civil servants should deliver services in a fair, effective, impartial and courteous manner.

   iv. *Open accountability*: Civil servants are accountable for their decisions and actions and should be willing to subject themselves to appropriate scrutiny for this purpose.

v. *Devotion to duty*: Civil servants should maintain absolute and unstinting devotion towards their duties and responsibilities at all times.

vi. *Exemplary behaviour*: Civil servants should treat all members of the public with respect and courtesy and at all times should behave in a manner that upholds the rich traditions of the civil services.

III. **Recruitment and Conditions of Service**: Recruitment and conditions of service of persons appointed to the 'Public Services' shall be governed by Rules made under this Act. The following principles of recruitment should be included for all appointments not routed through the UPSC or SSC:

i. Well-defined merit based procedure for recruitment.

ii. Wide publicity and open competition for recruitment to all posts.

iii. Minimisation, if not elimination, of discretion in the recruitment process.

iv. Selection primarily on the basis of written examination or on the basis of performance in existing public/board/university examination with minimum weightage to interview.

An independent agency should audit the recruitments made outside the UPSC and SSC systems and advise the government suitably. This audit should be conducted under the supervision of the UPSC.

IV. **New Conditions of Appointment**:

(1) A civil servant, other than those recruited or inducted for a short-term appointment, shall hold office for 20 years from the date of initial appointment.

(2) The relationship between the civil servant and the Government of India during the time he/ she holds office shall also be governed by the rules made in this

regard. All public servants shall be subjected to two intensive reviews on completion of 14 years and 20 years of service respectively. Their further continuance beyond 20 years will depend on the outcome of these reviews. It should be expressly provided that all new recruitments shall be for a period of 20 years and their continuance beyond 20 years would depend on the outcome of the intensive reviews.

V. **Fixation of Tenures:** All senior posts should have a specified tenure. The task of fixing tenures for various posts may also be assigned to this independent agency - Central Civil Services Authority.

VI. **Dismissal, Removal etc. of Civil Servants:** After the repeal of Articles 310 and 311 (as recommended in the Report on 'Ethics in Governance'), safeguards against arbitrary action against government servants should be provided in the new law. These safeguards should include:

   i. No penalty of removal and dismissal should be imposed, except by an authority, which is at least three levels above the post which the government servant is holding.

   ii. *Other penalties* - apart from dismissal and removal - may be imposed by an authority which is at least two levels above the current post of the government servant.

   iii. No penalty may be imposed, unless an enquiry is conducted and the accused government servant has been given an opportunity of being heard.

   iv. The Head of an organization should have powers to lay down the details of the enquiry procedure, subject to the general guidelines which may be issued by the Government from time to time.

VII. A performance management system should be mandatory for every organization in the government.

VIII. **Constitution of the Central Civil Services Authority:**

i. The Central Government shall, by notification in the Official Gazette, constitute a body to be known as the Central Civil Services Authority to exercise the powers conferred on, and to perform the functions assigned to it, under this Act.

ii. The Central Civil Services Authority shall be a five-member body consisting of the Chairperson and four members (including the member-secretary). The Authority should have a full time Member- Secretary of the rank of Secretary to Government of India. The Chairperson and members of the Authority should be persons of eminence in public life and professionals with acknowledged contributions to society. The Chairperson and members of the Authority shall be appointed by the President on the recommendations of a Committee consisting of the Prime Minister and the Leader of the Opposition in the Lok Sabha. (Explanation:- Where the Leader of the Opposition in the Lok Sabha has not been recognized as such, the Leader of the single largest group in the opposition in the Lok Sabha shall be deemed to be the Leader of the Opposition).

IX. **Functions of the Central Civil Services Authority:** The Central Authority shall discharge the following functions:

i. Review the adoption, adherence to and implementation of the Civil Service Values in the departments or organizations under the Central Government and send reports to the Central Government.

ii. Assign domains to all officers of the All India Services and the Central Civil Services on completion of 13 years of service.

iii. Formulate norms and guidelines for appointments at 'Senior Management Level' in Government of India.

iv. Evaluate and recommend names of officers for posting at the 'Senior Management Level' in Government of India.

v. Identify the posts at 'Senior Management Level' in Government of India which could be thrown open for recruitment from all sources.

vi. Fix the tenure for posts at the 'Senior Management Level' in Government of India.

vii. Submit an annual report to Parliament.

X. Creation of Executive Agencies in Government: Government should be authorized to create or reorganize some or all of the existing Departments into 'Executive Agencies'. The role of the Ministries should primarily concern policy formulation while implementation should be left to the Executive Agencies.

Each one of the above mentioned features of the proposed law has been separately discussed by the Commission in its Tenth Report and suitable recommendations have been made. These recommendations are equally relevant to the State administrative structure. In fact, the Commission specifically recommended creation of State Civil Services Authority on the lines of the Central Civil Services Authority at paragraph 8.7(d) of its Report. The Commission reiterates that each State Government needs to enact a similar Civil Services Law in order to provide appropriate legislative backing to the reform measures in respect of all personnel holding civil posts in the State. However, the Commission is also of the view that it is advisable to achieve a national consensus on this issue and have some kind of uniformity among different States on enactment of this Law. This issue may be taken up for deliberations / discussions among States at an appropriate forum such as the Inter-State Council, before the law is enacted by each State.

Recommendations

(a) The Commission reiterates that the recommendations in its Tenth Report pertaining to the Civil Services Law and Civil Services Authority should be implemented by the State Governments both in letter and spirit.

(b) In order to provide appropriate legislative backing to these reforms, each State Government should enact a Civil Services Law for all the personnel holding civil posts in the State (on the lines of the proposed Union Law). However, in order to evolve a national consensus and ensure a measure of uniformity among States, the matter may be taken up for deliberations at the Inter-State Council.

Appointment and Security of Tenure at the Senior Levels in the State Government

In the present system of State administration, top level assignments such as Heads of Departments and Regional/Zonal Heads are manned by officers of the All India Services. The supporting positions are held by senior officers of various State services. The Chief Secretary is the senior most officer of the State administration and assists the Chief Minister/ Council of Ministers in all matters of governance. Then there are Principal Secretaries who are in-charge of various departments such as Home, Industries, Finance, Forests, Agriculture, Health, Public Works Department (PWD), Water Resources etc. who work in conjunction with the respective Ministers.

The Director General of Police, Engineer-in-Chief, PWD, Principal Chief Conservator of Forests, Engineer-in-Chief, Irrigation, Director General of Health Services, Director, Agriculture and Director Industries are some other important functionaries who work as Agency Heads. The issues concerning appointments to these highest levels of administration and the security of their tenure have been points of debate since Independence. Often, the process of such appointments is found to be lacking in transparency and objectivity. Transfers are frequent and often coincide with the change in the political regime; the duration of tenure is thus uncertain. All this leads to instability of the administration and lack of faith in the system among the common people. There is need to introduce methods which would impart greater credibility to the appointments process; it should be impartial and merit based. It should also appear as to be so in the eyes of the stakeholders and the public. Selection of officers having unimpeachable conduct, integrity and professional competence is an essential requirement of good governance.

The Commission has examined the issue of security of tenure and a transparent and objective appointments process in its Reports on "Public Order" and "Personnel Management". For the appointment of Director General of Police, the Commission has recommended that the State Police Performance and Accountability Commission comprising inter alia the Home Minister as the Chairman and Leader of the Opposition in the State Assembly, Chief Secretary and others as its Members would recommend a panel of names to the State Government for appointment. The tenure for the Director General of Police and the Chief of the Crime Investigation Agency would be for at least three years and in case of their removal the State Government would need to seek the clearance of the State Police Performance and Accountability Commission or the State Investigation Board, as the case may be.

For appointments to the posts of the Chief Secretary and the Principal Conservator of Forest, the Commission communicated the following interim suggestions to the Government in December 2007:-

(i) There should be a collegium to recommend a panel of names to the Chief Minister/ Cabinet for these two posts. For the post of Chief Secretary, this collegiums may consist of (a) a Minister nominated by the Chief Minister, (b) the Leader of the Opposition in the State Legislative Assembly and (c) the incumbent Chief Secretary. For the selection to the post of Principal Chief Conservator of Forests the collegiums may consist of (a) The Minister Incharge of Forests, (b) the leader of Opposition in the State Legislative Assembly and (c) the Chief Secretary.

(ii) There should be a fixed tenure of two years for both these posts.

(iii) The selection for the post of Chief Secretary and Principal Chief Conservator of Forests should be widened to include all officers above a specified seniority (e.g. 30 years). All officers with seniority higher than a prescribed limit should be eligible to be a part of the panel.

Subsequently, in its Report on 'Refurbishing of Personnel Administration' (the Tenth Report), the Commission suggested a detailed procedure for placement of officers at the middle and top management levels in the Union Government. It calls for the constitution of a Central Civil Service Authority by law, which will be an independent five member body consisting of persons of eminence in public life and professionals with acknowledged contributions to Society. This Authority will be empowered to deal with a large number of issues concerning civil services such as assignment of domain to officers, preparing panels for posting at the levels of Joint Secretary and above, fixing tenures for senior assignments and such other matters that may be referred to it by the Union Government. The Commission is of the view that there should be a similar Civil Services law and a State Civil Services Authority for each State. The mandate and functions of the State Body would largely coincide with those prescribed under the proposed Union Civil Services Law. This Authority should deal with issues of appointment and tenure of higher officials of all ranks in the State Governments including the Chief Secretary, Principal Secretaries, Engineer-in-Chiefs and the Principal Chief Conservator of Forests. However, till the time the proposed law is enacted and the State Civil Service Authority is constituted, recommendations made at above may be immediately adopted by all the State Governments.

Recommendations

(a) After enactment of the State Civil Services Law on the lines of the proposed Union enactment, the proposed State Civil Service Authority should deal with matters concerning appointment and tenure of senior officers of all ranks in the State Governments (including the Chief Secretary, Principal Secretaries, Engineer-in-Chiefs, other Agency Heads and Principal Chief Conservator of Forests).

(b) Till the time that such an Authority is constituted, the following mechanism may be adopted for appointment of the Chief Secretary and Principal Conservator of Forests in the States:-

- There should be a collegium to recommend a panel of names to the Chief Minister/Cabinet for these two posts. For the post of Chief Secretary, this collegium may consist of (a) a Minister nominated by the Chief Minister, (b) the Leader of the Opposition in the State Legislative Assembly and (c) the incumbent Chief Secretary. For the selection to the post of Principal Chief Conservator of Forests the collegiums may consist of (a) The Minister In-charge of Forests, (b) the leader of Opposition in the State Legislative Assembly and (c) the Chief Secretary.
- There should be a fixed tenure of atleast two years for both these posts.
- The selection for the post of Chief Secretary and Principal Chief Conservator of Forests should be widened to include all officers above a specified seniority (e.g. 30 years). All officers with a seniority higher than a prescribed limit should be eligible to be a part of the panel.

(c) As regards the appointment and tenure of the Director General of Police, the recommendations made by the

Commission in its Report on 'Public Order' at para 5.2.3.7 should be implemented.

Regional Level Administration

The East India Company treated the District as the focal point of its revenue administration within British India. In 1786 the districts were reorganised into regular fiscal units each under a Collector. In 1787, leaving aside a few districts, the Collectors were vested with magisterial powers; they could try criminal cases within certain limits. The Cornwallis Code of 1793 divested the Collector of his major judicial functions, but he still remained the most powerful functionary of the Company on Indian soil. He was responsible for collecting various types of taxes and revenue; he was the government treasurer in-charge of local funds and he was the Magistrate, responsible for the maintenance of law and order, superintendence of the police and the management of jails and in-charge of relief in times of epidemics and disasters for the territories under his charge.

Towards the beginning of the 19th century, it was felt by the Company that keeping an eye on districts spread over far flung areas was becoming difficult and there was need to create an intermediate level of functionaries who could effectively supervise and control functioning of 4-5 districts. The Company did not want this intermediate functionary to have direct powers / responsibilities for the departments which were assigned to the Collectors, yet, he was expected to be powerful enough to have supervisory control over them. Thus, the institution of the Divisional Commissioner was born in 1829. Initially, Divisions were created in the permanent settlement areas of the British Empire consisting of modern day Bengal, Orissa, Assam, and Bihar. Later, the scheme was extended to NWFP and Avadh.

Gradually, the Division became an important hub of the British Administration around which almost all major departments of the government positioned their senior level officers, intermediate in rank between the official at the district level and the Agency Head located at the State headquarters. The range DIG of Police, Conservator of Forests and the Superintending Engineer of the PWD were among the first positions which were sanctioned at the divisional level immediately after placement of the Commissioner in the division. With the expansion in the number of government departments, the establishment grew in size. Posts of the Regional Directors of Health Services, Education, Agriculture and Animal Husbandry and Deputy/Assistant Commissioners of Transport, Excise and Commercial Taxes are the other important positions which got created at the Divisional Headquarters in course of time in the post-Independence era.

Theoretically, these positions serve two purposes:-

(a) A regional officer supervises the functioning of departmental officers posted in the districts (usually 4-5 in a division) and then he sends a consolidated report for this entire area to the State Government.

(b) Existence of these senior positions opens up promotional avenues for the departmental officers and hence serves an important purpose in cadre management.

In actual practice, the efficacy of the system varies widely across the States. In some of the States, the Division has been recognized as an established unit of field administration. The regional officers have been given substantial powers to exercise effective supervision and control over the district formations; the Headquarters too give considerable value and weight to their reports. But, there are States where regional units work more like post offices - doing only nominal work.

In the post 73rd/74th Constitutional Amendment scenario, the situation is different. The district has now been recognized by the Constitution as the third tier of government with local institutions, both rural and urban, vested with substantial functions and powers with respect to the matters listed in the 11th and 12th Schedule. In the transferred domain, the machinery of the State Government including the District Collector and his offices, have a limited role. The Commission has dealt with these facets of district administration in its report on 'Local Governance' (sixth Report). As recommended therein, all the development functions pertaining to the subjects listed under the Eleventh/Twelfth Schedule of the Constitution have to be dealt by a District Council consisting of representatives from both urban and rural areas. The District Collector would now be the ex officio Chief Officer of this body and would have a dual responsibility. He will be accountable to the District Council in respect of transferred matters, but will report to the State Government on regulatory/other matters which do not stand delegated to the District Council. Also the offices of the line departments of the State Governments working at the District and Sub-District levels pertaining to these subjects would be merged with the District Council and the appropriate Local Government Institutions.

In the past few decades, most of the State Governments have carried out large scale reorganization of the districts; geographically the districts have become compact and smaller. There have been rapid advances in technology leading to tremendous improvement in connectivity and accessibility (both physical as well as electronic). Hence, the Commission feels that there is no need to have any intermediate level of administration in the form of regional/divisional offices between the two units of Government - District and the State. Having such a layer in between the two tiers adds only to red-tapism and delays.

With regard to issues of promotions and cadre management, (which may get disturbed if the regional offices are wound up), the Commission feels that this problem can be taken care of by identifying suitable departmental posts in the major Districts and at the State Headquarters to be manned by the senior officers who are presently eligible to head the regional offices.

Recommendations

(a) In view of the emergence of District as the key unit of field administration - as the third tier of government - and with rapid advancement in physical and electronic connectivity between the State Headquarters and the Districts, there is no need to have an intermediate level of administration between the two units of government.

(b) In order to take care of cadre management issues arising out of this step, suitable posts should be identified by respective departments, in the major districts and at the Headquarters to be manned by senior officers who are presently eligible to head the regional offices.

Lokayukta and the Vigilance Set-up

Vigilance is an important facet of public administration. It is of critical significance in keeping a check on the integrity of the employees and for controlling government expenditure. The subject of vigilance can be discussed in two different perspectives.

(a) Existing Legislation, statutes and regulations

(b) Institutional set-up

Before 1947, it was the Indian Penal Code (IPC) which provided the legal base for initiating action against corrupt government employees. The chapter relating to offences by public servants contained in Sections 161 to 165 provided the legal interpretation on which cases of corruption were lodged against public servants.

The Prevention of Corruption Act 1947 was the first specific Act in this direction. Subsequently, the Criminal Law Amendment Act of 1952 and 1964 brought some changes in the above law (with regard to enhancement of punishment, expanding the definition of 'public servant' and 'criminal misconduct' and 'enhancing the powers of investigating officers'). Finally in 1988, a vastly modified enactment - Prevention of Corruption Act 1988 was put on the statute.

Currently, in most of the States, the vigilance setup consists of the following:-

(i) The Vigilance Commission and the Investigation Bureau

(ii) Lokayukta

In a majority of the States, the institution of Lokayukta is only a recommendatory body whereas the actual power of instituting corruption cases against public functionaries rests with the State Government (Vigilance Department). In Karnataka, the Vigilance Commission has been placed under the overall control of the Lokayukta.

Vigilance Commission/Vigilance Commissioner in the State

Currently, all the States have an Office of the Vigilance Commissioner which is usually headed by a senior IAS / IPS officer. There is also a Vigilance Bureau which is the investigating arm of the vigilance setup. The State Government consists of a large number of departments whose work is highly specialized and of technical nature. In order to obtain a composite view on various vigilance issues, it is desirable for the Government to have requisite technical expertise in the office of the Vigilance Commissioner. As such, the Commission is of the view that the organization of the Vigilance Commissioner in the State should be structured on the pattern of the Union CVC; particularly in the larger States. The State Vigilance Commission should be a three Member Body with Members who have been experts in their respective fields. In smaller States, however, the requirement of a multi Member Body may not be there.

As regards the Lokayukta, the Commission's views have been summarized in Para 2.8.4.1 of the Commission's Report on Ethics in Governance.

Recommendations

(a) The recommendations made by the Commission in its Fourth Report (on Ethics in Governance) and its Sixth

Report (on Local Governance) for action by State Governments should be implemented expeditiously.

(b) The organization of the Vigilance Commission/ Commissioner in the State should be structured on the patterns of the Central Vigilance Commission. In larger States, the State Vigilance Commission should be a three Member Body with Members who have been experts in their respective fields. In smaller States, it may continue to be a single Member Body.

(c) The laws regarding the Lokayukta would need to be amended to incorporate the changes suggested in the Report on 'Ethics in Governance'.

Human Resource Development, Capacity Building and Training

Capacity Building in public administration needs to be characterized by several key considerations:

- Developing strategic human resources policies
- Investing in professional and executive development; proactive bridging of insufficiencies of knowledge and skills, preventing obsolescence both individual and organizational.
- Establishing flexible human resource systems to meet socio-technological and environmental changes in the public service, particularly in view of changing conceptions of the role of the State
- Transforming cultural attributes of the personnel, relating to their personality, character and behaviour.
- Establishing performance management systems that provide motivation and rewards for improved functioning
- Improving decision-making systems so as to provide full scope for the skills and capacities of civil servants

Training is universally recognized as a critical component of human resource development. It has become even more important in recent years due to rapid quantitative and qualitative changes taking place in all dimensions of public administration across the world. Citizen-centricity of programmes, use of ICT, primacy of Right to Information and emphasis on programmes of social sector development and on issues of environmental protection and conservation are rapidly making the classical bureaucratic skills obsolete. Economic policies which rely heavily on globalization and corporatisation have given a new direction to the paradigm of governance. The representatives of the Government now have to interact with a new class of awakened stakeholders; civil society, academics and technologists, which is quite different from the passive recipients of services of the earlier era. The new regime of public service management calls for an advanced set of knowledge, skills and attitudes from civil servants. But, the prevailing perception is that the Government functionaries lack the required professionalism and sensitivity to meet the higher expectations that the people have from the public services.

The Commission believes that in order to raise the overall quality and effectiveness of government functioning, capacity enhancement of government personnel is an issue of critical importance. The Commission has examined it in detail in its Report on 'Refurbishing of Personnel Administration' (Tenth Report) particularly with respect to All India and Group 'A' Central Services. Some of the important recommendations of this Report are:

a. Every government servant should undergo a mandatory training at the induction stage and also periodically during his/her career. Successful completion of these trainings should be a minimum necessary condition for confirmation in service and subsequent promotions. Mandatory induction trainings should be prescribed for Group D staff also before they are assigned postings.

b. A monitoring mechanism should be set up for overseeing the implementation of the National Training Policy (1996).

c. All civil servants should undergo mandatory training before each promotion and each officer/official should be evaluated after each training programme. Successful completion of the training programmes should be made mandatory for promotions.

d. The objective of mid-career training should be to develop domain knowledge and competence required for the changing job profile of the officer. To this end, mid career learning opportunities relevant to specific domains or specializations should be made available for officers.

e. Public servants should be encouraged to obtain higher academic qualifications and to write papers for reputed and authoritative journals.

f. A strong network of training institutions at the Union and State levels needs to be built up to cater to the training requirements of civil servants. However, instead of spreading resources over a large number of institutions, a few institutions should be identified for capacity building and up gradation.

g. The composition of governing bodies of the national training institutions such as thc Lal Bahadur Shastri National Academy of Administration, Sardar Vallabhbhai Patel National Police Academy, Indira Gandhi National Forest Academy and also the State Administrative Training Institutes should be broadened by inducting eminent experts. The governing bodies should be adequately empowered to enable them to discharge their functions efficiently.

While generally reiterating and re-emphasizing the above recommendations, the Commission would like to analyse a few issues which are of specific relevance to the State and District administration.

At the State level, there are more than three dozen provincial service cadres dealing with subjects such as - General

Administration, Police, Finance, Agriculture, Excise, Transport etc. which have continuous training needs.

In many of the States, the practice of putting new recruits on mandatory induction training is in vogue only in case of a few of the organised services, such as the Civil, Police, Forest and Finance Services. But even this training leaves much to be desired in terms of the duration of the course, its content and practical exposure. Probationers belonging to many of the other services are straightaway given field assignments. The concept of midcareer training and skill upgradation of senior State service officers has not found roots in the personnel policy of the State Governments.

Similarly, the importance and need of imparting training to Group 'C' and 'D' government officials too, has not been adequately recognized by many State Governments. In fact, it is this large body of officials which interacts frequently with citizens and thus the 'image' of the government depends significantly on how these functionaries conduct themselves both professionally and personally. Because of widespread poverty, illiteracy and excessive centralization of power, there prevails a culture of deference to public authorities. Over a period of time, the public servants develop a sense of superiority. This underscores the importance of making available training opportunities to them. Such trainings will upgrade their professional knowledge and skills and also bring about change in their mindset and attitude so that they become an effective instrument of service to the people. In States like Gujarat where such trainings have been conducted periodically, independent evaluations have revealed that they have brought change in the attitude and professional output of Government officials. Therefore, regular and well-designed trainings of Government officials at these levels should be a major thrust area in the training policy of State Governments.

Almost all the States have an Apex Training Institute/Academy (commonly known as the State Administrative Training Institute) whose primary responsibility is to cater to the training needs of the State administration. However, it has not been able to do so effectively. Firstly, the capacity of many Institutes is far too inadequate vis-a-vis the annual intake into the various Services. Secondly, the training effort in most of the States is disjointed, ad-hoc and not demand driven. There is disconnect between the training programme chalked out by the Institute and the skills/attributes requirement and the overall career development plan of the personnel of various departments. This is due to the fact that such training modules are often not part of the larger human resource development plan of the State. Therefore, there is need to reorganize the entire training system with a clear focus and strategy. Steps are needed to identify and assess the training needs of Government personnel at all levels. The content of the training programmes should be derived from such assessed needs. Thirdly, there is very little attention given to mid-career training needs of officials; which could enable them to respond appropriately to the rapid changes taking place in different sectors of public management. This needs to be addressed.

Adequate capacity building of the training institutions is one of the key factors responsible for the quality of training. As recommended by the Commission in its Tenth Report, the composition of governing bodies of the State Administrative Training Institutes should be broadened by inducting eminent experts. The governing bodies should be adequately empowered to enable them to discharge their functions efficiently.

Equally important is the process of selection of faculty which needs to be rigorous and transparent, in terms of attracting the most suitable professionals to join as trainers. Whereas a fair proportion of professionals may come from the open market and the academia, departmental officers who are deputed to such institutes should be selected on the basis of their competence and motivation for such assignments. Very often, 'unwanted' officers are pushed into training institutes. A scheme of incentives to attract talented and dedicated officers to this field would be necessary.

In addition, training activities have usually been subjected to insufficient budgeting because of the low priority accorded to it. For a meaningful HRD programme this sector needs to be given a higher priority in budget allocation. This could be done easily if a certain percentage of all scheme funds is earmarked for training and related activities. It is also not necessary for all trainings to be formally institutionalised. A large part of trainings can also be provided 'in situ' under the supervision of the head of the organization with appropriate support from a team of experts.

The Commission is of the view that every State should formulate a comprehensive human resource development policy with training as its main constituent. While doing so the broad parameters of the National Training Policy, 1996 may be kept in mind. Such a policy should address the issues raised in the preceding paragraphs. Simultaneously, a suitable monitoring mechanism to supervise the implementation of such policy may also be set up.

The Commission feels that there is need to somewhat disperse the existing unitary institutional arrangement and set-up adequately equipped training centres at the regional and the district levels (their number will depend on the specific requirement of the State). The Apex Institute should concentrate on all aspects of training of Class I and Class II officers, (both pre-induction as well as mid-career programmes). The Regional Institutes could look after the shorter training needs of the Class II officers and also run foundation courses for Class III recruits. It would also be desirable to have district level training organizations which could take care of the mid-career training needs of Class III employees. The district centre should also have proper facilities for skill / behavioral training of Class IV employees.

The Commission is further of the view that the State level apex training institute (the ATI) should be truly professional and autonomous and have an overall integrative and coordinating role for the entire training/orientation activity running in the State. It should act as the primary resource centre for level II and level III Training Institutes. It would also provide training to those who will work as trainers at the Regional and District Institutes. In course of time, it can undertake projects of distance learning and become a virtual academy of training for the entire State.

The State Administrative Training Institutes should have embedded in them Centers dealing with Good Governance and documentation and institutionalization of good practices - so that these are institutionalized and disseminated across States.

Recommendations

(a) The Commission reiterates its recommendations pertaining to capacity building and training made in the Report on 'Refurbishing of Personnel Administration' (Tenth Report).

(b) Every State should formulate a comprehensive Human Resource Development Policy with training as an important component on the lines of the National Training Policy, 1996. Simultaneously, a suitable monitoring mechanism to supervise the implementation of such policy may also be setup.

(c) In addition to the apex level training body called the Administrative Training Institute (ATI), adequate numbers of Regional Training Institutes should also be established at different places across the State. The Apex Institute should take care of the training needs of the Class I/Class II officers of the State services, whereas the Regional Training Institutes should deal with the mid-career training needs of Class II officers and induction training of Class III employees. Steps should also be taken to set-up district level training organizations which could take care of the mid-career training needs of Class III employees. The district centre should also have proper facilities for skill/behavioral training of Class IV recruits.

(d) In this arrangement, the apex body, the ATI should have an overall integrative and coordinating role for the entire training/orientation programme running in the State. It should act as the primary resource centre for Regional and District Training Institutes. It should also provide training to those who will work on their faculty. In course of time, the ATI can undertake projects of distance learning and become a virtual academy of training for the entire State.

(e) The State Administrative Training Institutes (ATIs) should have embedded in them, Centers of Good Governance.

STATE PUBLIC SERVICE COMMISSION

Articles 315 to 323 of the Constitution deal with Public Service Commissions both at the Union and the State level.

Article 320 of the Constitution of India lays down the functions of the State Public Service Commission. The functions of the State Public Service Commission are:

(i) It is the duty of the State Public Service Commission to conduct examinations for appointment to the services of the State.

(ii) The State Public Service Commission will be consulted by the State Government on the following issues:-

(a) on all matters relating to methods of recruitment to civil services and civil posts;

(b) on the principles to be followed while making appointments, promotions and transfers to civil services and posts;

(c) on all disciplinary matters of a person serving the government of a State in a civil capacity, including memorials or petitions relating to such matters;

(d) on any claim by a person, who is serving or has served the government in a civil capacity that any cost, incurred by him in defending legal proceedings instituted against him in respect of acts done or purporting to have been done in the execution of his duty, shall be paid out of the consolidated fund of the state;

(e) on any claim for the award of a pension in respect of injuries sustained by a person while serving under the government in a civil capacity and any question as to the amount of any such award.

(iii) The State Public Service Commission functions as an advisory body. It is the duty of the State Public Service Commission to advise on any matter, referred to it by the government.

In the early years of Independence, State Public Service Commissions throughout the country functioned well primarily on account of the fact that:

(a) There was objectivity in selection of competent and experienced people as Chairman and Members of the Commission. The government treated the Public Service Commission as a sacrosanct institution and the Chair-man and Members were either very senior government servants (drawn usually from the ICS) or academicians of high standing in their field.

(b) The Commissions enjoyed excellent reputation for objectivity, transparency and fairplay.

But in recent years, this Constitutional body has suffered extensive loss of reputation in many States, mainly on account of (a) charges of corruption, favoritism and nepotism in matters of recruitment and (b) use of archaic processes and procedures in its functioning which leads to inordinate delays. For example, the civil services examinations conducted by a State Public Service Commission take a minimum time period of one and half year to complete. In some cases, it may take even longer.

The following issues need to be examined in this context:-

(i) Appointment of Chairman and Members - issue of qualifications

(ii) Role and functions of the Public Service Commission

(iii) Its composition / strength

Appointment of Chairman/Members

Currently, the Chairman/Members of the State Public Service Commission are appointed by the Governor in accordance with provisions described in Article 316 of the Constitution.

This Article says

'316 (1) The Chairman and other members of a Public Service Commission shall be appointed, in the case of the Union Commission or a Joint Commission, by the President, and in the case of a State Commission, by the Governor of the State:

Provided that as nearly as may be one-half of the members of every Public Service Commission shall be persons who at the dates of their respective appointments have held office for at least ten years either under the Government of India or under the Government of a State, and in computing the said period of ten years any period before the commencement of this Constitution during which a person has held office under the Crown in India or under the Government of an Indian State shall being included.'

The Article provides for two kinds of membership for this body. As far as possible, one half of the strength has to come from government service (serving or retired). But, the qualification needed, for this category has not been explicitly defined. On a plain interpretation of the words, any person who has worked in the government for a period of ten years in any capacity is eligible to be appointed as the Chairman or a Member of the State Commission. Often, junior employees have been appointed on this august body and have been given the onerous task of (a) making direct recruitment to regular Class I / II, posts under the State Government and (b) presiding over the meetings of the departmental promotion committees to clear senior level promotions. Weak on merit and professional ability, such appointees have not been able to do justice to their work.

With regard to the second category of Members, the situation is even more ambiguous. The Constitution does not stipulate any qualification for them. The appointees could be from any field and with any qualification. In practice, this distorts the entire selection process. Choice, often, is made in favour of persons who do not have the appropriate background, training or experience. Fairplay and good traditions have thus become casualties.

As a result, there has been considerable erosion in the reputation and credibility of the Public Service Commissions in some States. This issue was also discussed in detail by the first ARC, and it made the following recommendations to improve their working and standards: -

1. In making appointment to a State Public Service Commission the Governor should consult the chairman of the Union Public Service Commission and the Chairman of the State Public Service Commission.
2. At least one member of the State Public Service Commission should belong to a different State.
3. The minimum academic qualification for membership of a Commission should be a university degree.
4. A member selected from among government officers should have held office under a State Government or the Union Government for at least ten years; and should have occupied the position of a Head of Department or Secretary to Government in a State or a comparable position in an institution of higher education.

5. Members selected from non-official should have practiced at least for ten years in any of the recongnised profession like teaching, law, medicine, engineering, science accountancy or administration.

The Commission is of the view that the intention behind creation of an autonomous Public Service Commission as a Constitutional authority was to create a body of achievers and ex-administrators who could select meritorious candidates for recruitment and promotion to various civil service positions under the State Government with utmost probity and transparency. There is need to take steps to ensure that only persons of high standing, intellectual ability and reputation are selected as Chairman and Members of the Public Service Commission.

Strength of the Public Service Commissions

The Constitution does not prescribe any limit on the strength of the Public Service Commission. By tradition, the size of this Body in the States has remained small. The Union Public Service Commission had a slightly larger strength.

The current position in this regard can be seen in Table 2.2

In recent years, some of the States such as Kerala and Tamil Nadu have increased the strength of their Public Service Commission to disproportionately large numbers. As discussed and recommended in the subsequent paragraphs, this Institution will need to confine itself to the recruitment of candidates only for higher level posts leaving the recruitment at junior levels to the subordinate recruiting bodies. Therefore, the Commission is of the view that there needs be a limit on the strength of the membership of the State Public Service Commission.

The Commission is of the view that both (a) the matter of appointment of Chairman/Members and their qualifications and (b) the matter of prescribing a limit for the strength of the Commission, are complex issues. There is need to evolve a national consensus on these two issues among the States through discussions/deliberations at the Inter-State Council.

Table 2.2 : Composition of the Public Service Commissions

Name of the State	Sanctioned Posts (Chairman + Members)	In position	Vacancy
Assam	1 + 6	Chairman - 1 Member - 5	1 Vacant
Bihar	1 + 6	Chairman - 1 Member - 4	2 Vacant
Chhattisgarh	1 + 4	Chairman -1 Members - 3	1 Vacant
Himachal Pradesh	1 + 3	Chairman - 1 Member - 2	1 Vacant
Karnataka	1 + 9	Chairman - 1 Members - 7	2 Vacant
Kerala	1 + 17	Chairman - 1 Members - 17	--
Madhya Pradesh	1 + 4	Chairman - 1 Members - 3	1 Vacant
Maharashtra	1 + 5	Chairman - 1 Members - 5	--
Manipur	1 + 2	Chairman - 1 Member - 2	--
Rajasthan	1 + 5	Chairman - 1 Members - 5	-- --
Sikkim	1 + 2	Chairman - 1 Member - 2	--
Tamil Nadu	1 + 14	Chairman - 1 Members - 14	--
Tripura	1 + 3	Chairman - 1 Member - 2	1 Vacant
Uttarakhand	1 + 4	Chairman - 1 Member - 2	2 Vacant
Uttar Pradesh	1 + 7	Chairman - 1 Members - 7	-- --
West Bengal	1 + 6	Chairman - 1 Member - 5	1 Vacant

Note: The UPSC consists of one Chairman and ten Members.
Source: Information received from various States.

Recommendations

(a) Steps should be taken to ensure that persons of high standing, intellectual ability and reputation are selected as Chairman/Members of the State Public Service Commissions. A limit should also be imposed on the strength of its membership.

(b) There is need to evolve national consensus among States on the issues of (i) appointment of Chairman/Members and (ii) limit on the membership of the Commission, through discussions/deliberations at the Inter-State Council.

Functions of the Public Service Commission; its relationship with the junior recruiting bodies

As mentioned above, Article 320 deals with the functions of the Public Service Commission. Article 320(3) describes matters on which Union Public Service Commission or the State Public Service Commission shall be consulted.

Currently a large chunk of employees in the State Government belong to Group 'C' (Class III) and Group 'D' (Class IV) categories. The Commission feels that the domain of the State Public Service Commission should be (a) recruitment of candidates for higher level posts (class I and Class II posts of various States Services) and (b) advising the government in senior level promotions through the Departmental Promotion Committee. The Commission should also handle recruitment / promotion to teaching posts in government Colleges and other fully funded units of the Universities. As regards recruitment of junior functionaries, the role of the State Public Service Commission would be to lay down the principles, norms and standards which need to be followed. The State Commission would act as a watch dog organization for public recruiting agencies like the Subordinate Service Commissions, Teachers Selection Commissions, District Recruitment Boards etc.

Such a reform, while ensuring adoption of public policies like those on reservations, would speed up recruitments, lead to adoption of common norms and procedures ensuring objectivity and encourage local aspirants for district and local level posts.

Recommendations

(a) The Public Service Commission should handle only (i) recruitment of candidates for higher level posts under the State Government (Class I and Class II positions of various State cadres), (ii) advising government on senior level promotions through the DPC and (iii) recruitment and promotions to teaching posts in government Colleges and fully funded units of the Universities.

(b) With regard to the appointment of junior level functionaries of the State Government, the role of the State Public Service Commission should be to lay down broad norms and standards. The recruiting organisations concerned such as the Subordinate Service Commission, the School Teachers Selection Commission and District Recruitment Boards should follow these norms and standards in their working. The State Public Service Commission would act as a watch dog.

3

District Administration

INTRODUCTION

Historically the district, in some form or the other has been the most important unit of administration in the Indian sub-continent. The evolution of district administration in Mughal times and those of the East India Company has to be understood in light of the fact that neither had a legislative wing. Executive commands originated from the Emperor or the Governor General, or from the provincial governors, and were executed by the subprovincial authorities, howsoever designated.

The British Paliament was the first legislature in respect of India in modern times and enactments created and gave substance to the district head of administration, known variously as the Collector (in respect of revenue administration), the District Magistrate (in respect of administration of criminal justice) or the Deputy Commissioner (in respect of General Aministration and special functions / powers under local tenancy laws.*

Until the 73rd and 74th amendments to the Constitution, the governance structure of India was two-tiered comprising the Union Government and the State Governments. At the district level, apart from discharging the responsibilities cast by specific enactments, the Collectors performed such administrative tasks

* In this report the terms "Collector", "District Magistrate" and "Deputy Commissioner" will be used interchangeably.

as were assigned to them by the State governments. After Independence, the single greatest accretion to the responsibilities of the district administrator came through expension of rural development programmes. As the number of activities, institutions and departments involved in rural development increased, the coordinating and synthesizing role of the Collector in the development efforts of the government assumed greater importance.

With the constitutionally mandated establishment of Panachayati Raj Institutions and Municipal bodies, it has become necessary to re-examine and re-define the role of the district administration. It is imperative that the devolution of decision making to local levels should face no impediments. It is equally imperative that the unique administrative experience, expertise and credibility of the office of the District Collector built up over a period of two hundred years is properly utilized.

STATE AND DISTRICT ADMINISTATION

The linkages and relationship between the State government and the District Collector cannot be examined in isolation from the linkages existing between the district offices and local bodies. There is a high degree of complementarity between them. This chapter, examines their functioning and tries to suggest an environment for a responsive and citizen friendly district administration in line with the principles of decentralization and subsidiarity.

The overall administrative structure presently prevailing at the district and sub-district levels in the country consists of the following three components:

(A) Administration of regulatory functions under the leadership of the Collector and District Magistrate, such as law and order, land revenue / reforms, excise, registration, treasury, civil supplies and social welfare. This domain also includes oversight over primary departments of the government e.g. agriculture, animal husbandry, and primary and school education.

(B) District / sub-district level offices of the line departments of the State Government and their agencies, such as PWD, irrigation, health, industries etc. which have had stronger accountability relationship with the State headquarters rather than with the District Collector.

(C) Local bodies (Panchayati Raj Institutions and Municipal bodies) which, after the 73rd and 74th amendment of the Constitution, have become the third tier of government and are to be empowered to handle subjects pertaining to development of the local areas as illustratively listed in the Eleventh and Twelfth Schedule of the Constitution.

THE INSTITUTION OF DISTRICT COLLECTOR/ DEPUTY COMMISSIONER

Till some years ago, in most of the States, the District Collector was the head of the government at the district level, responsible for a diverse portfolio of functions ranging from delivery of essential services, land revenue administration, execution of rural development programmes, disaster management, maintenance of law and order and collection of excise and transport revenue. As such, virtually all the instruments of the State Government that operated at the local levels did so in conjunction with the Collector's office either formally or informally. In this regard, structurally diverse arrangements were built up over time. The relationships and reporting structures range from the Collectors undertaking broad oversight/supervision of the activities undertaken by line departments- to specific day-today management of some services. For many State Government bodies, the Collector had an important role in determining how, where and what quantity of their services were to be delivered. In recent years, however, the departments have tended to function increasingly as vertical silos up to the State level and, as stated above, the gradual empowerment of local governments is changing the role played by the District Collector in matters of local development.

Evolution and Change

Till the 1960s, when programmes of rural development were at a nascent stage, the Collector's job seemed to be carefully organized with land reforms, revenue collection, law and order, food and civil supplies, welfare and relief/rehabilitation being the principal areas of his responsibility. The needs of the people were limited, their interaction with the government was infrequent and the bureaucratic set up seemed to be dedicated. Under these circumstances, the office of the Collector was a strong and effective institution.

In the years that followed, a large number of new projects/ schemes were initiated by various departments of the Government, with the Collector as the notional head of the District Monitoring Committee. Apart from making a formal review in monthly/ quarterly coordination meetings, the Collector had a somewhat limited role in such matters. Towards the beginning of the 1980s, the development of rural areas got a further thrust and the government initiated a large number of Centrally Sponsored/ State sector schemes in agriculture, rural development, primary education and healthcare. Though, separate instruments were created for their execution, the Collector, in most of the cases, was given the overall supervisory charge of the programmes in the districts. The Collector and his administration were expected to be omniscient and omnipotent; capable of providing solutions to all the problems.

But after the introduction of the Panchayati Raj system in the country (post 1993), most of the development functions have been taken away from the Collector's domain, although the State Governments feel it convenient to use this institution to exercise control over the PRIs.

Need for a Collector in the District

The post of District Collector has been the most important feature of field administration in India for the last two hundred years. Before Independence, when the economy was primarily agrarian, the Collector as head of the land revenue administration also enjoying wide powers under criminal laws, was considered the ultimate guardian figure - responsible for the well being of residents in his jurisdiction - the representative of the British Empire, capable of doing anything and everything. In the post Independence era, when the economy diversified, and the pace of industrialization and growth of tertiary activities picked up, other functionaries too gained in importance. But, even now, in most parts of the country, excepting metropolitan/mega cities, the Collector is the most recognized face of the administration; he is considered to be the principal representative of the government at the district level, who could be approached to solve virtually all problems ranging from land disputes, to scarcity of essential commodities, to inadequacy of relief in times of crisis, to community disputes and even to issues of family discords. As Rajni Kothari observed:

> "the office of the Collector as the Chief Representative of the Government in the District is, in many ways, unique and its supposed stature and authority have engendered a sort of institutionalized charisma that is in some ways unparalleled in modern administrative development. "

In this context, the Prime Minister's Address at the District Magistrate's Conference on May 20, 2005 is of particular significance:-

> "The Collector or the District Magistrate remains even today the linchpin of the administrative system in India more than a hundred years after the creation of this Institution by the British....
>
> Indeed, revenue collection is the least important of tasks today. You have become agents of change, of good governance and development administration at the very base of our democratic structure. The insights you gain during your tenure at the district level stands you in good stead throughout your career because it gives you a first hand

experience in dealing with the hopes and aspirations, the lives and livelihoods of our people. The State and Central Governments benefit immensely from this district level administrative experience very early in the lives of our administrators....

In this redefined role of the Government, the cutting edge of a Government's function is at the district and lower levels. I think someone said India lives in States, I could amplify that to say that India lives in districts. Therefore, the provision of education and health facilities for improving human infrastructure, provision of physical infrastructure, improving economic opportunities for marginalised sections of society, preparing the society at large to face the challenge of disasters - natural disaster as well as manmade disasters - and who can forget the role of terrorism in disturbing all civilised societies in the world that we live in. We have to be prepared to meet all this challenges. And these are all functions which are best performed by local bodies and district administrations. As we sit in Delhi and try to design a template for a humane, caring and prosperous India, we are aware of the criticality of your role in this process – your role in ensuring good governance at the grassroots, in promoting innovation, in improving service delivery, in enhancing public private partnerships and in ensuring outlays become outcomes. I believe that unless we reform governance from the village level upwards, there can be no real reform at the National level. And what I heard this morning gives me confidence that we have men and women in this room who can be trusted to be active agents of improving the quality of our governance in the years to come....

We have also had a major shift in our administration through the 73rd and 74th Constitutional Amendments, which sought to revitalise local bodies and create elected representatives down the line. Though this was expected to whittle down the powers of the Collector, our historical

> experience is that the role of the Collector has only been transformed into a more powerful one of coordinator, facilitator and a person who is responsible for inter-sectoral coordination of various activities that characterise the work of our grassroot administration....
>
> Many of the challenges that you face in your district, be it the education challenge, the water challenge, the health challenge or the employment challenge, the solution may lie in enabling people to handle change and improving service delivery. A Collector therefore can provide a leadership to this task of nation building...."

The Commission had examined the issue of whether there is any need to retain the office of the District Collector in its present form in its Report on Local Governance. There is a view that with the empowerment of PRIs/ULBs in the districts, there is need to devise an environment in which the institution of District Collector gradually loses importance and ultimately recedes into a district level land revenue functionary, responsible to the local bodies. This view is based on the belief that the strong traditions linked with this institution and its recognition in the public mind as the prime mover of governance at the district level would tend to impede growth of any other authority at that level.

The counter view is that the office of the District Collector has risen to this level of importance and utility through many national and local crises and it should not be weakened.

Though as per the new administrative and development environment, PRIs/ULBs are the third tier of government, they do not totally remove the Collector's responsibility in matters of local development. The declining significance of land revenue has also not lessened the importance of the Collector in the management of land records, the maintenance of law and order and general administration and as an effective grievance redressal authority. These have remained and will remain central and core areas of State activities at the district level even when there is full fructification of local self-government. The Collector will thus continue to be responsible for a multiplicity of tasks at the district level such as improving human capabilities, creating physical infrastructure, improving economic opportunities for marginalized sections of society and facing challenges posed by disasters. He will have a new role that is the role of a coordinator, facilitator and a person who is responsible for inter-sectoral coordination of various activities that characterise the work of our grassroots administration. He is the functionary who would provide overall leadership in the district in the task of nation building. Hence, the Collector would remain a key figure in the scheme of administration at the field level.

The Commission has therefore expressed its view in its Report on "Local Governance" that a representative District Government should be empowered while fully utilizing the institutional strength of the District Collector.

Redefining the Collector's Role:

A Wide Mandate

At present the portfolio of the Collector's office generally includes the following functions and activities (though there may be variations across the States):-

- acting as the Head of Land and Revenue Administration, including responsibility for District Finance (expenditure and audit);
- acting as the District Head of the Executive Magistracy and overall supervision of law and order and security and some say in the police matters;
- as Licensing and Regulatory Authority in respect of the various special laws such as Arms, Explosive and Cinematography Acts etc. in the District;
- conduct of elections – for Parliament, State Legislature and Local Bodies;
- as the Officer-in-charge of Disaster Management;

- as the guardian of public lands with the responsibility to prevent and remove encroachments which are often a source of tension between vested interests and the district administration;
- public service delivery, either by facilitating or directly delivering services assigned to the district administration from other departments. (In this respect, the Collector often acts as Chairman of the Board for Parastatals, or as Chairman or Member of various standing and inter-departmental committees);
- facilitation of interaction between civil society and the State Government;
- handling issues of local cadre management such as recruitment, in-service training and promotion; and
- as the Chief Information and Grievance Redressal Officer of the district.

The details of these functions are given in Table 3.1.

The District Collector/Magistrate has specific powers entrusted to him under several Union and State enactments. These statutory powers have to be exercised with care and

Box No. 3.1

Role of District Collector in the Health Sector

NRHM is a programme which falls under the domain of the Zila Parishad. In Uttarakhand the Collector is the Co-chairman of the District Health Society.

Under the scheme of Rogi Kalyan Samiti – the District Magistrate is the Chairman of the Board of Governance for management of the District Hospital – Guidelines of the MOHFW.

In West Bengal, the core team at the District (to monitor the working of ASHA) is headed by the District Magistrate.

In Orissa, the District Magistrate is the Chairman of the District Health Society.

responsibility. The Commission noted that some Collectors were not even aware of all the laws under which they are empowered.

The Collector is also the Chairman of a large number of Committees at the district level. A list of the Committees chaired by the District Collector in Anantapur District of Andhra Pradesh was obtained from the Collector and is given below as an illustration (the Collector indicated that the names of some Committees might be missing from the list):

1. Irrigation Development Board (IDB)
2. Vigilance & Monitoring Committee on SC/ST Atrocities
3. District Forestry Advisory Committee
4. AP Water, Land & Tree Act Implementation Committee (APWALTA Act)
5. District Rajak Welfare Committee
6. District Naibrambana Welfare Committee
7. District Joint Staff Council Committee – Employees Unions/Associations
8. AP Employees Welfare Fund District Committee
9. Registration of Existing & New Aquaculture Fish Ponds Committee
10. District Midday Meals Monitoring Committee (Primary Education)
11. District Selection Committee for Recruitment of Teachers
12. District BC Service Co-operative Society
13. District ST Sub-plan
14. District SC Service Co-operative Society Ltd.
15. District Task Force Committee of Mines & Geology
16. District Hospital Development Society
17. District Level Review Committee of Bankers
18. District Consultative Committee of Bankers
19. District Advisory Committee for Renewable Energy (NEDCAP)

Table 3.1: Functions of the District Collector/Deputy Commissioner

Sl. No	Functional Area	Role of Deputy Commissioner/ District Collector (DC)	Variances across Select States
1.	Revenue Administration	The Collector handles all matters connected with land reforms and revenue administration (including custody of government lands). He is assisted by an Additional Collector / Joint Collector. Collector is the officer-in charge of the district under the State Excise Act.	Similar across different States
2.	Executive Magistracy and Maintenance of law and order	As the Magistrate of the District, exercises functions and powers under various provisions of the Cr.PC. Is the Officer in overall charge of Law and Order and internal security in the district. Is the authority to issue custody/detention warrants under special anti-crime/security enactments e.g. NSA. Retains importance in Police matters too e.g. under Bihar Police Act 2007, the Collector is the Chairman of the District	Varies from State to State though Cr.P.C. functions are broadly similar.

		Accountability Authority which monitors issues concerning departmental inquiries and complaints of misconduct against junior policemen.	
3.	Licensing and Regulatory Authority	The Collector is the licensing and regulatory authority under various special laws such as Arms and Cinematography Acts etc. in the district.	Similar across different States
4.	Disaster Management	The Relief /Disaster Management branch of the Collector's office deals directly with these functions.	Similar across different States
5.	Elections	The Collector is the District Election Officer for Parliament, State Legislature and Local Bodies.	Similar across different States
6.	Food and Civil Supplies	In most States, the Collector has a direct role to play in the functioning of the Food and Civil Supplies Department at the district level. He oversees the implementation of the Public Distribution System and has powers to enforce provisions of the Essential Commodities Act and related Rules and Orders.	Similar across different States

Sl. No	Functional Area	Role of Deputy Commissioner/ District Collector (DC)	Variances across Select States
7.	Welfare	The Collector plays a very critical role in the execution of welfare programmes such as those relating to disability, old age pension etc. either through direct superintendence or through oversight.	Varies from State to State depending on the role envisaged in this regard for local bodies. In Maharashtra, Zila Parishad (ZP) has a stronger role in welfare activities unlike in Andhra Pradesh or Rajasthan.
8.	Census	The Collector is the principal Census Officer.	Similar across different States
9.	Coordination	One of the most important roles of the Collector is to coordinate activities of other agencies/departments at the district level	Similar across different States
10.	Economic Development (Agriculture, Irrigation, Industry, etc.)	Though, many activities/functions of these sectors stand transferred to PRIs and local bodies, the Collector still has some role in many of these programmes. He chairs meetings of various Committees of	Varies from State to State depending on the role envisaged in this regard for local bodies. In Maharashtra and

		Agriculture, Animal Husbandry, Veterinary, Sericulture, Handlooms, Textiles, Irrigation and Industries departments. Also reviews their activities in monthly/bimonthly meetings and coordinates among the departments.	Himachal Pradesh, the ZP has a stronger role in primary economic development activities unlike that in Andhra Pradesh or Rajasthan.
11.	Human Resource Development	Though, a major part of this subject (primary education) stands transferred to the PRIs, the District Collector/Deputy Commissioner has been retained as Chairman/Co-Chairman in some of the district level committees. have been given to PRIs in	Varies from State to State depending on the role envisaged in this regard for local bodies. In Maharashtra and Himachal Pradesh, powers
matters relating to health &			primary education.
12.	Rural Development	Though major activities of this department stand transferred to the PRIs/ULBs, in some States, the Collector still continues to be the nodal authority for some programmes. Under the National Rural Employment Guarantee Act, the Collector has been designated as the District Programme Coordinator in some of the States.	In Andhra Pradesh, the DC is the Executive Director of District Rural Development Agency. In Maharashtra and Himachal Pradesh, DRDA is under the ZP. In Himachal Pradesh, the ZPs have been

Sl. No	Functional Area	Role of Deputy Commissioner/ District Collector (DC)	Variances across Select States
			empowered to appoint Assistant Engineers in DRDA.
13.	Local Self Government (PRIs / ULBs)	The role of the District Collector/ Deputy Commissioner with regard to local self governing institutions varies across different States. Mostly these relate to the powers of the State Government *visà-vis* the PRIs. (Powers of suspension, resolution, supersession etc.)	In Andhra Pradesh, the DC exercises direct control over the Gram Panchayats; in Orissa, the DC is the CEO of the ZP; in Maharashtra, the DC has a limited role to play.
14.	Preparation of Development Plan	Though under Articles 243-ZD and 243-ZE, the planning functions in a district have been given to DPC/MPC, the Collector coordinates with departments/ agencies involved in execution of various works.	Similar across different States.
15.	Information Technology	The Collector exercises superintendence over the District NIC Centre.	Similar across different States.

20. District Statue Committee
21. District Official Language Committee
22. District Disaster Management Committee
23. District Executive Committee for 108 Emergency Services
24. District Level Minimum Wages Committee for Unskilled Labourers
25. District Horticulture Mission
26. District AIDS Prevention and Control Society
27. District Tourism Committee
28. District Negotiation Committee for Finalization of Market Value of Lands purchased for acquisition
29. District Committee on Regularization of Encroachments
30. District Arms Purchase Committee
31. District Road Safety Committee
32. District RTA Committee (Regional Transport Authority)
33. ATMA Committee (Agriculture)
34. District Level Committee for TRICOR
35. District Selection Committee for Recruitment of Doctors on Contract Basis
36. District Level Co-ordination Committee for Women Development and Child Welfare (ICDS)
37. District Selection Committee for recruitment of Anganwadi Workers and Anganwadi Helpers. (ICDS)
38. District Level Committee for Implementation of Girl Child Protection Scheme (ICDS)
39. District Level Committee for Anti Trafficking (ICDS)
40. District Level Committee for CM/PM package (Pasukranthi/Kaheera Kranthi)
41. Andhra Pradesh Micro Irrigation Project, Anantapur
42. District Food Advisory Committee

43. Anantapur Society for Employment and Training (ANSET)
44. Urban Market Value Anomalies Rectification Committee (Registration Department)
45. Management Committee for AP Study Circle for BCs
46. District Single Window Clearance Committee (Industries Department)
47. District Level Committee for Incentives (Industries Department)
48. District Level PMRY Committee (Industries Department)
49. District Industries Promotion Committee (DIC)
50. District Level Juvenile Welfare Committee

To give another example, as per the findings of a study report prepared by the CGG, Hyderabad for the Department of Administrative Reforms and Public Grievances, Government of India, a Deputy Commissioner in Assam is the Chairman of 43 district level committees. In its interactions with some of the Collectors, the Commission noted that many of them were not fully aware of how many committees they are required to preside over.

Besides, there may be other important organizations functioning in the district such as the Red Cross Society, a Degree College or Sports Associations which may be also headed by the Collector. Often, the Collector is appointed as the Chairman of a Committee to manage a major trust/endowment located in the district.

Such widespread functions without well defined roles result in lack of clarity and diffusion of the Collector's responsibilities.aAlso, after the establishment of PRIs / ULBs as the third tier of government, there is no need to assign any role/ function to the Collector in respect of activities which are transferred by the State Government to these bodies.aAs such, the Commission is of the view that there is need to redefine the role and responsibilities of the Collector in a clear manner.

His job profile should consist of (a) a well defined set of exclusive activities both statutory as well as non-statutory as a functionary of the State Government (b) the general work of coordination with various departments / agencies of the State and the Union Governments at the district level and (c) in the interim period till the time the local elected Institutions mature into District Government – as the Chief Executive Officer of the proposed District Council.

The main functions of the Collector may now include:

(i) Land and Revenue administration, land acquisition, custodian of government lands and properties, registration, recovery of public demand

(ii) Executive magistracy and maintenance of Law and Order, Internal Security, Prisons, Remand/ Juvenile Homes

(iii) Licensing and regulatory functions with respect to various special laws pertaining to Arms, Explosives, Cinemas etc.

(iv) Disaster Management

(v) Civil supplies, public distribution and social welfare

(vi) Excise

(vii) Transport

(viii) Mining

(ix) Labour Laws

(x) Elections

(xi) Legal Affairs

(xii) Census

(xiii) Protocol, general administration,

(xiv) Treasury management / district accounts office related work

(xv) Public Relations Department, NIC and other miscellaneous functions assigned by the State Government, coordination with civil society

(xvi) Coordination with line departments / other agencies of the State and Union Governments

(xvii) In the interim period – till the local institutions obtain adequate maturity – as Chief Officer of the proposed District Government

Land and Revenue Administration

The land revenue administration in a State operates at four administrative levels – district, sub-division, tehsil/taluka/block and village. The Collector/Deputy Commissioner is the head of the revenue administration at the district level and is the custodian of government land and properties under his jurisdiction. He is assisted by the Additional Collector(s) and other officers of the State Civil Service. The revenue work at the Collectorate is divided into various Sections headed by a Superintendent who in turn, is assisted by ministerial staff.

Each district comprises of revenue sub-divisions. The sub-divisional level revenue offices are supervised by Deputy Collectors/Extra Asst Commissioners who are designated as sub-divisional officers under whom other subordinates such as officials in charge of revenue circles work. Sub-Divisional level officers of various departments such as Food and Civil Supplies, Excise, Social Welfare etc. work as branch officers of their district establishments.

Within each (sub) division, there exist a number of blocks/ talukas/tehsils. The tehsil/block level revenue offices are headed by Tehsildars/COs. It is at this level that there is a direct interface of the government with the public and the image of the Revenue Administration largely depends on the efficient and effective functioning of these officials. At the village level, the States usually, have a designated revenue official called Patwari/ Revenue Karamchari. In some States, the Executive Officer of the Gram Panchayat or GP Secretary may double up as the Patwari to handle revenue functions as well.

The revenue functions performed by the Revenue/Regulatory Department in Andhra Pradesh are given in the Table 3.2 below:

Table 3.2 : Function of the Revenue Department

Functions relating to Revenue Collection

- Water Tax
- Non-Agricultural Land Assessment Act, 1963
- Miscellaneous arrears
- Dues by courts
- Road cess
- Loans
- Public Premises Act.
- Irrigation sources Inspection
- Joint Azmoish (a survey assessment at the spot)
- Land Disputes
- Revenue sadassu (administrative meeting of the beneficiary group, officials and farmers) (Kisan Darbar/Sabha)
- Jamabandi

Functions relating to Land Records

- Pahanis/Adangals Maintenance
- Inspection and booking of crops
- Certified copies of Land Records and Khasra Pahanis
- Inspection of survey stones and their maintenance
- Maintenance of Government Land Registers
- Maintenance and Updation of Land Records
- Permanent Settlement Register / Sethwars
- FMBs
- Village Maps
- Village Accounts
- Demand Collection & Billing

Functions relating to the Record of Rights

- Pattadar Pass Book and Transfer Deeds
- Maintenance of Form I-A and I-B Registers
- Form 17 Registers

(*contd.*)

- Sanction of Succession & Transfer of Registry
- Amendments
- Record of Rights (ROR) Appeals
- Disposal of Form X claims

Functions relating to Land Reforms

- Andhra Pradesh Fragmentation and Consolidation of Holdings Act, 1956
- Andhra Area Tenancy Act, 1956
- Inam Abolition
- Atiyat
- Agricultural Land Ceiling Act
- Urban Land Ceiling Act
- A.P Estate Abolition Act
- Jagir Abolition Regulation
- Land Transfer Regulation

Functions relating to Land Use Management

- Assignment of Government Land for Agriculture and House site purpose.
- Land Acquisition for public purpose.
- Disposal of Government land by alienation, transfer and lease.
- Protection of Government Lands, tanks from unauthorised encroachments and eviction Homestead Act
- A.P. Assigned Lands (POT) Act, 1977.
- Assignment Committee Meetings.
- Disposal of ceiling surplus lands.
- A P Land Protection Act, 1982.

Land Title Management System

States have passed their own Land Revenue Acts which govern the land title management system. But the system of maintaining land records remains unchanged from the pre-Independence era. The State Revenue Law has created the 'Land Revenue' machinery consisting of functionaries such as the Commissioner, the Collector, Assitant Collector, Tahsildar, Revenue Inspector, Patwari etc. The village is the basic administrative unit and the Patwariais charged with the responsibility of maintaining the land records in the village. The land title management system basically consists of two components – (i) Survey of lands and (ii) Settlement procedure. Survey deals with actual measurement of land and converting them into maps, whereas Settlement deals with issues of ownership and other details. At the State level, the overall guidance and policy direction for land management is provided by the Revenue Department. The responsibility for measuring lands and registering the title holder at that point of time is entrusted to the Survey and Settlement Department, which during the period of these operations has its legally empowered functionaries up to the taluka level. Once, the survey and settlement operations are over, the newly created permanent revenue records are handed over to the Collector's office. Thereafter maintenance of records and carrying out necessary changes in the rent registers / other revenue documents on the basis of transfer deeds (sale/purchase gift etc.) become the task of the Collector, who discharges this through the 'tahsildars', revenue inspectors, and 'patwaris'.

The system of land records management varies from State to State depending upon their historical evolution and local traditions. Several departments are involved in managing land records in most of the States, and the citizen has to approach more than one agency for complete land records, e.g. Revenue Department for textual records and mutations; Survey & Settlement (or Consolidation) Department for the maps; Registration Department for verification of encumbrances and registration of transfer, mortgage, etc; the Panchayats (in some States) for mutation, and the municipal authorities for urban land records. These departments work in a stand-alone manner, and updating of records by any one of them makes the records of the others outdated. Thus, the records are usually outdated and do not reflect the ground realities. Also, there is no integration of textual and spatial records, making it difficult to give maps-to-scale with the Records of Rights (RoRs). Further, the most important activity for updating the records, i.e., survey has been neglected in most of the States. Original survey for cadastral mapping has not taken place in many parts of the country.

The Commission in its Eleventh Report has made the following recommendations:

Recommendations

a. Surveys and measurements need to be carried out in a mission mode utilizing modern technology to arrive at a correct picture of land holdings and land parcels and rectification of outdated maps.

b. This needs to be accompanied by an analysis of the existing mechanism for updating land records – which varies from State to Tate – to be supplanted by an improved and strengthened mechanism which ensures that all future transactions in titles are immediately reflected in the land records. Such a system should be able to detect changes in titles through various means – namely, succession, will, partition, gift, survivorship etc. and update records accordingly.

c. The dispute resolution mechanism with regard to land titles needs to be strengthened in order to be compatible with the demands made on it.

d. In case of urban areas, a similar exercise needs to be undertaken especially since measurements and surveys have not been done in many of such areas and even record of titles is not available in most cities.

The Commission would like to reiterate these recommendations. The Commission would also like to emphasise that the tasks mentioned above should be one of the primary duties of the District Collector.

Maintenance of Law and Order, Executive Magistracy, Prisons, Remand/Juvenile Homes, Cinemas, Arms and Explosives, Special Security Enactments

The Collector is the Magistrate of the district and he exercises extensive powers under various Sections of the Cr.P.C. Through powers given to him under Sections 106 to 124 of the Cr.P.C., he and the magistracy of the district can bind the people to maintain peace, security and good behaviour. He also exercises powers for maintenance of public order and tranquility through Sections 129 to 148 of the Cr.P.C. Though the recent amendments in the Police Acts by various States have removed the clause which placed the police of the district under the general control and direction of the District Magistrate, the Collector still continues to be recognized by people as the overall in-charge of law and order in his jurisdiction. Deployment and movement of armed forces in the district in times of emergency and crisis is done under his guidance. He is the authority who issues various kinds of licenses in the district (under Arms, Explosives, Cinematography Acts etc.). In many States, it is the Collector who is the overall supervisory authority responsible for proper management of jails and remand/juvenile homes in the district. He is also the authority empowered to issue detention orders / custody warrants under Special Security/Anticrime laws.

Disaster Management

Disasters both natural as well as man-made such as floods, drought, forest fires, earthquakes, factory fires, major accidents, environmental mishaps and riots etc., pose a big threat to the lives and properties of the people in the districts. Some districts are more prone to specific types of disasters than others and hence they require measures for continuous vigilance monitoring and prevention. The Collector is the Chairman of the District Disaster Management Committee (DDMC), which is responsible for making advance, plans to mitigate the effect of calamities and for providing both immediate as well as long term assistance to the affected people. The assistance may be in terms of rescue, immediate shelter, availability of food and emergent healthcare. The Collector is authorized by the government to grant gratuitous relief to the affected families and to take such measures as are necessary to reduce hardships caused by the disaster.

Civil Supplies, Public distribution and Social Welfare

The Collector oversees the arrangements for provision of essential commodities to citizens through the Public Distribution System (PDS). The PDS operates through a chain of fair price shops that issue rationed quantities of wheat, rice, sugar, kerosene, etc. at subsidized rates to various categories of less privileged people through ration cards. The District Food and Supply Officer controls and supervises the activities of these shops under overall superintendence of the Collector. This department has the responsibility to ensure that basic commodities such as foodgrains, sugar, oil, coal, etc. remain available to the people at the reasonable prices in the district. It has powers to penalize the hoarders of essential commodities, take steps to deal with adulteration in diesel/petrol/other commodities and to ensure proper usage of weights and measures etc.

Excise, Transport, Mining, Labour Laws, Elections and Legal Affairs

The Collector provides substantial contribution to the State budget through excise and transport revenue. He is the controlling officers for subordinate formations of these two departments in the district. For excise functions, he is assisted by Assistant/ Deputy Excise Commissioners/Superintendent and Excise Inspectors whereas the District Transport Officer, one or two Motor Vehicle Inspectors and Enforcement Officers help him in collection of transport revenue.

The Collector is the Chief Mining officer of the district and exercises powers to grant prospecting license and mining lease under provisions of the Mines and Minerals (development and regulation) Act, 1957. The Collector has also been vested with powers under some labour laws such as Bonded Labour (Abolition) Act 1976 and Workmen's Compensation Act, 1923.

For elections, the Collector is the District Election Officer (DEO) and is responsible for (a) preparation / updation of electoral rolls and (b) for holding free and fair elections in his jurisdiction. Under election laws, he is the Returning Officer (RO) for the Parliamentary elections. In other cases, his juniors function as Returning Officers; but he still remains the District Election Officer.

The Collector is the principal officer of the State Law Department at the district level and in this capacity he has a major role in the appointment of Government Counsels for District Courts.

Census, Protocol, General Administration, Treasury Management/District Accounts Office related Work

The Collector is the overall in-charge of the Treasury in the district and is responsible for sending detailed accounts of financial transactions taking place in the district to the office of the Accountant General. He is also responsible for census, protocol and other related works.

Exercising Functions and Powers under various Union and State Laws

The Collector exercises several functions and powers under a large number of Union and State Laws on a diverse range of subjects such as those dealing with Land Acquisition, Tenancy of Land, Abolition of Debt Bondage, Money Lending, manufacture and sale of liquor and opium, settlement in Forests, distribution of essential commodities, Arms & Explosives, encroachment on government land, granting license for minor minerals, conduct of Exams, recovery of Public Demands, grant of Homestead, Workmens Compensation and regulation of *Sarais* and Inns.

Public Relations Department, NIC, Other miscellaneous functions assigned by the State Government/coordination with civil society

The Collector is the head of the public relations department of the government at the district level and is responsible for disseminating information on the working of the government to the print and electronic media and the general public.

Coordination with line departments/other agencies of the State/Union Government

Coordination among various departments of the State Governments is one of the major activities of the District Collector. Most of the State Governments give due regard to the views of the Collector whenever there is need for inter-departmental interaction at the field level. Even other agencies look to him for guidance and support for effective implementation of their programmes and activities.

As Chief Officer of the Proposed District Government

As per recommendations made earlier, each district would ultimately need to have a District Council comprising of representatives of both rural and urban bodies. The District Collector would function as the Chief Officer of this Council. The District Collector-*cum*-Chief Officer would have dual responsibility and would be fully accountable to the elected District Government on all local matters, and to the State Government on all regulatory matters not delegated to the District Government.

The Commission believes that the functions described in the above categories are of critical importance to the effective functioning of the government at the field level andathe workload involved in the domain of these activities demands considerable time and attention of the District Collector and his direct subordinates. The State Government should ensure that the responsibility of the District Collector is neither diluted nor diverted from these activities.

Implementation of Right to Information Act at the District Level

The Right to Information Act, 2005 is a landmark legislation which is increasingly being viewed as an important tool for empowerment of the poor and the weak. Availability of information to the general public and clarity about functioning of governmental institutions are essential components of good governance. This Act promotes transparency, accountability, predictability and participation. A whole set of institutions has been created at the national as well as at the state level to ensure that organizations of the government comply with the provisions of the Act and enhance citizen centricity in governance. It is now more than three years since the law was enacted. There is a common perception that the impact of this legislation has not percolated in a significant way beyond the State capital. The Commission feels that the functioning of the lower level officials of the State and District Administration should be much more responsive and proactive to the needs and concerns of the citizen. There is need to strengthen the compliance machinery at the district level to enforce provisions of the RTI Act and to reduce the element of delay and subjectivity in the functioning of the lower level formations of the government. This could be done by creating a special RTI Cell in the office of the Collector, whose functions could be reviewed by the Collector himself at regular periodicity.

Experienced Officers as District Collectors

Currently in many States, IAS officers are posted as Collectors/District Magistrates soon after they get their senior scale i.e., on completion of about four years of service. Since the duration of the institutional training for All India Service officers itself is of two years, his entire repertoire of public administration consists of two years of work either in the field as Sub Divisional Magistrate or as an Under Secretary in the State Secretariat, when he, is catapulted to this post of immense responsibility.

A Collector/District Magistrate functions as the repre-sentative of the government at the district level and coordinates the activities of officers of other departments of the State Government, many of whom would have put in significantly larger number of years in the government service. Increased political consciousness, high expectations of the public and the complex requirements of modern day administration demand that officers should have, apart from ability, experience both in the field and Secretariat and the maturity to work in this important assignment. In other words the experience of officers posted should be commensurate with the problems and complexities of the district and to that extent there is a strong case for posting officers of sufficient seniority as Collector/District Magistrate particularly in districts with large populations and a history of administrative complexities.

The Commission is, therefore, of the view that while officers could usually, be posted as Collectors/District Magistrates in their early career, in complex and problemprone districts, an IAS officer should be posted as Collector/District Magistrate only on completion of 10-12 years of service.

Recommendations

(a) There is need to realign the functions of the Deputy Commissioners/District Collector so that he concentrates on the core functions such as land and revenue Administration, maintenance of law and order, disaster management, public distribution and civil supplies, excise, elections, transport, census, protocol, general administration, treasury management and Coordination with various agencies/ departments.

(b) The Commission reiterates its recommendations regarding the Land Title Management System made in its eleventh Report on e-Governance. It should be one of the primary duties of the District Collector to perform the task envisaged in the aforesaid recommendations.

(c) There is need to strengthen the compliance machinery at the district level to enforce provisions of the RTI Act and to reduce the element of delay and subjectivity in the functioning of the lower level formations of the government. This should be done by creating a special RTI Cell in the office of the Collector, whose functions should be reviewed by the Collector at regular periodicity.

(d) Officers may be posted as District Magistrates early in their career, but in complex and problem-prone districts an IAS officer should be posted as DM only on completion of 10-12 years of service.

(e) Steps should be taken to ensure that the Collector plays an effective coordination role in activities and programmes of other departments at the district level.

Modernizing the Office of the District Collector

The Commission feels that the organizational arrangement of the Collector's office, currently, is not in tune with the requirements of the job. This office has a large interface with the citizens, and hence needs to be more efficient and citizen friendly. Modernization is a basic requirement.

Some important steps that could help this process are:

- **Management Information Systems / IT tools /E-Governance**

  For effective monitoring and evaluation of programme/ projects which are directly under the charge of the Collector, there needs to be computerized/MIS attached to his office. On the basis of these, the Collector could undertake monthly or quarterly review of performance. This cell could also function as the nodal e-governance cell for other officers located in the district by using its capacity to coordinate, and develop relevant IT solutions.

- **Grievance and Public Feedback Cell**

  Grievance redressal of citizens and implementation of citizen charters should be a integral part of the Collector's office. This district grievance cell should be linked with the field offices and also with public kiosks located in the farflung areas of the districts. There should be computerized monitoring of complaints received in this cell.

- **A Vigilance Cell**

  Currently, vigilance is a neglected component of the Collectors functioning. In view of the fact that on an average, there are more than ten thousand employees working in a district under various departments of the State Government, there is case for setting up an exclusive vigilance cell at this level. This cell could work under overall supervision of the district Collector who will maintain appropriate liaison with the office of the State Vigilance Commission/Commissioner.

- **Tours Inspection Notes and Institutional Memory**

  It is largely due to elaborate inspection notes and personal observations of the District Collectors that we have a large collection of valuable District Gazetteers which describe almost all aspects of district administration in pre Independence India. The tradition continued till around 1960. There is need to revive it. This could be done by creating and strengthening a cell for this purpose in the District Collectorate.

- **Civil Society & Media Cell**

  The emergence of civil society groups in various sectors of governmental activity, now requires that there should be an appropriate forum where civil society groups could interact with representatives of the government. A specialized cell could take care of this necessity. Simultaneously the increasing role of media in society and governance requires the Collector to handle public issues promptly and effectively. At the same time, the Collector's office could develop partnerships with them on public education efforts.

Process Re-engineering and use of Information Technology

The provision of service delivery at the district and sub-district level provides a fertile ground for innovative use of information technology. There have been a number of experiments in different sectoral areas in this regard such as Jan Seva Kedras in Ahmedabad, e-district model of Tiruvarur in Tamil Nadu,

Mahiti Shakti Kendras in Panchmahal, Gujarat, Saukaryam in Vishakapatnam, Lok Mitra in Hamirpur, Himachal Pradesh etc.

By and large, e-Governance initiatives at the district and sub-district levels have been individual driven, particularly by the concerned Collector. The scale and quality of replication of successful initiatives has been weak. To create the necessary impetus and enable uniformity/standardisation, the role of the STATE assumes critical importance.

The state must provide a holistic approach and broad framework for enabling e-governance at the district level. The recent effort of the Department of Administrative Reforms and Public Grievances to evolve an e-District framework is a step in the right direction. States must use this forum to prepare an e-District Plan for their State. At the same time, a thorough review of current processes involved in different services delivered must be undertaken to streamline the delivery system and reduce the human interface.

The following steps are important in this context:

- Development of an e-District framework applicable to all districts based on which ICT initiatives may be undertaken by respective districts.
- Comprehensive classification of rules, guidelines and procedures is necessary for efficient service delivery and better understanding among both the officers and the general public.
- Delegation of adequate powers and responsibilities needs to be done so that unnecessary file movements and resultant delays may be avoided.
- Standardization of application forms and categorization of nature of applications and petitions based on priority and frequency.
- Codification and classification of common grievances with processing time mentioned and separate records may be maintained department-wise for tracking them.

- Introducing a IT based mechanism for feedback and grievance redressal wherein public grievances are attended to within specified timelines in a transparent manner. Every functionary must be made accountable for the effective and timely redressal of public grievances through a systematic monitoring process.
- Developing a reliable central district database through which data collection from the grassroot level with the help of local revenue administration machinery can be done. The database must contain block and circle-wise information on population, PHCs, PDS outlets, Police stations, schemes implemented, fund sanctioned, beneficiaries under the scheme etc.
- Undertaking computerisation of land records for provision of information and services pertaining to land related matters such as computerized copy of mutations, ROR etc.
- Providing e-governance services through the front-end service delivery nodes for rendering important services such as:
  - Payments of user charges (telephone, electricity, water supply and other bills), fees, taxes etc.
  - Online submission and tracking of applications (alongwith the name of officer with whom pending).
  - Online invitation of tenders and transparency in the process of selection of suppliers and contractors.
  - Complaints and grievances sent online to concerned departments, which after a fixed date gets automatically reported to the next higher authority
  - Scheme related information like list of beneficiaries, criteria of selection, entitlements under schemes etc.
- Making the National Identity Cards a tool for service delivery and issue of certificates

Box 3.2

SCORE – eRegistration in Bihar

A case study of Muzaffarpur Registry office Muzaffarpur, Bihar has the busiest Registration office in the State with an inflow of about 150-200 documents per day. The project on digitized registration of documents was initiated by the Department of Registration, Government of Bihar for this office in December 2005. The main objective of the project was to make the Registration of documents simple, transparent and hassle free and to deliver the deed to the parties the same day.

It was done by adopting the following strategy:-

- Calculation of the stamp duty and registration charges on computerized valuation of property (based on pre-determined circle rates).
- Depositing the above calculated amount in a designated bank which is linked digitally with the Registry office. The payment advice of the bank gets displayed instantly on the computer of the Registrar.
- Collecting Rs.20 per page of the document to cover costs.
- Hardware taken on hire with a technician in tow. Software developed by the NIC.
- An Autonomous District Society formed under the Collector to take care of the day to day management problems.

Results achieved:-

- Unambiguous computation of stamp duty and registration charge; scope of exploitation reduced significantly.
- Buying stamps is no longer compulsory; the process has become convenient.
- Registered deed made available to the parties the same day. In the past, it used to take six months to a year. Copies of any document available without delay.
- Registrar's powers to withhold registration on minor grounds curtailed.

Overall impact

Remarkable increase in citizen satisfaction

- Networking all branches in the District Collector's office with district and subdistrict offices would help ensure information sharing and facilitate convergence of services and delivery mechanism.

Most of the issues having a bearing on the effective and efficient district administration like security of tenure, transparent transfer posting policy, performance management, outcome evaluation, effective citizen centric administration, use of information technology, process re-engineering etc have been extensively dealt by the Commission in its previous Reports summarized in Chapter 1. Reports on Refurbishing Personnel Administration, Ethics in Governance, Citizen Centric Administration and e-Governance are particularly relevant in this regard. The issue of capacity building, training and human resource management has been dealt separately in this Report in the chapter on Personnel Management which also covers the steps required to be taken in this regard at the district level.

Documenting best practices/innovations

In many States and districts, officers have taken initiatives which have considerably improved performance of government programmes in the district. Be it the social audit of NREGA, simplifying procedures for registration of propertyor issuing various Certificates, Officers have shown ingenuity and innovativeness. Such initiatives have resulted in better implementational practices and improvement in the overall tenor of governance at the field level. With appropriate modifications, it is possible to replicate these innovations and practices in other areas too. However, many of these ideas and initiatives are forgotten when the officer is transferred out of his assignment. The Commission feels that there is need to document such innovations and institutionalise such innovations and practices.

Recommendations

(a) The Commission reiterates its recommendations on the issues of personnel management, performance and outcome evaluation, effective citizen centric administration, use of information technology, process re-engineering etc. made in its earlier Reports on "Refurbishing of Personnel Administration","Ethics in Governance", "Citizen Centric Administration", "Public Order", "Disaster Management", "Conflict Resolution" and "e-Governance". These recommendations should be expeditiously implemented where applicable to the district administration.

(b) The following steps should be taken to modernize the office of the District Collector:-

- Management Information System (MIS) should be set-up in the office of the Collector for effective monitoring and evaluation of programmes/ projects under his direct control.
- A computerized District Grievance Cell should also be set up in the Collectorate.
- An exclusive Vigilance Cell should be set up at the district level under overall supervision of the District Collector. This Cell should also maintain appropriate liaison with the office of the State Vigilance Commission/ Commissioner.
- A forum should be established at the district level to interact with civil society groups and media on important public issues.
- Immediate steps should be taken to introduce process re-engineering and increased use of information technology.

c) Innovations and best practices initiated by officers should be documented adequately and institutionalized through changes in rules/laws wherever required.

FUNCTIONAL AND STRUCTURAL REFORMS

Institutions of Local Governance at the District Level

After the 73rd and 74th Amendments PRIs have emerged as the third tier of government at the district and sub-district levels. But, in many States, these institutions have grown parallel to the existing administrative machinery of the State Government. Barring Kerala, Karnataka and Maharashtra where field offices of many departments have been placed under the control of Zilla Parishad, other parts of the country still remain department-centric. While Maharashtra and Himachal Pradesh have brought the DRDA under the Zilla Parishad, in Andhra Pradesh this body still functions under the Chairmanship of the Collector.

At the intermediate level i.e. at the block or taluka level, there is a relatively better integration of departments with the PRIs. The Block Development Officer (BDO), who is formally under the control of the Public Relation department, is the principal officer who coordinates development activities at the block level. The nature of relationship between the BDO and the extension officers of line departments varies from State to State – from direct supervision to coordination. While this administrative arrangement applies to line departments like Agriculture, Panchayati Raj and Rural Development, Education and Animal Husbandry, etc., many technical departments such as Health Engineering and Industry work independently of the PRIs.

At the village level, this problem does not exist given that most departments do not extend themselves to this level. There are exceptions, however, such as Kerala where the typical Gram Panchayat has a population of more than 20,000.

The Commission is of the view that the local bodies (PRIs/ULBs) and ultimately the District Council will have to play a primary role in planning, development and service delivery functions pertaining to the subjects listed in the Eleventh and Twelfth Schedule of the Constitution. Though in many States, the subjects technically stand devolved to the local bodies, the administrative set-up has not been re-aligned appropriately to equip them for becoming effective self-governing institutions.

The Commission has already recommended in its Report on Local Governance that each district should have a District Council comprising of representatives of both rural and urban bodies. It observed that:-

> "there must be a single elected District Council with representatives from all rural and urban areas, that will function as a true local government for the entire district. In such a scheme, the District Council will be responsible for all the local functions, including those listed for them in the Eleventh and Twelfth Schedules. The DPC in its present form will be redundant, once a District Council comes into existence as envisaged by the Commission. Planning for the whole district – urban and rural – will become an integral part of the District Council's responsibility. The role of the District Collector/DM also needs to be reviewed in the context of the District Council and the District Government. There are two broad views that have emerged over the years on this issue. Strong advocates of local governments empowerment argue that the District Collector's institution is redundant in a democratic milieu with empowered and effective local governments and should, therefore, be dispensed with. Pragmatists argue that the Collector's institution served the country well for some two centuries and has been the pillar of stability and order in a diverse and turbulent society. Therefore, the institution of District Collector must remain in the current form for some more time. Eventually, the District Council should have its own Chief Officer. Meanwhile, as an interim mechanism, there is merit in utilising the strength of the Collector's institution to empower local governments. The Commission is of the considered view that a golden mean between these two positions is desirable and the District government must be empowered while fully utilising the institutional strength of the District Collector.

The Commission believes that these two objectives can be realised, by making the District Collector function as the Chief Officer of the District Council. In such a case, the Collector's appointment should be in consultation with the District Council. The District Collectorcum - the Chief Officer would have dual responsibility and would be fully accountable to the elected District Government on all local matters, and to the State Government on all regulatory matters not delegated to the District Government."

With regard to the existing parastatals, the Commission observed that, "the parastatals should not be allowed to undermine the functions and authority of the PRIs. Some of the existing committees may need to be subsumed in the Panchayats and some of them may be restructured to have an organic relationship with them (Panchayats). The Union and the State Governments should not normally set up special committees outside the PRIs. However, if such specialised committees are required to be set-up because of professional or technical requirements, and if their activities coincide with those listed and devolved, they should function under the overall supervision and guidance of the Panchayats. Similarly, Community level bodies should not be created by decisions taken at higher levels. If considered necessary the initiative for their creation should come from below and they should be accountable to PRIs."

The Commission also examined various important issues pertaining to Centrally Sponsored Schemes in depth and observed that,

> "The role of the Panchayats vis-a-vis the Centrally Sponsored Schemes is not yet in line with the commitment of the 73rd Amendment. The CSSs have to shed their separate vertical identity and be part of the overall development plan of the Panchayati Raj system. The Commission feels that there has to be territorial/jurisdictional/functional convergence in their implementation. The centrality of PRIs in these schemes must be ensured if they are to deal with matters listed in

> the Eleventh Schedule. The Gram and Ward Sabha at the lowest level and the Panchayat Samiti and Zila Parishad at the higher levels have to be the structures looking after all their activities in terms of implementation, monitoring and social audit. Even while formulating such projects, the Union and State Governments need to include elements of flexibility so that they could be moulded as per local conditions and requirements. The Ministries concerned should only issue guidelines and the implementational flexibility should be left to the local bodies."

In addition to the developmental functions, the Commission also recommended devolution of some of the basic regulatory functions to the PRIs. It observed that,

> "Since Panchayats are an integral part of the government at the local level, their activities cannot be confined solely to development programmes. If public convenience and effective enforcement of a law or regulation warrants decentralization of regulatory functions, it would be most appropriate to devolve such functions to the local bodies. There are many areas where the rationale for devolving regulatory powers to the local governments is very strong. To begin with tasks like issuing birth, death, caste and residence certificates, enforcing building byelaws, issuing of voter identity cards, enforcing regulations pertaining to weights and measures would be better performed by local governments. The Commission in its report on Public Order stressed the importance of community policing in creating an environment which enhances community safety and security. The Gram Panchayats can play an effective role in community policing because of their close proximity with the people. In most of the developed countries, policing is a municipal job and there is no reason why it should not be so in India. The process of democratic decentralization cannot be complete without the gradual transfer of the functions and powers of the village police from the State Government officials in the village to the Village Panchayats. In due course,

with the implementation of the reforms suggested in this Report, the PRIs would be in a position to efficiently handle many more such functions. Therefore, regulatory functions which can be devolved to the Panchayats should be identified and devolved on a continuous basis."

Accordingly, the Commission made comprehensive recommendations on issues like creation of District Councils, position of parastatals, centrality of PRIs in the implementation of the Centrally Sponsored Schemes, role of Panchayats in service delivery and in important sectors such as education, health, water supply and sanitation etc; personnel management capacity building in local institutions, accountability and transparency, modernisation and use of technology in local bodies etc. in its Report on Local Governance.

The Commission reiterates that these recommendations should be implemented in both letter and spirit.

Implementation of the above recommendations would mean complete restructuring of the existing format of the Collector's office and line departments of the State Governments. While doing so the following aspects need to be kept in mind:

- The need to conform to the Constitutional mandate envisaged for urban and rural local bodies under the 73rd and 74th Amendment and deepen democratic and administrative decentralization
- Clarity in functional allocation and subjects and mapping them to specific institutions
- Streaming multiple accountability lines that exist within and across the Collector's office, line departments, other parastalals/agencies and local bodies
- Need for coordination between various structures and convergence in service delivery functions

In the light of the above considerations, the Commission again reiterates that there is need to restructure the entire administrative machinery at the district level in the following way:

- There should be an integrated command at the district level in the form of the District Council.
- The District Collector would have dual responsibility in the new set up:
    - As the Chief Officer of the District Council fully accountable to it on all local matters.
    - As the representative of the State, he would be reporting to the State Government on all regulatory matters not delegated to district government (District Council).

Till the time, the institution of the District Council as envisaged by the Commission is given shape, the Zilla Parishad will continue to remain the most important unit of selfgovernment at the district level.

Recommendations

a) There should be an integrated governing structure at the district level in the form of the "District Council" with representation from both urban and rural areas. The Council will act as the "District Government".

b) The District Collector should have a dual role in this government structure. He should work as the Chief Officer of the District Council and should be fully accountable to the District Council on all local matters.

c) The District Officer would also be fully accountable to the State Government on all regulatory/other matters not delegated to the District Government.

Line Departments of the State Government at the District / Sub-District level

Apart from the departments / functions which fall directly under the domain of the District Collector, there are many other departments of the State Government which too have their offices at the district/sub-district levels. These offices can be classified into two categories.

The first category consists of the offices whose activities/ functions coincide with the activities and functions assigned to the PRIs/ULBs under 11th/12th Schedule of the Constitution such as the Office of the District Superintendent of Education, the Office of the Executive Engineer (Minor Irrigation, water management and watershed development) DFO (Social forestry and farm forestry) and Office of the District Soil Conservation.

The main purpose of the 73rd and 74th Constitutional Amendment is to establish and empower the institutions of local governance. Once the activities mentioned in the 11th/12th schedule are transferred by the State Government to them, there would be no justification for the above branch offices to continue their separate existence at the district/sub-district level. The functions, funds and functionaries of these offices need to be transferred immediately to the appropriate local government institutions.

The second category of offices of the State Government existing at the district/ sub-district levels, belongs to the departments which execute State wide projects. Such departments will have to work in coordination with the Collector. These branch offices will continue to exist at the district level. The Collector will also have to play a coordinating role between these line departments and the District Council to the extent their activities impinge on the functions and responsibilities of the District Council.

With these functional and structural changes, the role of line department and its Head of the Departments (HOD) and their relationship with the proposed District Council would also need to be clarified. The role of the line departments in supporting the District Council will have to be clearly spelt out. While the District Council and local government institutions at the sub-district level are given clearcut roles in planning and implementation of development schemes, the line departments may be in a position to provide valuable technical support in this process. Briefly stated, what is envisaged is that the District Council shall be responsible for administrative approval and implementation in respect of all matters coming within its purview with the technical support and guidance of the concerned technical department of the government. In this scheme of things, the Agency Heads of the line departments will have to devote more attention to technical aspects of their work than they are able to do at present, burdened as they are with an enormous volume of administrative work, including work on personnel matters. Each Head of the Department will function as a nodal technical agency advising government on the one hand and monitoring and guiding the work of the District Councils on the other. He will have to assess the trends as they emerge and advise on policies, measures and programmes in time, to counteract negative aspects and encourage the positive ones. He will have to appraise and evaluate the projects and programmes proposed for technical approval as well. Adequate time and attention will need to be devoted to training and orientation programmes for constant upgradation of the skills of the technical personnel of the departments.

Recommendations

a) District/sub-district offices, whose activities/functions coincide with the activities and functions transferred by the State Government to the PRIs/ ULBs need not exist as separate entities at the district and sub-district levels. Functions funds and functionaries of such offices should be transferred to the appropriate local government institutions.

b) Line departments such as the Departments of Water Resources and PWD (Roads) or the Department of Health engaged in execution of State-wide projects need to maintain their separate offices at the district/sub-district level. On important issues, they will need to coordinate with the District Collector. They will also need to coordinate with the District Council to the extent their activities impinge on the powers and functions of the Council.

c) The line departments and their Agency Heads should provide technical support and guidance to the District Councils in planning and monitoring implementation.

4 Administration of the Union Territories

EVOLUTION OF STATES AND UNION TERRITORIES

At the time of Independence, India comprised of nine Governors' provinces (Madras, Bombay, West Bengal, United Provinces, Bihar, East Punjab, Central Provinces; Assam and Orissa) and five Chief Commissioners' provinces (Delhi, Ajmer-Merwara, Panth Piploda, Coorg and Andaman & Nicobar Islands). In the wake of Partition, the country faced the gigantic problem of consolidation, since nearly two-fifths of the area in British India consisted of 562 principalities and princely States, varying in size from a few square miles to an area as large as Hyderabad with 17 million people. Within a short span the earlier principalities and princely States integrated with the Indian Union.

In 1950, when the Constitution was adopted, the country consisted of four types of Provinces/Territories: Part A, B, C and D (Table 4.1).

There were nine States headed by Governors (Part A States) and nine headed by Raj Pramukhs (Part B States). Ten (Part C States) were administered by the President through Chief Commissioners. Then, there were Part D Territories which were administered by the President through a Chief Commissioner although there was no provision for a legislative body or a Council of Ministers.

Table 4.1 : State set-up at the Commencement of the Constitution

Part A	Part B	Part C	Part D
1. Assam	10. Hyderabad	19. Ajmer	29. A & N Islands
2. Bihar	11. J & K	20. Bhopal	
3. Bombay	12. M.P.	21. Bilaspur	
4. M.P.	13. Mysore	22. Cooch-Behar	
5. Madras	14. Patiala & East Punjab States Union	23. Coorg	
6. Orissa		24. Delhi	
7. Punjab		25. H.P.	
8. The United Provinces	15. Rajasthan	26. Kutch	
	16. Saurashtra	27. Manipur	
9. West Bengal	17. Travancore-Cochin	28. Tripura	
	18. Vindhya Pradesh		

Soon the demand for a redrawing of the State boundaries on the basis of regional and linguistic identity gathered strength. The State of Andhra was created in 1953. The government also appointed a States Reorganisation Commission in 1953. On the recommendations of this Commission, the Indian Union was divided into 14 States (consisting of Andhra Pradesh, Assam, Bihar, Bombay, Jammu & Kashmir, Kerala, Madhya Pradesh, Madras, Mysore, Orissa, Punjab, Rajasthan, Uttar Pradesh and West Bengal) and 6 Union Territories (consisting of Andaman and Nicobar Islands, Delhi, Himachal Pradesh, Laccadive Minicoy and Amindivi Islands, Manipur and Tripura).

During the course of the next 15 years, some more restructuring took place. Bombay was divided into Maharashtra and Gujarat (1960), Nagaland was carved out of Assam as a separate State (1961). Punjab was divided into two new States viz. Punjab and Haryana (1966). Their joint capital Chandigarh was declared a Union Territory under an Administrator, which post is held ex-officio by the Governor of Punjab. The jurisdiction of the Punjab and Haryana High Court extends to all the three entities.

In January 1971, Himachal Pradesh which was a Union Territory got the Statehood. In April 1970, a separate Autonomous State of Meghalaya was created within Assam.

The process of reorganization continued in the 1970s and 1980s. In 1972, as a result of the North-Eastern Areas Reorganization Act, 1971 which came into force in January 1972, Meghalaya, Manipur and Tripura emerged as three separate States in the northeast. Arunachal Pradesh and Mizoram were made Union Territories. In 1972, the Union Territories were seven in number: Andaman and Nicobar Islands, Delhi, Laccadive Minicoy and Amindivi Islands (in 1973 they were renamed as Lakshadweep), Goa, Daman and Diu, Mizoram, Arunachal Pradesh and Dadra and Nagar Haveli.

The territory of Dadra and Nagar Haveli was in Portuguese occupation until its liberation by the people in 1954. From 1954 to 1961 the Territory functioned almost independently by what was known as "Free Dadra and Nagar Haveli Administration". The territory was merged with the Indian Union in 1961 and since then it is being administered by the Government of India as a Union Territory under the charge of an Administrator.

In 1975, Sikkim became the 22nd State of the Indian Union. In 1986, the Constitution 53rd Amendment Act inserted a new article 371G conferring full statehood on Mizoram. The North-East Frontier Agency (NEFA) which was renamed as Arunachal Pradesh and made a Union Territory in 1972 also got a full statehood in December 1986.

The territory comprising of Goa, Daman and Diu was since 1510 under the Portuguese continuously for about 450 years (except for a brief period during the later half of the 17th century when Shivaji conquered a few areas in and around Goa). On liberation from the Portuguese in 1961, it was made a composite Union Territory along with Daman and Diu. This continued for

26 years. In 1987, Goa was declared as the 25th State of the Indian Union by an Act of Parliament and Daman and Diu was made a separate Union Teritory. It is governed by an Administrator. The State of Goa and the Union Territories of Dadra and Nagar Haveli and Daman and Diu come under the jurisdiction of the Bombay High Court.

Puducherry, Karaikal (located 150 km to the south of Puducherry on the east coast), Mahe (located on the Malabar coast) and Yanam (located close to east Godavari district of Andhra Pradesh) were parts of the French settlement in India for 138 years since 1816. These territories merged with the Indian Union in 1954 and since then have been a Union Territory. Currently, it is governed by a Lt. Governor with the support of a Council of Ministers. The jurisdiction of the Tamil Nadu High Court extends to these territories.

Before Independence, Delhi was one of the six Chief Commissioner's provinces (others provinces were British Baluchistan, Ajmer Mewar, Coorg, Andaman and Nicobar Islands and Panth Piploda). In 1950, when the Constitution came into existence, it was made a Part C State. On reorganization of States in 1956, Delhi became a Union Territory under the direct control of the President through the Chief Commissioner. In 1966, under the Government of Union Territories Act 1966 an Executive Council was created for the Capital. This arrangement continued till the "Government of National Capital Territory Act, 1991" was passed and Delhi got a legislative assembly and a Council of Minsters. The subjects of Public Order, Police, NDMC, DDA and Land Resource Management (Entries 1, 2 and 18 of the State list) were however kept outside the purview of the Assembly and the Chief Minister. The Lt. Governor exercises exclusive powers over these matters.

Administration of the Union Territories

The administration of the Union Territories is governed by provisions described in Part VIII of the Constitution (Articles 239 to 241). Article 239 (1) reads,

"(1) Save as otherwise provided by Parliament by law, every Union territory shall be administered by the President acting, to such extent as he thinks fit, through anadministrator to be appointed by him with such designation as he may specify.

(2) Notwithstanding anything contained in Part VI, the President may appoint the Governor of a State as the administrator of an adjoining Union territory, and where a Governor is so appointed, he shall exercise his functions as such Administrator independently of his Council of Ministers."

Article 239-AA empowers Parliament to create a legislature and a Council of Ministers for the Union territory of Puducherry. Article 239-AA deals with special provision for the National Capital Territory of Delhi (viz. creation of a legislative assembly / Council of Ministers for the National Capital Territory). The legislative assembly has been given powers to make laws with respect to any of the matters enumerated in the State List or in the Concurrent List as applicable to Union Territories except matters with respect to entries 1, 2 and 18 of the State List and Entries 64, 65 and 66 of that List in so far as they relate to the said Entries 1, 2 and 18.

Article 239-AB deals with the powers of the President in case of failure of the Constitutional machinery in the National Capital Territory (analogous to Article 356). Section 239-B describes the power of administrator to promulgate ordinances during recess of legislature (analogous to the powers of the Governor in a State to promulgate ordinances).

With regard to the other five Union Territories, the administration is governed by

(a) special enactments passed by Parliament, or

(b) by regulations made under Article 240 of the Constitution.

Article 240 of the Constitution reads as under,

"Power of President to make regulations for certain Union territories –

(1) The President may make regulations for the peace, progress and good Government of the Union territory of – (a) the Andaman and Nicobar Islands; (b) Lakshadweep; (c) Dadra and Nagar Haveli; (d) Daman and Diu; (e) Puducherry"

In recognition of the similarity of location and issues involved, the UTs may be considered under three groups, namely:

- Largely urban Union Territories (Delhi & Chandigarh)
- Island Territories (Andaman & Nicobar Islands, Lakshadweep)
- Territories in the Mainland (Puducherry, Daman & Diu, Dadra & Nagar Haveli)

However, since, each of the seven Union Territories has some distinct characteristics, issues of governance in each of them has been separately discussed in this Report.

THE NATIONAL CAPITAL TERRITORY OF DELHI

Due to its strategic location, Delhi has been a seat of power of several empires in its long history; the earliest architectural relies dates back to the Maurya period (300 B.C.) After Independence, a major change came about: Delhi became the seat of the Union Government in a federal polity. The evolution of administration in Delhi has been conditioned by the fact that Delhi remains the seat of both the Union Government and the local government.

At the time of Independence, Delhi was a Chief Commissioner's province and when the Constitution became effective, it became a part C State with its own Legislative Assembly. It became a Union Territory in 1956 and was governed by an Administrator appointed by the President under Article 239 of the Constitution and designated as a Chief Commissioner.

A year later, two landmark legislations, the DMC and the DDA Acts were enacted to plan and promote the growth and development of the city. The erstwhile Delhi Transport Undertaking and the Delhi Electric Supply Committee were amalgamated into the newly created Delhi Municipal Corporation. (These two bodies were again separated from the MCD in 1971 and 1976 respectively and the work of water supply and drainage was transferred to an autonomous Board, the Delhi Jal Board, in 1988). The NDMC looking after Lutyens' Delhi (an area of 43 sq Kms) and the Cantonment Board looking after the Cantonment remained separate entities.

Delhi Metropolitan Council (1966-1990)

In the 1960s public opinion grew for providing a democratic set up for Delhi. In partial fulfilment of this demand, the Delhi Administration Act, 1966 was enacted. The Act provided for a deliberative body called the Metropolitan Council having recommendatory powers. This was headed by a Lt. Governor as the Administrator to be appointed by the President of India under Article 239 of the Constitution. There was an Executive Council consisting of one Chief Executive Councillor and three Executive Councillors. The Metropolitan Council was a unicameral body consisting of 56 elected members and 5 others nominated by the President.

Article 239A, which was inserted in the Constitution by the Fourteenth Amendment Act (1962), provided for creation of local legislatures or Council of Ministers or both for some of the then Union Territories (which later became States) viz., Himachal Pradesh, Manipur, Tripura, Goa, Daman and Diu, Mizoram and Arunachal Pradesh and the present Union Territory of Puducherry. However some of the other Union Territories viz., Delhi, Andaman and Nicobar, Lakshadweep, Dadra and Nagar Haveli, Chandigarh were excluded from the purview of this Article.

The *Metropolitan Council* - remained the deliberative wing of the Delhi Administration, devised as a compromise between a representative body with full legislative and financial powers and administration by the President through his nominee. The important functionaries of the Metropolitan Council were: the administrator, Presiding Officer, Leader of the House, Leader of the Opposition, Whips, Members, Secretary and Secretariat.

The Lt. Governor presided over Delhi Administration and its deliberative wing, the Delhi Metropolitan Council. Under Section 11 of the 1996 Act, he was required to summon, from time to time, the Metropolitan Council to meet at such time and place as he thought fit, with the condition that six months should not intervene between its last sitting in one session and the date appointed for its sitting in the next session. He also had powers to prorogue the Metropolitan Council. He could also dissolve the body after obtaining prior approval of the President. Although the power to summon and prorogue the Council vested in the Lt. Governor, he exercised this power on the recommendation of the Executive Council.

Leader of the House

The Chief Executive Councillor, who along with three other Executive Councillors, was appointed by the President of India under section 28(1) of Delhi Administration Act to assist and advise the Lt. Governor in the exercise of several of his functions in relation to matters enumerated in the State List or the Concurrent List of the Seventh Schedule, functioned as Leader of the House in the Metropolitan Council.

Leader of the Opposition

The Leader of the largest recognized party in the Opposition having a strength of 15 or more members was recognized as the Leader of the Opposition in the Metropolitan Council although there was no specific provision either in the Delhi Administration Act or in the Rules of the Metropolitan Council in this regard.

Whips

There was no provision either in the Delhi Administration Act or in the Rules of Procedure of the Metropolitan Council with regard to the post of Whips in the House. However, in practice the Chief Whip and Whip of the Ruling party were nominated by the Leader of the House and the Whips of other parties by Leaders of the respective parties in the Council.

Members

The Metropolitan Council consisted of 61 members of whom 56 were elected and five were nominated. As in the case of other Members of Parliament and State Legislatures in India, the term of office of the Members of the Metropolitan Council was five years.

The Delhi Administration Act, 1966 suffered from several shortcomings. The Council had no legislative powers and had only an advisory role in the governance of the city. There was, therefore, a continuous demand for creation of a full-fledged State Assembly with a Council of Ministers to aid and advise the Lt. Governor. Accordingly, on 24th December, 1987, the Government of India appointed the Balakrishan Committee to go into the various issues connected with the administration of the Union Territory of Delhi and to recommend measures for streamlining the administrative set up. In its Report submitted in 1989, that Committee recommended that Delhi should continue to be a Union Territory but should be provided with a Legislative Assembly and a Council of Ministers with appropriate powers to deal with matters concerning the common man. The Committee also recommended that with a view to ensuring stability and permanence, the arrangements should be incorporated in the Constitution to give the National Capital a special status among the Union Territories.

Present Form of the Delhi Assembly

On the basis of these recommendations, Parliament passed the Constitution (Amendment) Act in 1991, which inserted Articles 239 AA and 239 AB in the Constitution providing, inter alia, for a Legislative Assembly for Delhi. A comprehensive legislation passed by Parliament called "The Government of

National Capital Territory of Delhi Act, 1991", supplemented the Constitutional provisions relating to the Legislative Assembly and the Council of Ministers and matters related thereto. The strength of the Assembly was to be 70 – all chosen by direct election from as many constituencies. At present 13 of the seats are reserved for Scheduled Caste candidates. The Constitution also lays down that the strength of the Council of Ministers shall not be more than ten percent of the total number of members in the Assembly i.e seven.

The Assembly has the power to make laws with respect to all the matters in the State List or in the Concurrent List of the Constitution of India except Entries 1 (Public Order), 2 (Police), and 18 (Land), and entries 64, 65 and 66 relatable to the said entries of the State List.

The President appoints the Chief Minister and on the advice of the Chief Minister appoints other Ministers. The Ministers hold office during the pleasure of the President. The Chief Minister and the Council of Ministers aid and advise the Lt. Governor in the exercise of his functions in relation to matters with respect to which the Legislative Assembly has power to make laws.

The Lieutenant Governor has the powers to summon, prorogue or dissolve the Assembly. He can also address the Assembly or send messages to it. The Lt. Governor addresses the first session of the Assembly after each general elections and the first session of each year. Like members of other State Legislatures and Parliament, the members of the Delhi Legislative Assembly too are empowered to vote in the election of the President of India. They are also subject to the Tenth Schedule of the Constitution, which contains provisions regarding disqualification on grounds of defection.

The Government of National Capital Territory of Delhi Act 1991 provides for special provisions in case of Finance Bills to be considered by the Delhi Legislative Assembly. In terms of these provisions, a Bill or amendment shall not be introduced into, or moved in, the Legislative Assembly except on the recommendation of the Lieutenant Governor, if such Bill or amendment makes provision for any of the following matters, namely:-

(a) The imposition, abolition, remission, alteration or regulation of any tax;

(b) The amendment of the law with respect to any financial obligations undertaken or to be undertaken by the Government of the Capital;

(c) The appropriation of moneys out of the Consolidated fund of the Capital;

(d) The declaring of any expenditure to be expenditure charged on the Consolidated Fund of the Capital or the increasing of the amount of any such expenditure;

(e) The receipt of money on account of the Consolidated Fund of the Capital or the Public Account of the Capital or the custody or issue of such money or the audit of the accounts of the Capital;

Similarly, the annual financial statement pertaining to estimated receipts and expenditure of the Capital for a particular year shall not be laid before the Assembly unless the previous sanction of the President has been obtained.

Governance Issues and Challenges

As discussed above, Delhi, due to historical reasons and being the National capital has a unique and complex governance structure,conditioned primarily by the fact that there are two governments functioning concurrently in the same city It is a Union Territory but at the same time it also has a Legislative Assembly consisting of elected members and an Executive consisting of the Chief Minister and the Council of Ministers. As per provision of Article 239AA(3)(a), the legislative powers of the Government of the NCT are restricted. It can legislate on the subjects mentioned in the State List of the Seventh Schedule except those dealing with public order, police and land

and the related aspects of Entries at 64, 65 and 66. The Section reads:

> 239AA (3) (a) Subject to the provisions of this Constitution, the Legislative Assembly shall have power to make laws for the whole or any part of the National Capital Territory with respect to any of the matters enumerated in the State List or in the Concurrent List in so far as any such matter is applicable to Union territories except matters with respect to Entries 1, 2 and 18 of the State List and Entries 64, 65 and 66 of that List in so far as they relate to the said Entries 1, 2 and 18.

These subjects are directly under the control of the Union Government. The Police Act, 1978 which was specifically enacted for the National Capital Territory of Delhi, provides for a Police Commissioner who works directly under the Lt. Governor. The Chief Minister of the NCT and the Council of Ministers thus do not have any powers with respect to public order and functioning of the police in Delhi. Several other important functional powers concerning transferred subjects too, continue to vest in the Union Government or the Lt. Governor. For example Entry 5 of the State List consists of "Local Government, that is to say, the constitution and powers of municipal corporations, improvement trusts, district boards, mining settlement authorities and other local authorities for the purpose of local self-government or village administration." But in actual practice, the functions pertaining to the Municipal Corporation and Improvement Trusts are being handled by bodies which are exclusively under the control of the Union Government. The municipal functions in the city are being looked after by three agencies namely, the Municipal Corporation of Delhi (MCD), the New Delhi Municipal Council (NDMC) and the Delhi Cantonment Board all under control of the Union Government. There are as many 57 as Sections/ sub-Sections in the DMC Act, 1957 and 67 Sections/Sub-Sections in the NDMC Act, 1994 where the Union Government wields power directly. A major portion of the finances come to the Delhi Municipal

Corporation through the budget of the Delhi Government, whereas the NDMC receives funds directly from the Union Government (Ministry of Urban Development). The Delhi Development Authority, a body created under an Act of 1957 to carry out spatial planning of Delhi is also fully under the control of the Union Ministry of Urban Development. Though, the DDA Board has three representatives from the Legislative Assembly of the NCT, the overriding power vests in the Lt. Governor. The NDMC again is a nominated body which has two members of the Delhi Legislature on its board, but again the real powers rest with the Chairman of the Council who is an officer appointed by the Union Government. To sum up, these organisations are either directly under the control of the Union Government or are more accountable to it as compared to the Government of National Capital Territory (NCT) of Delhi.

The Delhi Jal Board, GENCO and TRANSCO (successors of Delhi Vidyut Board),Delhi Transport Corporation and Delhi Fire Services are some of the major organizations which function directly under the Delhi government.

This diarchy creates problems for effective governance of Delhi. They could be considered under the following five headings

(1) Role of the Government of the NCT in Municipal Affairs; - its relationship with the Municipal Corporation of Delhi

(2) Role of the Government of the NCT in spatial planning and land development; - its relationship with the DDA

(3) Status of the NDMC

(4) Role of the Government of the NCT in public order, security and enforcement of other laws

(5) NCR Planning Board.

Role of the Government of NCT in Municipal Affairs – Its Relationship with the Municipal Corporation of Delhi (MCD)

The MCD is the largest municipal authority within the jurisdiction of the National Capital Territory of Delhi. Out of a total area of 1483 sq.km., an area of approximately 1400 sq.km. fall within the jurisdiction of the MCD with an estimated 97% of the population of Delhi residing in the MCD area. The remaining areas are covered in almost equal proportion between the NDMC and the Delhi Cantonment Board. The MCD created by the Delhi Municipal Corporation Act, 1957 as amended has a strength of a maximum of 134 elected Councilors with a Mayor and a Deputy Mayor elected by these Councilors. In addition the Lt. Governor may nominate 10 persons with special knowledge and experience in municipal administration. Members of the Lok Sabha from Delhi and 1/5th of the Members of the State Legislative Assembly are also Members of the MCD. It is divided into 12 Zones which are further divided into Wards. The MCD discharges its functions through a Standing Committee, a Wards Committee, various other Committees and the Commissioner. The Commissioner, who is the Chief Executive Authority, is appointed by the Union Government and is generally a senior IAS officer.

The obligatory functions of the MCD inter alia include the following:-

- registration of births and deaths;
- construction and maintenance of drains, drainage works and public latrines;
- removal and disposal of garbage;
- regulation of places for the disposal of the dead;
- reclamation of unhealthy localities;
- measures for preventing the spread of dangerous diseases;
- establishment and maintenance of dispensaries and maternity and child welfare centres;
- maintenance and upgradation of hospitals;
- construction of streets and bridges;
- public vaccination and inoculation; the maintenance of municipal markets and slaughter houses; and

- establishment and maintenance of primary schools.

In addition, the MCD also has a vast range of discretionary functions, which *inter alia* include:

- furtherance of education by means other than schools;
- establishment and maintenance of libraries and museums;
- establishment of stadiums and gymnasiums;
- registration of marriages;
- survey of buildings and land; and
- construction of rest-houses, poor houses, infirmaries, shelters for the destitute and disabled, and asylums.

The MCD is authorized to impose a variety of taxes, fees and cess which includes property tax, fees for sanctioning and approving building plans, taxes on vehicles, theatres and cinemas and advertisement and hoardings, tax on consumption of electricity etc. The MCD is also authorized to levy education cess, toll tax, duties on the transfer of property, building taxes etc. A proportion of its budget is by way of release of funds by the Government of NCT, Delhi from its plan budget. Also the Delhi Government has to share a part of its tax collection with the MCD as per the recommendations of the Finance Commission appointed by the Delhi government. This is in accordance with the provisions of the Seventy-Fourth Amendment and Article 243Y of the Constitution.

243Y. (1) The Finance Commission constituted under Article 243-I shall also review the financial position of the Municipalities and make recommendations to the Governor as to—

(a) the principles which should govern—

(i) the distribution between the State and the Municipalities of the net proceeds of the taxes, Power to impose taxes, duties, tolls and fees leviable by the State, which may be divided between them under this Part and the allocation between the Municipalities at all levels of their respective shares of such proceeds;

(ii) the determination of the taxes, duties, tolls and fees which may be assigned to, or appropriated by, the Municipalities;

(iii) the grants-in-aid to the Municipalities from the Consolidated Fund of the State;

(b) the measures needed to improve the financial position of the Municipalities;

(c) any other matter referred to the Finance Commission by the Governor in the interests of sound finance of the Municipalities.,

There are several provisions in the DMC Act which place this body under the control and superintendence of the Union Government. Section 338A of the Act (general superintendence, etc., of the Union Government), Section 54(appointment of the Commissioner), Section 347D (appeal to the LG against the orders of the appellate tribunal), Section 349A (powers of the Union Government to make bye-laws) and Sections 485, 486, 487, 488, 489 & 490 (powers of the Union Government to require production of documents) are some of the important provisions which places this body under the domain of the Union Government to carry out inspections to issue directions, enforce compliance and power to dissolve the Corporation on default in performance of the duties. In all, there are 57 Sections/sub-Sections in the DMC Act through which the Union Government wields power over this body.

There is growing realisation that once an elected legislature has been established for this Territory, the Delhi Government should have full responsibility and powers with regard to provision of municipal services in the area. Further reasons are (i) Municipal functions come under Entry 5 of the State List of the Seventh Schedule which is a transferred subject (ii) a substantial part of the MCD funds comes from the plan budget of the GNCT of Delhi (iii) the citizens of Delhi democratically elect legislators for the GNCT and the principle of subsidiarity demands that municipal bodies should be linked to the nearest tier of Government.

In fact the present government of NCT has been urging the Union Government that the municipal affairs of the Capital (minus the NDMC and Delhi Cantonment area) need to vest in the government of NCT.

The contrary view is that the National Capital Region of Delhi is an entity distinct from a full fledged State. It is primarily a Union Territory with slightly enlarged powers which find expression through a democratically elected Assembly and a Council of Ministers. Delhi being the seat of the Union Government, the final authority in respect of its overall development, land use planning and development, allocation, provision of basic services, public order, enforcement of other laws, crime control and security needs to vest in the Union Government. The demand for the development of the city as a model metropolis which could take care of the interests of the entire Nation, institutions of National/ International importance, foreign establishments and provide top grade amenities to its citizens, also dictates that the management of the city should remain with the Union Government. The Municipal Corporation being the key urban service provider in the city should be in a position to work in a wider perspective and hence needs to stay with the Union Government.

During the last two decades, this issue has been examined in detail by four high powered committees;

(1) Balakrishnan Committee, 1989

(2) Virendra Prakash Committee, 2001

(3) Omesh Saigal Committee, 2006 (on restructuring of the MCD)

(4) Ashok Pradhan Committee, October 2006 (on multiplicity of institutions in the NCT dealing with urban development and civic amenities).

The following views of various Committees on some of the major urban governance issues of the NCT are given below:

- **Balakrishnan Committee**: Split MCD into 8 Municipalities. 7 to be co-terminus with the existing districts and 1 for the area covering NDMC

  Issue of Control: Did not suggest any change in the existing Constitutional structure. But for better coordination it recommended that a senior officer of the NCT government should be designated as the Commissioner of Local Bodies.

  Issue - Introducing the Mayor-in-Council system in the MCD: Did not agree

- **Virendra Prakash Committee**: Split the present organization into 4 smaller Municipal Corporations one each for Central Delhi, West Delhi, South Delhi and Shahadra. The Committee also suggested having 2 Municipal Councils, one each for Narela and Nazafgarh.

  Issue of Control: Did not suggest any change in the existing Constitutional structure. But for better coordination it recommended setting up a State Level Coordination Board under the Chairmanship of the Minister of Urban Development of the GNCT

  Issue - Introducing the Mayor in Council system in the MCD: Did not agree, as it would create an authority parallel to the Chief Minister.

- **Saigal Committee:** The thrust of the Saigal Committee recommendations was on internal restructuring of the MCD, not on its split up (paragraph 7.8.3 of the Report). It recommended

  (a) To keep intact the present MCD as an umbrella organization; some kind of a holding municipal structure. At the second tier create empowered and autonomous Janpad Parishads (11 in number). Each Janpad will have a separate fund and all the taxes under section 113(1) and

(2) of the DMC Act should be collected and retained by the Janpad. At the third tier will be the Ward Sabhas (S. 134).

The Committee did not recommend splitting of the MCD into smaller and independent Municipal Corporations.

As a passing reference, it wrote that "Even if the government decides to create more than one corporations each of them should have the above mentioned three tier empowered structure".

Issue of Control It recommended that except for Section 503 (Grant of exemptions to diplomatic missions) all other powers should be exercised by the GNCT.

Appointment of the Municipal Commissioner should be made by the GNCT in consultation with the Union Government.

Issue - Introducing the Mayor in Council system in the MCD: Did not agree, as it would create an authority parallel to the Chief Minister It will aggravate the issue concerning 'multiplicity of authorities'.

- Pradhan Committee: The thrust of the Pradhan Committee recommendations too is on restructuring of the present MCD. The emphasis is on strengthening of zone.

  It recommended empowerment of the existing Zonal Deputy Commissioners further and even upgrading the post to the level of Joint Secretary and simultaneously designate the MCD Commissioner as Principal Commissioner in the grade of Additional Secretary, GOI.

The jurisdiction of each municipal zone should be coterminus with Police and Revenue Districts and as and when the geographical area of a Police District undergoes a change the jurisdiction of MCD zone should follow suit to maintain geo convergence.

As a passing reference, it commented that "Many ills besetting the MCD today are its own unmanageable size . . . justified to bring about a change in the administrative structure. Ideally, the Corporation should be split into smaller compact bodies for specific areas and jurisdiction having separate elected bodies". It also suggests that powers of enforcement of building regulation should be given to Revenue Deputy Commissioners. Suggests enlarged role for them.

The Commissioner of MCD should be appointed by the GNCT.

Issue of control The MCD should function under the Government of National Capital Territory of Delhi, with the Union Government having powers to issue directions through the Lt. Governor, Delhi and in the event of their noncompliance to supersede the body. Also, the Central Government to have overriding powers in respect of buildings regulations.

***Issue** - Introducing the Mayor in Council system in the MCD:* Was silent on this. The MCD should confine its functions to core activities (as mentioned in 12th Schedule). Should shed its functions relating to management of hospitals and schools.

- **Recommendation of the GNCT**: The GNCT should have complete control over transferred subjects and hence over MCD. The MCD should be split up into 3 independent Municipalities.

  (a) Trans Yamuna (East) – 32 Wards

  (b) North Delhi – 48 Wards and

(c) South Delhi – 54 Wards.

Does not support the Model of Zonal empowerment.

Issue of Control: The MCD/Successor bodies should completely be placed under the direct control supervision and superintendence of the GNCT in all respects without any stipulation and reservation.

All powers being exercised by the Union Government with regard to MCD either directly or through Hon'ble Lt. Governor should be transferred to the GNCT.

Does not support Mayor-in-council system.

The GNCT should have complete control over transferred subjects and hence over MCD. The MCD should be split up into 3 independent Municipalities.

(a) Trans Yamuna (East) – 32 Wards

(b) North Delhi – 48 Wards &

(c) South Delhi – 54 Wards.

Does not support the Model of Zonal empowerment.

Issue of control the MCD/Successor bodies should completely be placed under the direct control supervision and superintendence of the GNCT in all respects without any stipulation and reservation.

All powers being exercised by the Union Government with regard to MCD either directly or through Hon'ble Lt. Governor should be transferred to the GNCT.

Does not support Mayor-in-council system.

The Commission is of the view that since Delhi is the national capital with people from all parts of the country being its residents, some responsibility for its orderly growth and security must lie with the Union Government. At the same time, there is no reason to burden the Union Government with matters of local import which are best addressed by the elected government of the Territory and the elected Municipal Corporation. In other words, a balance has to be struck between the imperatives flowing from Delhi's status as the national capital and as the seat of its own elected government. The existing balance is heavily tilted towards the Union Government at the cost of the functional ability of the Government of the NCT. The Commission has sought to restore a more workable balance on the principle of subsidiarity.

In the scheme of the DMC Act 1957 the Union Government has the powers of general superintendence over the Corporation. When the Act was passed, the only proximate elected government was the Union Government and powers that might normally have been exercised by a State Government vested in the Union Government. For example, Section 330 A provides:-

> "Notwithstanding anything contained in any other provision of this Act, the Commissioner shall exercise his powers and discharge his functions under this Chapter, under the general superintendence, direction and control of the Central Government".

Section 349A of the Act deals with the powers of the Union Government to make byelaws: -

> "the Central Government may, by notification in the Official Gazette, make bye-laws for carrying out the provisions of this chapter".

Provisions contained in Chapter XXIV of the Act deal explicitly with the issue of control of the Union Government over the Municipal Corporation. They endow powers on the Union Government to call for records to inspect, to give directions and ensure their compliance and to dissolve the body (Sections 485 to 490).

Section 490A of the Act deals with the delegation of powers by the Union Government. It reads:

> "The Central Government may, by notification in the Official Gazette, direct that any power exercisable by it under this Act shall, subject to such conditions, if any, as may be

specified in the notification be exercisable by the Government or any of its officers or by the Commissioner or any other authority".

The Commission is of the view that a simple notification issued by the Union Government under Section 490A will bring the MCD within the domain of the GNCT. In order that, the Union Government retains some overarching role over delivery of municipal services in the National Capital Territory, a few provisions of the existing Act will need to remain as they are. For example, Sections 487 to 490 of Chapter XXIV will need to be retained in their present form. Section 54 which deals with the appointment of Commissioner will have to be suitably amended so that the Municipal Commissioner is appointed by the GNCT in consultation with the Union Government. Similarly, some provisions of Chapter XVI dealing with building regulations will need to be kept in the domain of the Union Government (for example Section 347). Section 503 (dealing with exemptions to the diplomatic missions) and Section 508 (special provisions as to the Red Fort area) will also need to lie with the Union Government. The Commission suggests that the Union Government should appoint an Expert Committee which would work out the details of the required legal changes in a time-bound manner.

Recommendations

a) The Municipal Corporation of Delhi (MCD), including appointment of the Commissioner and other functionaries should lie in the domain of the Government of the National Capital Territory (GNCT). This can be done by way of a notification under Section 490A of the Act, issued by the Union Government. However, the appointment of the Commissioner should be made by the GNCT in consultation with the Union Government.

b) In order that, the Union Government retains its overarching role over delivery of municipal services in the

National Capital Territory, some provisions of the existing Act should remain unchanged. For example, Sections 487 to 490 of Chapter XXIV will need to be retained in their present form. Provisions dealing with building regulations should be kept intact in the domain of the Union Government (for example Section 347). Section 503(dealing with exemptions to the diplomatic missions) and Section 508 (dealing with special provisions for the Red Fort area) should also vest with the Union Government.

c) The Union Government may appoint an Expert Committee which could work out the details of the required legal changes in a time bound manner.

Empowerment of the Mayor

The MCD discharges its functions through its general body called the Corporation and through a large number of subsidiary formations such as the Standing Committee, Wards Committees (one for each zone), various other subject specific Committees and the Municipal Commissioner. The Commissioner is the Chief Executive Authority of the Corporation. As per provisions of Section 35 of the DMC Act, at its first meeting each year, the Corporation elects one of its Members to be the Chairperson, known as the Mayor and another as Deputy Mayor. Their tenure is only for one year. By the time the Mayor starts understanding the problems of the city or the functioning of the Corporation, it is time for him to demit office. A short tenure therefore does not allow the position of the Mayor to grow in stature or authority.

Table 4.2 indicates the term and mode of the election of Mayors invarious States.

The Commission is of the view that a longer tenure is one of the factors necessary for empowerment of elected representatives. The tenure of the Mayor should be for 5 years; co-terminous with the election cycle of the Corporation and subject to the condition that he/she enjoys the confidence of the House. Hence, the Mayor of the MCD should be elected once every five years.

Table 4.2 : Terms and Mode of Election of Mayors in Various States

Sate	Election	Term
Andhra Pradesh	Indirect	Five years
Assam	Indirect	One year
Delhi	Indirect	One year
Gujarat	Indirect	Two-and-half years
Haryana	Indirect	One year
Himachal Pradesh	Indirect	One year
Karnataka	Indirect	One year
Kerala	Indirect	Five years
Madhya Pradesh	Direct	Five years
Maharashtra	Indirect	Two-and-half years
Odisha	Indirect	One year
Rajasthan	Indirect	Five years
Tamil Nadu	Direct	Five years
Uttar Pradesh	Direct	Five years
West Bengal	Indirect	Five years

The wider issue of empowerment of elected representatives in Urban / Rural Local Bodies has two additional dimensions viz. (a) the mode of election of the Mayor – whether he/she should be directly elected by the citizens or by the Councillors and (b) the way in which the elected representatives exercise powers.

These issues have already been discussed in detail by the Commission in its Report on Local Governance, and it has held the view that the Mayor should be directly elected by popular mandate through a city-wide election. The Mayor should function as both the Chief Executive and the Chairperson of the Council. The Commission further observed that "in smaller towns and cities, the elected Mayor can directly fulfil all executive responsibilities. But as cities grow larger, with vast population and an array of departments and complex functions, the Mayor needs the support and help of a group of persons to exercise executive authority under his overall control and direction. Therefore, some form of cabinet system with functionaries appointed by the Mayor exercising authority on his behalf in various departments of the executive branch is desirable. In systems where the chief executive is directly elected, and separation of powers is practised, the cabinet is often drawn from outside the legislature. But in a city government, the imperatives of separation of powers should be tempered by the need for greater harmony between the elected council and the Mayor. It is therefore desirable to draw the Mayor's cabinet or committee to discharge executive functions from the elected council. The Commission recommends that a Mayor's 'cabinet', chosen by the elected Mayor from among the councillors, should be constituted in all municipal corporations. The size of this cabinet should not exceed ten per cent of the strength of the council, or fifteen, whichever is higher. Such a cabinet will function directly under the control and supervision of the Mayor, and the final authority on any executive matter shall vest in the Mayor".

The Commission feels that the above observations and recommendations are of considerable relevance to the Delhi Municipal Corporation. Implementation of these recommendations will strengthen the element of citizen-centricity in the municipal administration of the city.

Recommendations

a) The Mayor of the MCD should be directly elected by popular mandate through a city-wide election. The term should be for five years.

b) The functions of chairing the Corporation and exercising executive authority should vest in the same functionary i.e. the Mayor. The Mayor should be the Chief Executive Authority of the MCD.

c) The Mayor should appoint a 'Cabinet'; choosing the members from amongst the elected corporators. The strength of this body should not exceed 10 per cent of the number of the elected Corporators or fifteen, whichever is higher. The "Cabinet" should exercise executive authority on matters entrusted to it by the Mayor, under his/her overall control and direction.

Issue of splitting up the MCD

The size of the Municipal Corporation of Delhi has been the subject of intense debate for last many years. There is a strong view that a large single municipal body providing civic services to more than 157 lakh people (2006) spread over an area of 1400 square kilometers is simply unsustainable and urgent steps must be taken to tackle this issue.

This issue was discussed in detail by both the Balakrishnan Committee and the Virendra Prakash Committee. More recently, the Committees under Shri Omesh Saigal and Shri Ashok Pradhan too went into this issue, but with a different perspective (emphasis on internal administrative restructuring).

Views in support of splitting up the MCD

Balakrishnan Committee

The Balakrishnan Committee's recommended the splitting up of the Corporation into eight smaller municipalities. The main thrust of the Committee's argument was:-

> 'The population being serviced by MCD is too enormous to be managed effectively and efficiently by a single monolithic organization. The large population as well as its spread over far flung areas have brought civic services almost to the breaking point. The common man living in far flung areas of Delhi faces great difficulty in approaching the office of the Corporation situated at one place for many of his daily needs and grievances'.

'The retention of the single Corporation in Delhi has created problems for certain sectorsof the population of Delhi like East Delhi since the discussions and proceedings in the meetings of the Corporation are, by and large, devoted to the problems of the Corporation as a whole and specific local needs tend to be lost sight of '.

'If there are a number of compact municipalities, apart from the obvious advantages of vicinity, the Councillors concerned will be taking direct and undivided interest in respect of their own areas. It might also be possible to infuse a sense of competitiveness between the various municipalities and such healthy competition among them may go a long way to ensure efficient municipal administration'.

'Hence the demand of the time is that the monolithic Municipal Corporation of Delhi should be abolished and the municipal services entrusted to separate municipalities set up at various centres in Delhi'.

Table 4.3 : Suggestion of the Balakrishnan Committee

Sl. No.	District	Population (in lakh)					
		1981	1991	2001	2006	2011	2021
1.	South		15.85	23.60	26.40	29.20	37.14
2.	South West		6.86	12.35	15.09	17.82	24.72
3.	West		13.17	19.44	22.81	26.17	34.99
4.	North West		17.53	28.73	36.61	44.49	63.82
5.	North		9.35	11.10	12.34	13.58	17.16
6.	Central		6.07	6.49	6.79	7.10	8.27
7.	East		10.54	15.31	17.20	19.09	24.40
8.	North East		10.46	17.21	19.88	22.55	29.69
	Total	62.20	89.83	134.23	157.12	180.00	240.19

It needs to be noted that when this Committee was deliberating on this issue, it had the census data of 1981 before it; the population of Delhi then was a meagre 62.20 lakhs (1981 census). During the period 1981-1991, the population showed a growth rate of 53 per cent and rose to 94 lakhs in 1991.

Virendra Prakash Committee

The Virendra Prakash Committee too, went by almost the same arguments:-

> "The weight of opinion accessed by the Committee is definitely in favour of the proposition that size does matter. Smaller size offers the benefits of (a) bringing governance closer to the governed; (b) reducing the span of control, leading to effective supervision and direction; (c) enhanced political and administrative responsiveness and accountability; (d) stepped upinvolvement of the people and civil society organizations; (e) diversity and competition in the municipal system enabling adoption of innovative ideas, techniques and technologies: (f) engendering ownership of the municipal body in citizen consciousness".

The Committee recommended setting up four municipal corporations and two municipal councils in place of the present MCD (Table 4.4).

When this Committee submitted its Report, the population of Delhi was still only 134.2 lakhs (2001 census). As against that it has a population of 157.12 lakhs in 2006 and a projection of 180 and 240 lakhs in 2011 and 2021 respectively.

Stand of the Present Delhi Government

The Delhi Government has, after due consideration, recommended to the Union Government that the present MCD may be split into three autonomous municipalities – one for the trans-Yamuna area since it has been historically neglected, is distinct from the rest of Delhi and would thus require special focus, and one each for North and South Delhi with large

Table 4.4 : Suggestion of the Virendra Prakash Committee

Sl. No.	Corporation / Council	Zone	Population (in lakh)				
			1991	2001	2006	2011	2021
I. Corporations							
1.	Central Delhi	City	5.03	5.49	5.58	5.67	6.31
		Sadar Paharganj	4.00	3.79	3.81	3.82	4.15
		Karol Bagh	5.36	6.12	6.63	7.13	8.72
		Civil Lines	6.68	9.56	11.22	12.89	17.25
		Total	21.07	24.96	27.24	29.51	36.43
2.	West	Rohini	8.09	13.85	17.78	21.71	31.31
		West	11.17	16.27	19.04	21.81	29.09
		Total	19.26	30.12	36.82	43.52	60.40
3.	South	Central	8.08	12.73	14.14	15.54	19.60
		South	8.14	10.91	12.29	13.68	17.54
		Total	16.22	23.64	26.43	29.22	37.14
4.	Shahadra	South Shahadra	10.54	15.31	17.20	19.09	24.40
		North Shahadra	10.46	17.21	19.88	22.55	29.69
		Total	21.00	32.52	37.08	41.64	54.09
II. Councils							
1.	Narela	Rural Narela	2.74	5.44	8.02	10.60	16.61
2.	Najafgarh	Rural Najafgarh	9.54	17.55	21.53	25.51	35.52
		Total	89.83	134.23	157.12	180.00	240.19

populations of 44.26 lakhs and 57.46 lakhs respectively. In order to effect this change, the proposal suggests extensive amendment of the Delhi Municipal Corporation Act, 1957.

Views opposing the split up

Saigal Committee 2006

In 2006, the Saigal Committee too went into the issue of reorganization of the MCD. It emphatically said no to the idea of creating multiple independent civic bodies in the Capital. The emphasis of the Report was on internal restructuring. It suggested a three tier structure in which the middle level corresponding to the present day 'Zone' was to be empowered significantly both financially and administratively; made into semi autonomous entities, enjoying powers to collect and retain taxes. Named as Janpads, they were to be the effective fulcrums of municipal administration in the National Capital Territory. At the lowest level of the structure were the Ward Sabhas. The MCD at the apex level was intended to operate as some sort of an Umbrella structure – a Holding Entity laying broad policy guidelines and providing technology and HRD support to the Zones and Ward Sabhas whenever necessary.

As a passing reference, The Saigal Committee commented that whatever be the number of municipalities in the city, there was need to put in place the above empowered three tier structure for effective and citizen friendly delivery of services.

Pradhan Committee 2006

The Pradhan Committee's views on this issue too, centred around restructuring of the MCD:

> "The other alternative is to empower the existing Zonal Deputy Commissioners further and even consider upgrading the post to the level of Joint Secretary and simultaneously designate the Commissioner as Principal Commissioner in the grade of Additional Secretary, Government of India / Principal Secretary. The jurisdiction of each municipal zone

should be co-terminus with Police and Revenue Districts and as and when the geographical area of a Police District undergoes a change the jurisdiction of MCD zone should follow suit to maintain geographical convergence. In this regard the Philippines experience is relevant, Manila, the capital city very much comparable to Delhi has been divided into several zones each with amunicipality headed by a Mayor and coordinated by the Manila City Government".

The Committee was of the view that with regard to enforcement of building regulations and to ensure better coordination, there was a need to empower the Revenue Deputy Commissioners.

The Committee also suggested that a separate Department of Local Self-Government headed by a Principal Secretary rank officer should be set up in the GNCT of Delhi to coordinate the affairs of the local bodies.

The Pradhan Committee too, commented that "Many ills besetting the MCD today are its own unmanageable size . . . justified to bring about a change in the administrative structure. Ideally, the Corporation should be split into smaller compact bodies for specific areas and jurisdiction having separate elected bodies". It did not however suggest any scheme for its split up, rather a considerable part of the recommendations dwelt on how to enhance effectivity at the middle level (zones), through better enforcement of regulations ,and through empowerment of Revenue Deputy Commissioners.

Experience of other cities

Municipal Governance in Bengaluru

Prior to 2006, the municipal services in Bangalore and outlying areas were being provided by a large number of municipal committees. Though, the main city remained under the charge of the Bangalore Mahapalike, (population – 43 lakhs area 226 Sq.Kilometer) due to a sudden expansion of the economy in the last 2 decades, the population of the areas lying on the fringes of the city grew phenomenally. In order to provide basic servicesto residents of these areas, 8 smaller municipalities (7 city municipal councils and 1 town municipal council) sprang up. The quality of the civic services and infrastructure provided by these small municipal bodies was primitive. The demand for municipal services was growing in a most haphazard manner and in absence of a coordinated plan, no concrete action seemed to be in sight. In order to tackle the dissatisfaction caused by (a) non-uniformity in services, (b) varying tax rates and (c) lack of coordination, a decision was taken by the Karnataka Government in 2006 to integrate these small municipal bodies and 111 villages of 65 gram panchayats lying on the fringes of Bangalore city with the Bangalore Municipal Corporation. As a solution to the infrastructural civic & administrative constraints of the expanding city, Brihut Bengaluru Maha Palike (BBMP) was born, covering a population of 54 lakhs spread over an area of 696 sq.kilometers.

Municipal Structure in Kolkata

Municipal services in Greater Kolkata are being provided by six municipal bodies. They are (i) Kolkata Municipal Corporation, (ii) Howrah Municipal Corporation (iii) New Barrackpore Municipaltiy, (iv) Chandan Nagar Municipal Corporation (v) Kalyani Municipality and (vi) Municipality at Sonarpur – Rajapur. The civic services provided by the later 5 bodies leave much to be desired vis-à-vis those provided by the Kolkata Municipal Corporation.

Municipal Structure in London

Under the London Council Act of 1963, the Municipal Administration in London consisted of 32 Boroughs. These boroughs were created in the metropolis to work as the principal local authorities responsible for running most of the local services in their areas. They functioned under an apex body called the Greater London Council. In 1986, Margaret Thatcher abolished the GLC and transferred its strategic functions to bodies controlled by the Central Government or Joint Boards. For next 13 years, there was no single elected body at the apex level for the whole of London.

The situation was largely reversed when the Greater London Authority (GLA) Act was enacted in 1999. A 23-member Greater London Authority headed by a directly elected Mayor came into existence in the city in the year 2000. Its main activities concern:

(i) Transport
(ii) Policing
(iii) Fire Services
(iv) Economic Development
(v) Planning
(vi) Culture
(vii) Environment and
(viii) Health

In 2007, the Act was amended enhancing the powers of the Mayor to include planning functions in relation to local development schemes and some other planning applications of strategic importance.

Municipal Structure in the City of New York

The city of New York is governed by a City Council. The New York City is a 51 Member body headed by a directly elected Mayor. The Mayor appoints several Deputy Mayors who are functional heads and assist the Mayor in his functions. There are 5 Boroughs and 51 City Councils in the territory. The City Councils are local bodies enjoying considerable power and discretion in providing services to the local citizens and can be compared with the boroughs of the Greater London Authority.

The Commission has taken into consideration all the above arguments, examples and experiments. It feels that the analyses made by the Balakrishnan and Virendra Prakash Committees are valid even today. The weaknesses in the functioning of a monolithic organization as pointed out by the Saigal and Pradhan Committees need to be addressed comprehensively. Bringing governance closer to those governed demands effective supervision and control, enhanced political and administrative responsiveness and accountability. Recognition of diversity and the need for having a system which supports equitable growth and development and also encourages competitiveness are essential ingredients of modern day administration. Keeping in mind the phenomenal growth of the NCT's population and the consequent stress on the infrastructure and municipal services which need to expand rapidly, the Commission is of the view that the present monolithic structure of the Municipal Corporation needs major restructuring. It may be visualized in two ways: (a) By outright splitting of the MCD into eight, six or three, independent municipalities as recounted in the preceding paragraphs or (b) by keeping the main body intact and by adequately strengthening and empowering the lower formations by granting effective functional autonomy to them.

The Commission notes that the multiplicity of organizations is one of the major problems being faced by the citizens of Delhi. Therefore any decision to split the present MCD into multiple autonomous municipal bodies will introduce further complexities on account of the (a) varying political complexion of the elected representatives of these bodies (b) varying revenue potential (c) different levels of aspirations of the local people (d) difference in the quality/extent of the existing infrastructure. These variations could in turn lead to complications with regard to (a) tax rates (b) inter-corporation movement of goods/services (c) availability of uniform civic amenities (d) issues of capacity building (e) building bye-laws etc. The Commission also recognizes that trying to put in place a mechanism which can enforce effective coordination among multiple bodies consisting of directly elected representatives is a difficult proposition.

Historically the city of Delhi has been a compact geographical and cultural unit; any attempt to divide it into multiple autonomous municipalities will destroy this compactness.

On consideration of the above pros and cons, the Commission is of the view that the municipal services in the NCT need to continue under the jurisdiction of a single municipal body viz. the MCD. However, to make its functioning more efficient, responsive and citizen friendly, it should be re-structured into an effective three tier institution i.e. the apex institution, the corporation, the zones and the wards. There is need to adequately strengthen and empower the middle tier – Zones/Janpads. In tune with the recommendations of the Saigal Committee, the Commission suggests that the zones should be given maximum possible financial and administrative autonomy. Each zone should have a separate fund and all the taxes collected under Sections 113(1) and (2) of the DMC Act should be collected and retained by the zones. Their powers with regard to enforcement of regulations and bye-laws should be enhanced appropriately. These Janpad Parishads will be democratic institutions.

(a) They will need to be politically linked with the "umbrella" Corporation

(b) The role and area of their operation must be clearly demarcated

(c) They should have autonomy in their area of operation

(d) They must have adequate powers to fulfill their role

(e) Their relationship with the apex body – "the corporation" must be clearly defined and the roles to be performed by each clearly spelt out

(f) Officers must have freedom and autonomy to fulfill their roles without day to day interference of the elected functionaries who are subjected to constituency pressures, still should be within the control of the elected people.

Each Zone/Janpad will have a Zonal Council/Janpad Parishad, with all the Councillors elected from Wards that comprise the Janpad as members. The MLAs and the MPs whose constituencies or a substantial part of it fall within the area of the Janpad will also be members. All these elected persons will have equal voting rights. Every Zonal Council/Janpad Parishad will elect a Chairman and a Deputy Chairman from amongst the Councillors. The Zone/Janpad will also have other members without voting rights and these can include the Deputy Commissioners both of revenue and police and 2 or 3 reputed persons in the Zone/Janpad area. Matters concerning their appointment, qualifications etc. can be prescribed by Regulations to be framed by the Nagar Nigam. In all other matters, except for matters that are discussed in the next chapter, their composition, functioning and powers will be analogous to that of the MCD under the present DMC Act, 1957 including the framing of a separate budget.

The third tier would consist of the Ward Sabhas. The MCD will be the apex level which will not delve into day-to-day functioning of the zones. It will act as a kind of a holding entity, responsible for giving overall policy directions, high level conceptual, technical and Human Resource Development (HRD) support to the Zones, whenever necessary. It will provide coordination among Zones and make laws/bye-laws for the whole of Delhi and also take up projects which run across multiple Zones. It will be the duty of this apex body to ensure that standards of development and civic amenities remain uniform throughout the city.

Recommendations

(a) The municipal services in the entire National Capital Territory (NCT) may be under the jurisdiction of a single municipal body viz. the current Municipal Corporation of Delhi (MCD).

(b) In order to provide efficient, responsive and citizen friendly services to the citizens, the MCD should be converted into a three tier institution with the Corporation at the apex. The middle tier i.e. the Zones should be adequately strengthened and empowered. The zonal body called Janpad Parishad/Zonal Council will primarily be a representative body consisting of elected Councillors (whose constituency falls majorly within the area of the Zone) and some nominated members. These Janpad Parishads/ Zonal Councils should be given considerable financial and administrative autonomy. Each Zone should have a separate fund and all the taxes under Sections 113(1) and (2) of the DMC Act should be collected and retained by them. Their powers with regard to enforcement of regulations and byelaws should also be enhanced appropriately. The third tier will consist of Ward Sabhas.

(c) The MCD should be at the apex level of the new structure. It will act as a kind of an Umbrella Organization – a Holding Entity, responsible for giving overall policy directions and high level conceptual technical and HRD support to the zones. This Apex body should not delve into the dayto- day functioning of the Zones. It should provide coordination among Zones & make laws/bye-laws for the whole of Delhi. It should take up projects which run across multiple zones. It will be the duty of this apex body to ensure that standards of development and civic amenities remain uniform throughout the city.

(d) Substantial changes will need to be introduced in the provisions of the existing DMC Act, 1957 to implement these recommendations. The Expert Committee suggested earlier at paragraph 4.2.6.16(c) may be asked to carry out this task within a period of two months.

Distinction between Urban and Rural Areas in the NCT

The DMC Act, 1957 is applicable to the whole of the NCT except New Delhi and Delhi Cantonment as per the definition of "Delhi" given in Section 2(10). But the Act differentiates between rural areas [Section 2(52)] and Urban Areas [Section 2(61)].

Section 507 of the Act refers to special provisions applicable to rural areas of the NCT (with regard to lower rates of taxation, fees and other charges).

Section 507; Notwithstanding anything contained in the foregoing provisions of this Act,-

(a) the Corporation with the previous approval of the Government, may, by notification in the Official Gazettee, declare that any portion of the rural areas shall case to be included therein and upon the issue of such notification that portion shall be included in and form part of the urban areas;

(b) the Corporation with the previous approval of the Government may, by notification in the Official Gazettee, - (i) exempt the rural areas or any portion thereof from such of the provisions of this Act as it deems fit, (ii) levy taxes, rates, fees and other charges in the rural areas or any portion thereof at rates lower than those at which such taxes, rates, fees and other charges are levied in the urban areas or exempt such areas or portion from any such tax, rate, fee or other charge.

The Commission is of the view that the traditional concept of "rural areas" which used to be characterized by low levels of income obtained through agricultural activities, does not hold good for Delhi. The land prices around NCT have shot up in geometric progression during the last few decades and it has brought unexpected prosperity even to small and marginal farmers living in the "rural areas" of the NCT. In this context, the Commission feels that there is no need to maintain this artificial distinction between "urban" and "rural areas" and the entire geographical area falling within the NCT should be declared as "urban" under the meaning of Section 2(61) of the DMC Act. The Municipal Corporation should realise taxes, levies and other charges accordingly from the residents of these areas.

Recommendations

a) There is no need to maintain the artificial distinction between urban and rural areas in the National Capital Territory. The entire geographical area falling into the

NCT should be declared as "urban" under the meaning of Section 2(61) of the DMC Act.

b) The Municipal Corporation should realise the taxes, levies and other charges accordingly from the residents of these areas.

New Delhi Municipal Council

The NDMC (an eleven member nominated body) in its present form was created by the New Delhi Municipal Council Act, 1994. It covers an area which includes Rashtrapati Bhawan, Prime Minister's Office, Embassies of foreign countries, residences of the Ministers and important dignitaries, and the offices of the Union Government. 80% of the buildings in this area are owned by the Government. As such, the NDMC is almost fully under the control of the Union Government. The Chairperson of the NDMC is a senior civil servant appointed by the Union Government in consultation with the Chief Minister of Delhi. The Council includes three Members of the Legislative Assembly, Delhi whose constituencies fall within the NDMC area, five nominated officers by the Union Government and two Members nominated by the Union Government in consultation with the Chief Minister who may be professionals, social workers and others representing particular interests. The Member of Parliament representing the New Delhi constituency is a special invitee to the Council meetings, but does not have the right to vote. The functions of the NDMC have been specified in the Act and are similar to those of the MCD. The Balakrishnan Committee on the Reorganisation of Delhi Set-up (1989) recommended the replacement of Punjab Municipal Act, 1911 as applied to the New Delhi Municipal Committee by a fresh enactment creating the New Delhi Municipal Council and the continuance of its special dispensation but on democratic lines.

The Union Government decided to retain the nominated character of the local body. The NDMC Bill was enacted in 1994. The Statement of Objects and Reasons spelt out that one of the important objects of the said Bill was to harmonise the law with the Constitution (74th Amendment) Act, 1992 with necessary exemptions and modifications under Article 243 ZB of the Constitution, wherever departure had to be made. It was also stated that the New Delhi Municipal Council consists of only 3% of the area and population of NCT of Delhi. Accordingly, it was felt that a different kind of local system had to be structured which took into account the special characteristics of New Delhi Municipal Council area which comprises the territory that has been described as Lutyens's Delhi and is the seat of the Government of India.

The Pradhan Committee went into this issue as well and recommended that there was no need to change the status-quo with regard to management of the NDMC.

In view of the fact that the Union Government owns 80 per cent of the land and buildings in the NDMC area, many of which are important Union Government offices and residences as well as a concentration of foreign diplomatic missions it would be appropriate that the present structure of NDMC is not disturbed.

Recommendation

There is no need to change the present governing structure of the New Delhi Municipal Council.

Delhi Cantonment Board

Set up under the Cantonment Act, 1924, the Delhi Cantonment Board consists of a Chairman, 7 elected and 7 official members. The Cantonment Board is empowered to exercise powers and perform civic functions such as provision of water supply, electricity, education, health etc. within its jurisdiction spread over an area of approximately 43 sq.kms. The responsibility for delivery of basic municipal services such as roads, drainage, sewerage, street lights, etc. within its area is with the Cantonment Board. The Board is also empowered to levy and collect various local taxes such as house tax, water tax, advertisement tax, profession tax, etc. in order to raise their own resources. Though, the overall control of the Cantonment area lies with the Union Government, some coordination between the Board and the Delhi Government is necessary. However, since it covers primarily the military area, the Commission does not wish to go further into this matter and propose any changes in its structure etc.

Role of the Government of NCT in Spatial Planning and Land Development ; its Relationship with the Delhi Development Authority

The Delhi Development Authority was created by an Act of Parliament in 1957 in order to promote and secure planned spatial development of Delhi. Major functions of the DDA include formulation of the master plan for the city. It is authorized to acquire, hold, manage and dispose of land and other property, to carry out building, engineering, mining and other operations, to execute works in connection with the supply of water and electricity, disposal of sewage and other services and amenities. The Union Ministry of Urban Development is the nodal ministry for the DDA. The mandate of the DDA is to acquire land for development of new areas notified as 'development areas' and once it is developed, hand it over to the relevant local authority with the DDA remaining as a lease administering authority. The responsibility of the DDA also includes overall planning of traffic and transportation. In the discharge of its functions, it has to coordinate with a large number of agencies, others under the control of the Delhi Government like PWD, some under the Union Government like the Ministry of Road Transport and also some with autonomous organisations such as the Delhi Metro Rail Corporation. In 1974, 'construction of housing units' was added to DDA's mandate.

The DDA has till date finalized three perspective plans for systematic growth and planned development of the capital region. The first master plan was Delhi – 1962, the second was the master plan for 2001 and the third master plan is Delhi 2021.

The performance of the DDA has been the subject of criticism by various bodies. The planning process has been described as inadequate and its implementation tardy, especially with regard to meeting the demand for housing and commercial space in Delhi. The Estimates Committee Report submitted in 1984, M/s. Tata Consultancy Service Report submitted in 1986 and the Report of the Committee on Reorganization of the Delhi set-up in December, 1989 clearly stated that the DDA had, over the years, drifted away from its main objective viz. planning and development of Delhi. The additional activities undertaken by the DDA led to a situation where its organizational structure became bloated, unwieldy and ineffective. Both the Estimates Committee and the Committee on Reorganization of the Delhi set-up had observed that DDA has been burdened with such a variety of functions that it has lost its direction and sense of priority. Consequent to the above recommendations the activities relating to the Inter State Bus Terminus (ISBT) and lotteries were taken away from it. But even now, the DDA continues to deal with a large number of activities in addition to its core function of planning and development.

There is a view that this organization should be brought under the management and control of the Government of NCT. This demand is based on the argument that since there is an elected legislature for the NCT, the effective control of land and land management should lie with this legislature and not with the Central Government or its representative the Lt. Governor.

In this context, it is relevant to note that though land is a subject under the State List of the 7th Schedule (Entry 18), under provisions of Article 239AA3(a), this subject has not been transferred to the Delhi Legislature and is still being managed by the Union Government through the Land and Development Office (Ministry of Urban Development) and the DDA.

Except for sending three Members of the Delhi Legislative Assembly to the DDA Board, the Delhi legislature has no control over its functioning. During interactions of the Commission with the Chief Minister, and senior officials of the GNCT it was urged that since the issue of land management is closely linked with the other functions entrusted to the Delhi Government it should have substantial control over this subject. It was also pointed out that the elected government feels severely handicapped due to lack of decision making powers in this respect, as well as due to the multiplicity of agencies existing in Delhi. The Commission is aware of the requirements of governance over the national capital city. It is also recognized that the Union Government must have control over macro-planning of the capital territory with regard to allocation of land and its management. It is felt that an effort must be made to strike a balance between these two divergent requirements so that the purpose of creating an elected Government is also served without substantially diluting control of the Union Government.

The Ashok Pradhan Committee went into this issue in considerable detail. The Committee recognized that there was lack of integration in the planning process in Delhi. It observed that "whereas DDA is responsible for spatial planning, the socio economic planning is the responsibility of the Delhi Government. As a result not only the planning for the entire city but also its execution suffers." The Committee pointed out the anomaly in the existing arrangement where the subject "land" under Entry 18 of the State list has been kept outside the purview of the Delhi Legislative Assembly, the agricultural land and gram panchayat land continue to be administered by the Delhi Government. Incidentally, it is the agriculture land which is acquired by the Delhi Government and handed over to the DDA for development and disposal but the Delhi Government does not have a say in the planning and disposal of the land, so developed. While referring to the historical evolution of governance in Delhi, the Committee observed that "it is necessary that this matter should be examined de novo to ascertain whether circumstances, conditions, considerations and rationale for which it was decided in 1956 and again in 1966 to exclude Delhi

Government from the control and management of land still exist and whether there is adequate justification today (with elected Assembly and Council of Ministers in position) to exclude land from the purview of the management and control of the Delhi Government and whether the existing arrangements in regard to 'land' (Entry 18 of the State list) conforms fully to the provision as contained in Article 239AA of the Constitution. The Union Government may consider confining its control and management of land (and buildings) in its possession through L&DO and leave the rest to the Delhi Government/ Administrator, Delhi." However, though the Committee makes a reference that "the ideal solution would be to transfer the subject 'land' to the Government of NCT of Delhi" it refrains from recommending such transfer. The Committee recommended that "the Chief Minister of Delhi should be the Chairperson of DDA (para 8.2.13 of the Report) which would enable him/her to bring about the desired coordination between the two areas of planning and contribute to the land development and its disposal by the DDA. However, all proposals and decisions of the Authority shall be placed before the Lt. Governor for approval before implementation. The proposed arrangement does not in any way compromise the position that land is and would continue to remain the responsibility of the Central Government and all its existing powers enjoined upon it in the DD Act, 1957 including powers to issue any directions to DDA shall continue to remain with it."

The Commission appreciates the complexities of the matter recognized by the Ashok Pradhan Committee, as discussed. The governance structure in Delhi has gradually evolved over a considerable period and has led to the establishment of a democratically elected government. Considering the importance of control over land in the national capital city, the Commission feels that the time has not yet come when this control could be completely handed over to the Delhi Government. At the same time, in order to remove bottlenecks in the governance and coordination between various activities related to land management, the Delhi Government should have a substantial say in this regard. It is felt that the desired objective could be achieved by adopting the recommendations of the Ashok Pradhan Committee. As such, the Commission is of the view that there is need to change the composition of the DDA and make the Chief Minister of Delhi, its Chairperson.

Section 3(3) of the DDA Act, 1957 indicates the composition of the Delhi Development Authority:

> "The authority shall consist of the following members, namely:- (a) Chairman who shall be the Lieutenant Governor of the National Capital Territory of Delhi, *ex-officio*;"

Other provisions 3(b) to (h) deal with other members of the body.

A simple replacement of the word "Lt. Governor" by the "Chief Minister of the NCT" will serve the purpose.

At the same time, the Union Government's control over macro-planning of land and its utilization needs to stay. The Union Government may continue to exercise its control by giving prior approval to any Rules / Notifications required to be framed under the relevant Act. (Section 4 which deals with the power of the Union Government to appoint two suitable persons as the Secretary and the Chief Accounts Officer, Section 9 dealing with submission of plans to the Union Government for approval, Section 12 dealing with the Union Government's power to declare any area as a development area for the purpose of this Act, Sections 15 and 21 dealing with acquisition / disposal of land, Section 22 dealing with Nazul land, Section 26 dealing with annual report, Sections 41,42, 52, 55 and 56 and 57 with regard to issues of control by the Union Government, returns and inspections, powers to delegate, powers of modification, power to make rules and power to make regulations etc and various other related sections which give powers to the Union Government will remain as they are).

Apart from changes in the composition and structure of the DDA and the provision with respect to control over its functioning, reform is also needed in the internal governance of the DDA to make it a more efficient, responsive and corruption free organisation. It has not been possible for the Commission to separately look into all such issues; however, it is observed that the Ashok Pradhan Committee has made some important suggestions regarding the functioning of this body which inter-alia includes (a) appointment of a full time member to look exclusively after planning, and (b) nominating experts under Section 3(g) of the DDA Act to bring in expertise from outside the realm of government so that new ideas and touch of professionalism could be bought to the planning process. These and other recommendations need to be considered and implemented urgently. The Commission would like to specifically mention the issue of transfer of developed area by the DDA to the Municipal Corporations. Any delay in this process affects the residents. The DDA and the MCD must ensure that as soon as the development of a particular area is completed, it is handed over to the MCD for performing civic functions.

With the restructuring of the DDA on the lines stated above; constituting a Metropolitan Planning Committee as per Article 243ZE of the Constitution may not be necessary.

Recommendations

a) The composition of the DDA needs to be changed. The Chief Minister of Delhi should be the Chairperson of this body in place of the Lt. Governor. This should be done by amending Section 3(3) (a) of the DDA Act, 1957.

b) As stated in paragraph 4.2.10.12, other powers of the Union Government as mentioned in various sections of the DDA Act should remain.

c) Steps should be taken urgently to improve the internal functioning of the DDA on the lines recommended by the Ashok Pradhan Committee.

Role of the Government of the NCT:- In Police, Law and Order

As stated earlier, the subject of Police and Law and Order, have not been devolved on the Delhi Government. This is being administered by the Ministry of Home Affairs, Government of India through the Lt. Governor of Delhi. The Delhi Government thus has no say in the Police Administration and maintenance of law and order within the capital city. However, as a democratically elected government they are often held responsible by the citizens for any lapses in this regard. There is no doubt that security is a critical area of governance and the Union Government must retain overall control over the law and order machinery of the country's capital city. At the same time, the requirement of having a Police force under the control of the Delhi Government to enforce a number of local and special laws lying within its domain cannot be ignored. Therefore, the unbundling of activities related to security such as the traffic management, local policing, enforcement of special laws etc. needs to be explored. During discussions with GNCT it was suggested that "since Delhi has a special status as the National Capital the security aspect can remain with the Home Ministry but traffic and law and order should be brought under the Delhi Government." In this regard, it would also be useful to draw inspiration from the recommendations made by the Commission on related issues in its Reports on "Public Order" and "Local Governance".

In its Fifth Report (dealing with Public Order), the Commission recommended farreaching reforms in the Police Administration. The Commission recommended separation of crime investigation from other policing functions. Subsequently, it was observed that the investigation agency would only be dealing with specified cases and a large number of cases under the IPC as well as State and special laws would still come under the domain of the law and order police. Interestingly, it was pointed out that out of the 50 lakh crimes registered each year in the States and Union Territories, only one third of these were

IPC crimes and the rest were offences under various special and local laws. Accordingly, the Commission recommended setting up a local police service in bigger cities with populations of more than one million to deal with offences under municipal and local laws. As regards special laws, the Commission recommended that their enforcement should be gradually entrusted to the respective department e.g. State Excise, Forest, Transport, Food etc. For management of traffic within the city limits, it was recommended that "the function of traffic control (alongwith traffic police may be transferred to the local government in cities having a population of more than a million)."

In addition, the Commission also recommended setting up of the Metropolitan Police Authorities in all cities with a population above one million. This authority should have powers to plan and oversee community policing, improve police citizen interface and suggest ways to improve quality of policing etc. The authorities should have nominees of the State Government, elected Municipal Councillors and non-partisan eminent persons to be appointed by the Government as Members with an elected Member as the Chairperson. This recommendation was also reiterated by the Commission in its Sixth Report on Local Governance.

The Commission feels that the above recommendations of the previous Reports need to be implemented in all the States and UTs. However, a distinction is required to be made in the case of Delhi due to its unique features. The Union Government may retain control over the broader aspects of security and law and order whereas traffic, local policing and enforcement of the special laws could be handed over to the Delhi Government. This could be done by bringing suitable amendments in the Delhi Police Act. In the long run some of these activities could be transferred to the Municipal Corporations.

The Virendra Prakash Committee recommended the following with regard to transfer of police functions to the MCD; "A persistent handicap from which urban authorities in Delhi have suffered gravely has been the non-availability of police force on time and in requisite strength for enforcing the will of the law on the law-breakers. Both the DMC and the DDA Act empower their executive authorities to direct police officers to take effective, specified action to abate nuisance; prevent unauthorized construction or illegal colonization, remove persons, materials and equipment involved in such unlawful activities and to maintain a vigil over any place where any development in contravention of the law was being carried out in order to ensure that it was not continued further. There is, however, the crucial proverbial slip between the cup and the lip in so far as availability of police force and the needs of enforcement authorities are concerned".

The Saigal Committee too supported the above recommendation of the Virendra Prakash Committee (para 10.20.3 and 10.20.4 of the Saigal Committee Report). It was of the view that there was no problem in appointing a senior police officer (may be of the rank of Special Commissioner) to assist the Principal Commissioner of the MCD for enforcement purposes.

In the light of these considerations, the Commission is of the view that powers of the Police with regard to traffic, local policing and special laws (such as Delhi Entertainment Tax Act, Cinematography Act etc.) may be handed over to the Delhi Government. As it will involve a major restructuring of the present Delhi Police establishment, it may be advisable to constitute a Task Force with representation from both the Union and the NCT Government to study the matter in depth and suggest appropriate restructuring including the required legislative changes.

Recommendations

a) The Union Government may retain control over the broader aspects of security and law and order whereas traffic, local policing and enforcement of the special laws could be handed over to the Delhi Government. In the long run some of these functions could be transferred to the Municipal Corporation.

b) As this will involve major restructuring of the present Delhi Police establishment, it may be advisable to constitute a Task Force with representatives of both the Union and the Delhi Government to study the matter in depth and suggest appropriate restructuring through legislative and administrative measures.

The Government of the NCT – Power to Raise Public Debt

Budget making is an important function of government. Depending on the extent of its financial resources and its plan for development, the government takes recourse to borrowing. The Borrowing is usually on the strength of its consolidated fund (created under the provisions of the Article 263(1) of the Constitution) or some other guarantee. The issue of borrowing either by the Union Government or by the State Government is specifically governed by Articles 292 and 293 of the Constitution which read as:

> 292. The executive power of the Union extends to borrowing upon the security of the Consolidated Fund of India within such limits, if any, as may from time to time be fixed by Parliament by law and to the giving of guarantees within such limits, if any, as may be so fixed.
>
> 293. (1) Subject to the provisions of this Article, the executive power of a State extends to borrowing within the territory of India upon the security of the Consolidated Fund of the State within such limits, if any, as may from time to time be fixed by the Legislature of such State bylaw and to the giving of guarantees within such limits, if any, as may be so fixed.
>
> (2) The Government of India may, subject to such conditions as may be laid down by or under any law made by Parliament, make loans to any State or, so long as any

limits fixed under Article 292 are not exceeded, give guarantees in respect of loans raised by any State, and any sums required for the purpose of making such loans shall be charged on the Consolidated Fund of India.

(3) A State may not without the consent of the Government of India raise any loan if there is still outstanding any part of a loan which has been made to the State by the Government of India or by its predecessor Government, or in respect of which a guarantee has been given by the Government of India or by its predecessor Government.

(4) A consent under clause (3) may be granted subject to such conditions, if any, as the Government of India may think fit to impose.

Currently, though the Delhi Government has a Consolidated Fund of its own, it is not permitted to raise public debt as the budget of the GNCT is treated to be a part of the Union Government's budget. During the course of its meeting with the Chief Minister and officials of the Government of NCT, it emerged that the Government has plans to create top class infrastructural facilities for Delhi, but finance is a big constraint. The budgetary support which comes to it from the Government of India (Home Ministry) for capital expenditure is inadequate.

In such a situation, it is realized that if the Government is permitted recourse to market borrowing, the development of the National Capital Territory could take off at a faster pace.

The Commission has discussed this issue in the context of PRI finance in its Report on Local Governance (6th Report) and has even recommended such powers to be given to the PRIs. (para 4.3.8.2) "For their infrastructure needs, the Panchayats should be encouraged to borrow from banks/financial institutions. The role of the State Government should remain confined only to fixing the limits of borrowing".

Keeping in mind the increasing need for high quality civic services and upgradation of infrastructure in the National Capital

Territory, the Commission is of the view that the Government of the NCT needs to have access to greater funding – beyond its own revenues or the grants given to it by the Union Government. The Delhi Government should be allowed to raise public debt by floating loans in the market, (just like the powers available to the States). This could be done by an amendment in Article 293; wherever the word "State" is mentioned, it needs to be replaced by the words "State and UT having a Legislature". This would be subject to limitations imposed by Articles 293(3) and 293 (4) of the Constitution.

Recommendation

The Government of the NCT needs to have access to greater funding; beyond its own revenues or the grants given to it by the Union Government. It should be allowed to have recourse to market borrowings. This could be done by introducing an amendment to Article 293 by replacing the word "State" with the words "State and UTs having a Legislature". Such borrowings would be subject to limitations imposed by Article 293(3) and 293 (4) of the Constitution.

National Capital Region Planning Board

The National Capital Region comprises an area of 33,578 square kilometers in the States of Haryana, Rajasthan, Uttar Pradesh and the National Capital Territory of Delhi. The coverage of the NCR is as follows:

NCR Limits

NCT Delhi	1,482 square kilometers
Haryana	Eight districts - Gurgaon, Rewari, Faridabad, Sonepat, Rohtak, Panipat and Jhajjhar & Mewat, comprising 13,413 square kilometers
Uttar Pradesh	Five districts - Ghaziabad, Bulandshahr, Meerut and Baghpat & Gautam Buddha Nagar, comprising 10,853 square kilometers
Rajasthan	Alwar district comprising 7,829 square kilometers

The NCR Planning Board was created through an Act of Parliament in 1985 with the concurrence of the Legislatures of Haryana, Rajasthan and Uttar Pradesh for preparing a plan for the development of the National Capital Region and for coordinating and monitoring the implementation of such Plan and for evolving harmonized policies for the control of land uses and development of infrastructure in the National Capital Region so as to avoid any haphazard development thereof. Section 8(f) of the NCR Planning Board Act empowers the Board to select, in consultation with the State Governments concerned, any urban area outside NCR having regard to its location, population and potential for growth, which may be developed as a Counter-Magnet Area (CMA) in order to achieve the objectives of the Regional Plan. The NCR Planning Board is a 21-member body with Union Minister of Urban Development as the Chairman. It also has 10 co-opted members.

The 21 members of the re-constituted Board and the 10 Co-opted members are as follows:-

Composition of the NCR Planning Board

1.	Union Minister for Urban Development	Chairman
2.	Minister for Power, Government of India	Member
3.	Minister for Communications & IT, Govt of India	Member
4.	Minister for Railways, Government of India	Member
5.	Minister for Roads and Highways, Govt of India	Member
6.	Chief Minister, Haryana	Member
7.	Chief Minister of NCT- Delhi	Member
8.	Chief Minister, Rajasthan	Member
9.	Chief Minister, Uttar Pradesh	Member
10.	Minister of State for Urban Employment and Poverty Alleviation	Member
11.	Lieutenant Governor, NCT – Delhi	Member
12.	Minister of Town and Country Planning, Government of Haryana	Member

(*contd.*)

13.	Minister of Urban Development, Government of Rajasthan	Member
14.	Minister, Urban Development, Government of U.P.	Member
15.	Secretary, Ministry of Urban Development, GoI	Member
16.	Chief Secretary, Government of Haryana	Member
17.	Chief Secretary, Government of Rajasthan	Member
18.	Chief Secretary, Government of NCT - Delhi	Member
19.	Secretary, Housing & Urban Development, Government of Uttar Pradesh	Member
20.	Chief Planner, Town & Country Planning Organisation, Govternment of India	Member
21.	Member Secretary, National Capital Region Planning Board Secretary	Member

Co-opted Members

1. Chief Minister, Madhya Pradesh
2. Secretary, Ministry of Commerce and Industry, Department of Industrial Policy and Promotion, Government of India
3. Secretary, Department of Expenditure, Ministry of Finance, Government of India
4. Secretary, Department of Power, Government of India
5. Secretary, Ministry of Roads and Highways, Government of India
6. Chairman, Railway Board, Government of India
7. Secretary, Department of Urban Development and Housing, Govt. of Punjab
8. Secretary, Department of Urban Development and Housing, Government of Madhya Pradesh
9. Principal Advisor (HUD), Planning Commission, Government of India
10. Vice Chairman, Delhi Development Authority.

One of the functions of the Board as defined in Section 7 (e) of the NCRPB Act is to arrange for and oversee the financing of selected development projects in the National Capital Region. For this purpose a National Capital Region Planning Board Fund has been created under Section 22 of the Act, which inter-alia is required to be utilized for (a) 'providing financial assistance to the participating States and the Union territory for the implementation of Sub-Regional Plans and Project Plans;' and

(b) 'providing financial assistance to the State concerned for the development of the Counter Magnet Area subject to such terms and conditions as may be agreed upon between such State and the Board.'

Development projects to be taken up in the National Capital Region and the Counter Magnet Areas (CMAs) would need to be identified by the Board, participating States of NCR, CMA and their implementing agencies. The Board may provide financial assistance to the participating State Governments and their implementing agencies including Local Bodies, Development Authorities, Housing Boards, Industrial Development Corporations or such other agencies of the State Governments as the case may be.

Depending on the availability of resources, the projects concerning:

(a) Land acquisition and development for creation of social and physical infrastructure,

(b) Upgradation and augmentation of existing infra-structure,

(c) Development of centres of art and culture,

(d) Infrastructure and other development projects in the Counter Magnet Areas,

(e) Pilot projects on rural development and

(f) Development of new townships can be taken up by the NCR Board.

A loan upto 75% of the project cost may be provided to the State / implementing Agency.

Assessment of the NCR Board

So far the NCR Board has provided financial assistance of around Rs.1800 crores for various schemes in the Region. However, because of the reluctance of State Governments at times, to allocate adequate funds, coupled with the lukewarm response of their implementing agencies, the outcome has not been satisfactory.

There is a view that in order to make this body more effective, there is need to add teeth to the organization and this should be done by (a) enhancing the funds at the disposal of the NCR Board, (b) allowing it to have a Special Utility Vehicle (SUV) which in times of necessity would be in a position to take up actual execution of sanctioned projects (if the Member State concerned or its implementing agency refuses to take it up), (c) to devise a mechanism which could ensure that the regional and sub regional plans approved by the NCR Board are dovetailed appropriately with the plans of the State Governments / Area Development Authorities, and (d) to ensure compliance with the decisions taken by the Board.

There is also a contrary view that since the Member States have active Area Development Authorities of their own with adequate technical support and infrastructure to implement projects in their jurisdiction, it may not be necessary to create a separate technical / implementational body for the exclusive disposal of the NCR board. In any case, major central agencies like the National Highway Authority of India (NHAI) and Delhi Metro development Corporation (DMRC) would always be available to assist the States in respect of high value/complex infrastructure and related projects. Creation of a support/ implementation agency under the NCR Board could also be interpreted as infringement at States powers to implement development plans.

Composition of the NCR Board

Currently, the NCR Board consists of 21 members as shown in Table No.4.10. The Commission is of the view that in order to have quick and binding decisions, the body needs to be pruned. Only the 6 Union Ministers and 3 Chief Ministers (Uttar Pradesh, Haryana and Rajasthan) need to be on this Board. The Chief Minister of Madhya Pradesh could be invited as a co-opted member whenever issues concerning Gwalior, a counter magnet city, come up.

In order to ensure compliance of the decisions taken in this meeting, the NCR Board could be supported by a Committee under the Chairmanship of the Secretary incharge of Urban Development in Government of India. Other Members of this Steering Committee could be Secretaries in charge of Commerce and Industry, Industrial Policy & Promotion, Expenditure, Power, Roads and Highways, Chairman, Railway Board (all from the Government of India), Chief Secretaries of Uttar Pradesh, Rajasthan, Haryana, Principal Advisor (HUD), Planning Commission, and Vice Chairman, Delhi Development Authority. Chief Secretaries of Punjab and Madhya Pradesh may be invited to the meeting whenever necessary.

Recommendations

a) The NCR Planning Board should remain a planning, monitoring and advisory body in charge of preparing the Master Plan for the NCR Region consisting of both regional and sub-regional Plans. It should have adequate financial resources at its disposal so that it could selectively provide financial assistance to a few schemes of importance.

b) The composition of the 21 member NCR Planning Board should be modified and only 6 Union Ministers and 3 Chief Ministers (Uttar Pradesh, Haryana and Rajasthan) may be members of the Board.

c) There should be an Executive Committee under the chairmanship of Secretary in-charge of Urban Development in Government of India with Secretaries incharge of Commerce and Industry, Industrial Policy and Promotion, Expenditure, Power, Secretary, Road Transport and Highways, Chairman, Railway Board (all from the Government of India), Chief Secretaries of the Governments of Uttar Pradesh, Rajasthan, Haryana, Principal Advisor (HUD), Planning Commission, and Vice Chairman, Delhi Development Authority as members.

d) Since the Chief Ministers of the three States are members of the Board, the decisions that are agreed to should be binding on the States concerned. The NCR approved regional plans/sub-plans should mandatorily be part of the Plans of State Governments. The NCR Planning Board Act should be amended accordingly.

CHANDIGARH

Originally built as the capital of Punjab, Chandigarh became a Union Territory, the joint capital of Punjab and Haryana, upon creation of Haryana in 1966. It is thus the seat of two governments and the UT Administration. The health and education infrastructure of the UT serves all three as also, to some extent, Himachal and Jammu and Kashmir. There is a composite High Court for the three entities in Chandigarh. The UT has a single district and a single tehsil.

The total area of the UT is 114 square kilometers of which 80 kms. are urban and served by a Municipal Corporation, while 34 kms. are rural and served by a three tier Panchayati Raj set up. The decadal growth rate of population in this UT has been 40%.

The Capital of Punjab (Development and Regulation) Act 1952 provides the structure for the management of urban governance. Enacted when the construction of Chandigarh was undertaken as a project, it combines State Government and municipal processes in its agencies – principally the Estate Officer and the Chief Administrator. Conceived as a special measure of limited duration until institutions of local self governance were established, it continues to be in force even though the development of Chandigarh is almost complete and a Municipal Corporation has come into existence. As a result both the UT Administration and the Municipal Corporation exercise municipal powers which can obviously lead to administrative confusion. Civic services to 90 per cent of the population of the UT (in urban areas) are provided by the Municipal Corporation while to the remaining 10 per cent (rural) they are provided by the State Government (UT Administration). A neat trifurcation of governance functions is not possible as the infrastructure (water, electricity, medical services, education) is planned for the UT as a whole. On a reference from the UT Administration, the Municipal Corporation has agreed to take over all 18 villages in the UT in a phased manner.

As the city was originally planned, there was to be a sixteen kms. deep green periphery around it. This is mandated by the Punjab New Capital (Periphery) Control Act 1952. However. The townships of Mohali and Panchkula in Punjab and Haryana respectively have both come up within the periphery. Within Chandigarh also the periphery is under pressure because of the need of land for further development.

Administrative Set-up

The Punjab Reorganization Act of 1966 provided, inter-alia, that all laws applicable in Punjab on 1.1.1996 would also continue to apply to the Union Territory. The UT is administered by the Union Government through an Administrator appointed under Article 239 of the Constitution. Since 1984 the Administrator has been the Governor of Punjab. Apart from the four posts of Advisor to the Administrator, Inspector General of Police, Conservator of Forests and Chairman of the Housing Board manned by AGMUT officers, all other posts are filled up either by deputation of officers from the Governments of Punjab and Haryana in the ratio of 60:40, or by direct recruitment by Chandigarh Administration.

At present the Administrator is advised by an Advisory Council which he nominates. This tends to be large, to accommodate various interests in the city, and at times unwieldy. The meetings also tend to be infrequent. There is no structured political input into decision making by the Administrator and political advice comes primarily through informal channels.

The Department Related Parliamentary Standing Committee on Home Affairs in the 121st Report on the Administration of Union Territories (2006), had inter alia made the following observation about Chandigarh:

> ". . . The Committee is of the view that the Municipal Corporation cannot solve all the problems of the people and the Advisory Council cannot help things to the extent people want their aspirations to be fulfilled . . . the Committee recommends that some kind of arrangement should be put in place in the UT of Chandigarh which should be easily accessible to the public and which could effectively and adequately redress their grievances".
>
> "The Committee notes that the Metropolitan Planning Committee can go a long way in solving the problems of the people of Chandigarh and fulfilling their aspirations. Even though the Metropolitan Planning Committee is not the ultimate solution to the elected legislative body, it can, to a large extent, address the problems of the masses. The Committee suggests that suitable legislation may be brought in at the earliest so that steps may be initiated for setting up of the Metropolitan Planning Committee."
>
> "The Committee understands that infrequent meetings of the Advisory Council to Administrator might be causing problems in redressing the grievances of the people. In the absence of a legislative body, at least, other bodies such as the Advisory Council should be given the necessary teeth to address the people's grievances. The Committee, therefore, suggests that necessary steps may be taken in that direction to ensure that the Council meet more frequently. The Committee also agrees with the view of the Home Secretary that members of the Advisory Council should be adequately empowered. It recommends that the Ministry of Home Affairs should take necessary steps to redefine the powers and functions of the members of the Advisory Council and steps may also be taken to give more powers to the Council as

such. As regards the suggestion of Home Secretary that the Council needs to be broad-based, the Committee has not received any concrete proposal from the Ministry. The Committee, however, feels that the issue needs to be deliberated upon and steps taken in this direction too."

"The Committee understands that the Zila Parishad and the Panchayati Raj Institutions (PRIs) in 18 villages would come to an end should the jurisdiction of Municipal Corporation of Chandigarh be extended to these villages. And in the absence of any demand from the 18 villages for extension of jurisdiction of the MCC into their areas and the orientation of MCC being urban, these villages may lose their rural identity without entailing any benefits and urban taxation of the municipality may add to their woes. The Committee, therefore, recommends that the rural identity of the 18 villages may not be disturbed."

Keeping in view the above facts and the recommendations of the Department-related Parliamentary Standing Committee, the Commission is of the view that there is urgent need to revisit the Capital of Punjab (Development and Regulation) Act and the Punjab New Capital (Periphery Control) Act, 1952 and examine if and how they are to be aligned with the changed circumstances. This issue needs to be examined urgently by the Ministry of Home Affairs and the UT Administration.

The Commission is further of the view that the required legislation for creating the Metropolitan Planning Committee should be attempted without further delay. It would, to a large extent, address the problems of the people.

As regards the Advisory Council, the Commission feels that a compact and cohesive body comprising of inter alia the Member of Parliament from Chandigarh, one MP each from Punjab and Haryana, the Mayor of Chandigarh and the Advisor to the Administrator would be able to provide the useful inputs to the Administrator and also be able to meet more frequently.

The Commission is further of the view that since the UT of Chandigarh is substantially urban and the 18 villages resemble urban habitats and are inextricably dependant on the urban infrastructure for their sustenance, the jurisdiction of the Municipal Corporation should extend over the entire Union Territory. The apprehensions of the 18 villages highlighted in the Report of the Parliamentary Standing Committee can be addressed by Ward/Area Sabhas as recommended in the Commission's Report on Local Governance. Also, till such time that the infrastructure in these villages comes at par with the urban areas of Chandigarh; they may be given necessary (local) tax relief.

Delegation of Administrative and Financial Powers

During the visit of the Commission to the Union Territory, it was pointed out that the proposals forwarded to the Ministry of Home Affairs for approvals often remain pending for long. It was stated that the present system of over-centralisation affects the administrative efficiency of the system because of long delays. Inadequate financial delegation to the Administrator is impeding faster execution of projects and hampers progress. This issue has become all the more important in view of the increasing demand for better infrastructure and facilities for the citizens of Chandigarh.

Equally important is the matter of delegation of administrative powers to the UT administration. The Administration does not have the power to create posts. Its powers to frame recruitment rules is also limited to Group B, C and D posts. The Commission has been given to understand that the Chandigarh administration is functioning with diminishing manpower as a certain proportion of posts are abolished each year in accordance with the direction of the Department of Expenditure. Chandigarh is a revenue surplus UT. The Commission feels that the UT Administration should have the competence to create certain categories of posts such as teachers, doctors and para-medical staff which are necessary for delivering vital services used by the people of the Region.

Recommendations

a) There is urgent need to revisit the Capital of Punjab (Development and Regulation) Act and the Punjab New Capital (Periphery Control) Act, 1952 and examine if and how they are to be aligned with the changed circumstances. This issue should to be examined urgently by the Ministry of Home Affairs and the UT Administration.

b) The Metropolitan Planning Committee should be constituted without further delay for comprehensive planning of the entire area covered under the jurisdiction of the Union Territory of Chandigarh.

c) The entire territory under the jurisdiction of the Union Territory of Chandigarh should be declared as urban area. However, in order to protect the interest of present villages in the process of development, Ward/Area Sabhas should be constituted as recommended by the Commission in its Report on Local Governance. Also, till such time that the infrastructure in these villages comes at par with the urban areas of Chandigarh, they may be given necessary (local) tax relief.

d) The present Advisory Council to the Administrator should be substituted by a more compact and cohesive body comprising inter-alia of the Member of Parliament from Chandigarh, one MP each from Punjab and Haryana, the Mayor of Chandigarh and the Advisor to the Administrator. Such a compact body would be able to provide the necessary inputs to the Administrator and also be able to meet more frequently.

e) The Union Government should suitably enhance the financial powers of the UT administration by notifying the delegation. Within such delegated powers, the UT Administration must be given full administrative and functional autonomy. In addition, the UT of Chandigarh should also have powers to create certain categories of posts such as teachers, doctors and para-medical staff which are necessary for delivering vital services used by the people of the region.

PUDUCHERRY

The Union Territory of Puducherry comprises four areas namely Puducherry, Karaikal, Mahe and Yanam, which are not geographically contiguous. Puducherry is located in the East Coast, about 162 kms. south of Chennai. This is the largest among the four regions and consists of 12 scattered areas interspersed with enclaves of Villupuram and Cuddalore Districts of Tamil Nadu. Karaikal is about 160 kms. south of Puducherry and is bound by Nagapattinam and Thiruvarur Districts of Tamil Nadu State. Mahe lies almost parallel to Puducherry 653 kms. away on the west coast near Kannur District of Kerala State. Yanam is located about 840 kms. north-east of Puducherry and is located in the East Godhavari District of Andhra Pradesh State. The territory of Puducherry was merged with the Indian Union on 1st November, 1954 in terms of the defacto agreement signed between the Government of India and the Government of France on 21st October, 1954. The dejure transfer of Puducherry took place on 16th August, 1962. The Treaty between India and France for the cession of the French possessions of Puducherry, Karikal, Mahe and Yanam provided, inter alia, that any constitutional change in the special administrative status of the Territory which was in force prior to 1st November, 1954 (the date on which the de facto possession of the Territory was transferred to the Indian Government), would be made after ascertaining the wishes of the people of the territory. The Union Territory of Puducherry is administered under the provisions of the Government of Union Territories Act, 1963.

The Union Territory of Puducherry is 479 Sq.Kms. in area and has a population of 9,74,345 according to the 2001 census. The density of population of the Union Territory is 2034 persons/ Sq.Km. The rural population is 3,25,726 persons (33.43%)

whereas the urban population is 6,48,619 persons which constitutes 66.57% of the total population.

As against the national pattern, the percentage of population in urban areas is much higher than the population in rural areas. The entire Mahe and Yanam regions have been classified as urban. 66% of the Union Territory is classified as urban as against the All India level of 25.7%. The Scheduled Caste population is 1,57,771 and accounts for 16.19% of the total population. There are no Scheduled Tribes in the UT of Puducherry (according to the 2001 Census Report). The decadal growth rate of population is 20.62%; the Territory has four districts and ninety eight village panchayats.

Administration

As indicated earlier, Puducherry is administered as a Union Territory within the Constitutional provisions of Article 239, Article 239A and the Government of Union Territories Act. In terms of Article 239A provisions for an elected legislature and Council of Ministers for Puducherry have been made. At present, the Legislative Assembly in Puducherry has 30 elected members with a Chief Minister and Council of Ministers. The legislature has the powers to legislate in respect of the subjects under the State and Concurrent lists of Schedule 7 of the Constitution. However, being a Union Territory, the administration is directly controlled and supervised by the Union Government through the Lt. Governor (Administrator) appointed for this purpose particularly with regard to the administrative and financial matters. In order to discharge the legislative and administrative functions, the Rules of Business of the Government of Puducherry was framed in 1963 under the Government of Union Territories Act, 1963. In terms of Rules 49-58 of the said Rule, the Administrator has the powers to refer any draft Bill to the Union Government, before it is introduced in the legislature of the Union Territory and in that case the advice of the Union Government shall be awaited before the introduction of any such Bill.

The Administrator shall refer to the Union Government every Bill which:

(a) If passed by the Legislative Assembly, is required to be reserved for the consideration of the President under sub-section (2) of Section 21 or, as the case may be, under the second proviso to Section 25, of the Act;

(b) Relates to any matter enumerated in the Concurrent List in the Seventh Schedule to the Constitution;

(c) Attracts the provisions of Article 304 of the Constitution as applicable to the Union territory; (restriction of trade and commerce among States)

(d) Relates to any matter which may ultimately necessitate additional financial assistance from the Central Government through substantive expenditure from the Consolidated Fund of the Union territory or abandonment of revenue or lowering of the rate of any tax;

(e) Pertains to any matter relating to Universities;

(f) Affects or is likely to affect the interests of any minority community, Scheduled Caste or Backward Class.

Also, subject to the provisions of any instructions which may from time to time be issued by the Union Government, the Administrator shall make a prior reference to the Union Government in the Ministry of Home Affairs or to the appropriate Ministry with a copy to the Ministry of Home Affairs, in respect of the following matters, namely:

(a) All important cases raising questions of policy;

(b) Cases affecting the relations of the Central Government with any State Government, the Supreme Court or any High Court or the Court of Judicial Commissioner;

(c) proposals for appointment of the Chief Secretary, Development Commissioner, Finance Secretary, Law Secretary, Inspector General of Police and appointments to posts which carry an ultimate salary of Rs. 2,000/- per month or more;

(d) Inter-sectional alteration in plan schemes; and

(e) Non-delegated financial powers.

When a matter is referred by the Administrator to the Union Government or any other authority under these Rules, further action thereon shall not be taken except in accordance with the decision of that Government or authority.

Further, the Government of Union Territories Act (Section 23) provides that, a Bill or an amendment shall not be introduced into, or moved in the Legislative Assembly except on the recommendation of the Administrator, if such Bill or amendment makes provision for any of the following matters, namely:

(a) Imposition, abolition, remission, alteration or regulation of any tax;

(b) Amendment of the law with respect to any financial obligations undertaken or to be undertaken by the Government of the Capital;

(c) Appropriation of moneys out of the Consolidated fund of the Capital;

(d) Declaring of any expenditure to be expenditure charged on the Consolidated Fund of the Capital or the increasing of the amount of any such expenditure;

(e) Receipt of money on account of the Consolidated Fund of the Capital or the Public Account of the Capital or the custody or issue of such money or the audit of the accounts of the Capital.

Similarly, the annual financial statement pertaining to estimated receipts and expenditure for a particular year shall not be laid before the Assembly unless the previous sanction of the President has been obtained (Section 27).

Strengthening, Legislative, Financial and Administra-tive Power of the UT Administration (Puducherry)

There has been a consistent demand for granting statehood to Puducherry with special category status. The Legislative Assembly of Puducherry had passed several resolutions to this effect. However, the Government of India has not agreed to this demand mainly on the following grounds:-

(i) It is not eligible to be considered for a special category status as per the guidelines of the Planning Commission.

(ii) It is not a viable State economically. Out of its total budget of about Rs. 1050 crores in the year 2007-08, the UT had a revenue deficit of over Rs. 439crores.

(iii) It consists of four geographically, culturally and linguistically separate segments. While Puducherry and Karaikal are Tamil speaking, Mahe is Malayalam speaking and Yanam is Telugu speaking.

(iv) The per capita income of Puducherry is almost double that of neighbouring Tamil Nadu. Therefore, it cannot be said that development has suffered for want of Statehood.

While it is not within the purview of the Commission to examine this issue, it strongly recommends that the elected government should have adequate powers and authority with regard to governance and development of the Union Territory as per the aspirations and requirements of the people.

To this end, there is need to delegate much more administrative and financial powers to the Union Territory government as indicated in the following paragraphs.

Financial and Administrative Delegation

In terms of the Delegation of Financial Powers Rules (DFR), 1978, Government of India has been delegating financial powers under various categories to the Administrator / Government of Puducherry Administration. Under Rule 13 of the DFR, the Administrator has been given full powers with respect to the contingent and miscellaneous expenditure, whereas in case of sanction of a scheme/ project under Rule 18 of the DFR, he can sanction schemes valued up to Rs.10.0 Crore.

Currently, the non-plan allocation to the Union Territory stands at Rs.439 crores. For the last several years, the allocation has remained at this level whereas for other States and Union Territories there has usually been an increase of 10% per annum. There is a demand that this amount needs to be suitably enhanced.

As already stated, the Commission is of the view that the elected government in Puducherry must have unfettered powers with regard to its development and governance as per the needs and aspirations of the local population. The control of the Union Government in the legislative and executive domain of the UT Assembly needs to be reduced. Various requirements of the legislative Bills to be referred to the Union Government and the discretion of the Administrator in this regard needs to be reconsidered and suitably minimized. This would require more delegation of administrative and financial powers to the Government which should be revised once in five years. The Council of Ministers should be free to discharge its functions within such delegation with freedom and discretion.

Panchayats in Puducherry

In the Union Territory of Puducherry, there are only two tiers of Panchayat namely, Village Panchayats and Commune Panchayats (Middle level Panchayats) and no District Panchayats. There are 10 Commune Panchayats and 98 Village Panchayats and they are governed by the Puducherry Village and Commune Panchayat Acts, 1973. The 73rd Constitutional amendment was implemented in Puducherry by a Notification dated 24th April, 1993 of Ministry of Rural Development, Government of India. In addition, a second notification was issued on 13th April, 1994 by the Ministry of Home Affairs, Government of India stating that Article 243-ZD of the Constitution shall apply to the UT of Puducherry with the modification that the 'intermediate-level' shall substitute the word 'district-level' in the said Article.

The Commission has recommended a slew of measures in its Sixth Report on "Local governance" to strengthen and empower local government institutions, which needs to be implemented on priority.

Power to Raise Public Debt

Similar to Delhi, the Puducherry Administration, though having a Legislative Assembly is not permitted to raise public debt which does not seem to be appropriate. This issue has been examined in detail earlier in this Chapter while dealing with GNCT of Delhi. The Commission feels that Puducherry should be treated at par with Delhi and the recommendations made therein should equally apply in the case of Puducherry.

Recommendations:

a) There should be enhanced financial and administrative delegation of powers to the Government of Puducherry. The Council of Ministers should be free to discharge its functions effectively within such delegation.

b) The delegation of powers should be made as suggested in Table No. 4.13 and revised once in five years.

c) Recommendations made by the Commission in its Report on "Local Governance" (6th Report) may be implemented on priority in order to strengthen and empower the PRIs in Puducherry.

d) The Puducherry Administration should be given the powers to raise public debt in order to finance its development projects and plans.

ANDAMAN AND NICOBAR ISLANDS

The territory of the Andaman and Nicobar Islands comprises of a group of 572 islands, islets and rocks lying in the south-eastern part of the Bay of Bengal. It has a total geographical area of 8249 sq. kms. and 38 of its islands are inhabited. There are three districts, namely North and Middle Andamans, South Andamans and Nicobar. The total population of the UT as per the 2001 census is 3,56,152 with a population density of 43 per sq. km. Most of the people are from mainland, particularly the West Bengal, Andhra Pradesh, Tamil Nadu, etc. giving the territory the sobriquet "Little India". Andamans is also home to indigenous tribes, four of which are Negritos, namely the Great Andamanese, Onge, Jarawa and Sentinalese who live in forests in the Andaman group of islands and two are Mongoloid tribes, namely the Nicobarese and Shompens living in the Nicobar Islands. Some of these tribes are on the verge of extinction and some, particularly the Sentinalese, are still hostile. Their prime mode of livelihood is hunting and fishing.

Administration in Andaman & Nicobar Islands

When the Islands became a Union Territory in 1956 an Advisory Council to the Chief Commissioner (CCSE) with four members nominated by the Union Government was constituted. In 1961, the CCSE was supplanted by the Home Minister's Advisory Council (HMAC), comprising three ex-officio and three non-official members. The number of nonofficials later rose to seven. In 1963, a new advisory committee to the Chief Commissioner (CCAC) was constituted in addition to the HMAC. Originally this body consisted of six members. Later on, the strength was increased to 12 in 1972-73 and 20 in 1977, with direct election of the members. In 1979 a 30 members indirectly elected Pradesh Council was constituted. In 1981, a Pradesh Council presided over by the Administrator with 24 elected Pradhans of Gram Panchayats, the Member of Parliament, the Vice-President of the Port Blair Municipal Board, 3 nominated tribal members and a woman nominee as members was formed. When the three tier panchayat system with 67 Gram Panchayats at the village level, 7 Panchayat samities at the block level and

3 Zila Parishads at the district level came into existence in 1994, the provision for the Pradesh Advisory Council was repealed.

Coordination Mechanism at the Union Level

The Administration of the Union Territory of Andaman and Nicobar Islands is controlled and supervised by the Ministry of Home Affairs, Government of India through the Lt. Governor (Administrator) appointed under Article 239 of the Constitution and in terms of the Government of Union Territories Act, 1963. However, considering the special nature of these far flung territories, a special body called Islands Development Authority was set up in the Planning Commission for the Andaman and Nicobar Islands and Lakshadweep in 1986. There is also the Home Minister's Advisory Committee whose task is to advise regarding legal, administrative, financial and other matters relating to the Union Territory.

Home Minister's Advisory Committee

As per a notification of the Ministry of Home Affairs dated 21.11.1996, the meetings of the Advisory Committee are presided over by the Minister of Home Affairs and in his absence by the Minister of State in that Ministry. The Committee currently consists of the following members:-

(a) Lt. Governor, Andaman & Nicobar Islands

(b) Member of Lok Sabha representing the UT

(c) Five Members from Zila Parishad

(d) Chairman of Municipal Council and two other Members of the Council

(e) Two members to be nominated by the Minister of Home Affairs on the recommendation of Lt. Governor to represent Nicobar Group of Islands, one of these to be a woman member.

(f) One woman member to be nominated by the Minister of Home Affairs on the recommendations of the Lt. Governor from the among the Members of the Zila Parishad if there is no woman in (c) above.

(g) Secretary to the Islands Development Authority as a permanent invitee.

The terms of reference of the Committee are inter alia:

1. General questions of Policy relating to the Administration of the Territory.
2. All legislative proposals concerning the Territory in regard to matters in theState list.
3. Such matters relating to the Annual Financial Statement of the Union in so far as it concerns the Territory and such other financial question as be referred to it by the President.
4. Any other matter on which it may be considered necessary or desirable by the Minister of Home Affairs that the Advisory Committee should be consulted.

Only three meetings of the Committee have been held since its reorganization in 1996, the last being on 20.12.2006.

Islands Development Authority

The Islands Development Authority (IDA) was constituted in August, 1986 under the Chairmanship of the Prime Minister to formulate policies and programmes for an integrated development of Andaman and Nicobar Islands and Lakshadweep with the following terms of reference:

1. To decide on policies and programmes for an integrated development of the islands, keeping in view all aspects of environmental protection, as well as the special technical and scientific requirement of the Islands.
2. To review progress of implementation and impact of the programmes of development.

The IDA cell in the Planning Commission serves as its Secretariat. A Standing Committee under the Chairmanship of

Deputy Chairman, Planning Commission was also constituted in October, 1990 to follow up on the decisions of the IDA. The terms of reference for the Standing Committee inter alia include preparation of perspective plans for both the Islands, identifying appropriate programmes within the special requirements and limitations of the Islands and monitor and review the progress of development activities and plans. It is also required to facilitate interaction with Union Ministries and agencies and provide technical and other support required for the development of these Islands. Since its inception in 1986, only 12 meetings of the IDA have been held.

KEY ADMINISTRATIVE AND DEVELOPMENT ISSUES

Need for restructuring existing institutions

Due to its geographical location and its unique features, providing good governance to the A & N Islands is a major challenge. Its strategic security concerns, preservation of natural resources, development, empowerment of local governments, involvement of local people in the administration, protection of the endangered tribes, transport and connectivity are major issues of governance to be reckoned with. There is need to balance the conflicting nature of many of the concerns. The present institutional set-up, both at the UT and the Union levels has not been able to adequately meet these administrative challenges. On the other hand, there continues to be a growing demand for people's voice and representation in the governance of the Islands which is lacking mainly due to the absence of strong institutions of democratic governance and adequate decentralization of power. There has also been a demand for a Legislative Assembly on the pattern of Delhi and Puducherry.

The Commission during its visit to the Andaman Islands had occasion to discuss some of the key administrative issues with the Lt. Governor (Administrator), officers of the Administration, the Member of Parliament, Panchayat and Zila Parishad members as well as members of the public and the media. While it may not be feasible to have an elected Legislative Assembly in this territory (because of security and other considerations), the Commission feels that it is important to restructure and strengthen the institutional arrangements both at the Union and UT levels in the interests of administrative expediency, efficiency and closer involvement of the inhabitants so that they have a voice in the Island's administration and governance.

At the UT level, a three-tier Panchayati Raj system is in place and the Commission's recommendations on Local Self Governance in its sixth Report would further strengthen them. But between these PRIs and the Home Minister's Advisory Committee/ IDA there is a great hiatus and hence there is need for an effective local but high level consultative institution. The Commission feels that this could be in the form of an Administrator's Advisory Council comprising the Chief Secretary, the local Member of Parliament, Chairpersons of Zila Parishad and Port Blair Municipal Council and senior representatives of the Ministries of Home Affairs, Tribal Affairs, Environment, Forests and Defence and the Planning Commission. With relevant terms of reference and frequent meetings, this Committee should be able to provide an intermediate platform for meaningful consultations and suggestions for the consideration of the Administrator and the Union Government.

Since the issues facing the Islands are multi-faceted and require large financial and special manpower resources, the Union Government will necessarily have to continue to play a leadership role in facilitating the Islands' future development and ensuring security of this strategic area. Neither the Home Minister's Advisory Council (because of infrequent meetings) nor the Island Development Authority has been able to fully realize this mandate. Even though very important directions have emanated from the IDA by the Prime Minister, the fact is that these meetings are burdened with far too many items of somewhat routine nature which do not require the intervention of such a high level body. For example, in the last meeting the agenda items included issues like settling contractors' bills, fixing prices of aracanut, building houses for old settlers, etc. The Commission, therefore, feels that these two high level Committees may be replaced by more functional bodies. The IDA could be replaced by a multi-disciplinary task force under the Deputy Chairman, Planning Commission which would lay down the road map for the Andaman & Nicobar Islands Administration both for medium term and long term perspective plan and monitoring its implementations. The Home Minister's Advisory Committee may be replaced by a Committee under the Chairmanship of the Union Home Secretary with officers of suitable seniority from the Ministries of Environment and Forests, Tribal Affairs, Finance, Defence, Shipping and Planning Commission to examine and give prima facie administrative approval to important proposals. Some of the key issues which would need to be kept in mind while preparing any plans or proposals for the Andaman & Nicobar Islands are listed below.

Security concerns

The security significance of these Islands stems from the fact of its close proximity to other countries and to an important international sea route. Its proximity to the Malacca Straits and growing Chinese presence in the area highlights its importance (Aceh in Indonesia is only 40 nautical miles away from Indira Point, the tip of the Great Nicobar Island). These Islands have a vast coastline (1/4th of the total coast line of the country) and because of isolated and scattered islands and adverse weather conditions, surveillance is inconsistent. The seas around these islands are not adequately patrolled which makes poaching of timber and marine produce and illegal immigration fairly easy. There have been, reports of smuggling weapons meant for Myanmar and the North-East. Even though the South-Eastern Naval Command was created some years ago, the Indian Navy has very few ships stationed in the Islands. In fact the Armed Forces often rely on the shipping services of the UT Administration.

Carrying Capacity of the Islands

Despite the fact that several islands are uninhabited and there are occasional proposals to inhabit some of these in a planned manner, there is also a point of view that the carrying capacity of the islands has perhaps already been exceeded. This issue, therefore, needs to be addressed in the light of the following considerations:

(a) Over 90 per cent of the Islands is under reserve forest cover and the Supreme Court has issued directives placing severe restrictions on exploitation of the forests in the light of the Forest Conservation Act, 1980. A balanced view between defence requirements, development and preservation of forests needs to be taken. A minimum percentage below which the reserve forest area shall not be reduced may be fixed by law, as applicable to these islands only.

(b) Because of the topography and climatic reasons the islands are not self sufficient in any kind of food other than sea food and this situation is not likely to change. There will be an increasing dependence on supplies shipped from the mainland to sustain the population.

(c) Power generation is almost entirely diesel based.

(d) There are no rivers on the islands, and all water supply is based on stored rain water. This constraint places severe limitations on the kinds of economic activities that can be undertaken and the number of people who can be sustained.

(e) Sustaining a supply chain for 38 islands, taxes the shipping infrastructure. There is a significant drop in the quality of supplies away from Port Blair and further increases in density of population will impose heavy costs.

(f) The encouragement of tourism also impinges on carrying capacity and needs to be carefully balanced.

Issues of Connectivity

The airport at Port Blair can take only single aisle jet aircraft and because of the topography, these aircrafts can take off only in one direction. In any case, air services cater to only a small segment of the traffic and the bulk of passengers, both to and from the mainland and between the islands, rely on shipping services, which are heavily subsidized.

Affordable passage between the Island and the mainland remains a necessity to prevent a sense of isolation and promoting integration. In the last meeting of the Island Development Authority, one of the important agenda items pertained to need for reforms in the shipping services since they are the lifeline of the Islands. The setting up of a new Corporation by the Ministry of Shipping for managing and maintaining the shipping State and District Administation Administration of the Union Territories services and all related activities for the A&N Islands and Lakshadweep was discussed in detail. Earlier an Expert Committee had gone into this issue but an urgent decision after carefully weighing the pros and cons still needs to be taken.

Endangered Tribes

The Andaman & Nicobar Islands have about 30,000 tribals and in the past they have suffered as their habitat shrank and land was increasingly appropriated for government use, etc. In the last meeting of the Island Development Authority, the Prime Minister had directed that there is need to evolve a sensitive approach towards tribals especially the primitive tribal groups. There is need to learn from the experience of the implementation of the policy on Jarawa tribes while formulating the policy on other primitive tribal groups. The Ministries of Home Affairs and Tribal Affairs need to work in close coordination in this connection.

Human Resource Development

Within the Island, opportunities for wage employment are mainly in the government sector and it is not likely that recruitment in this sector can keep pace with the increasing population. Educated youth will, therefore, need to look at the mainland for economic opportunities. As competitive pressures on the mainland are far higher than in the Islands, it would be desirable that adequate number of seats in institutions of learning, particularly higher learning, in the mainland are earmarked for students from the Islands. This would acclimatize them suitably, integrate them emotionally and provide wider opportunities of employment, including in the Islands where a number of technical posts (for example doctors) is not easy to fill up.

The above issues should be addressed and put in the form of a medium and long term perspective plan by the proposed Committee of the Planning Commission in consultation with the Advisory Council of the Lt. Governor.

Administrative and Financial Delegation

During the visit of the Commission to the Islands, the issue of administrative and financial delegation was strongly raised by the Administrator and the UT Administration officials. It was emphasized that there is a need to give due weight for the development of the islands under the UT apart from the focused attention on security measures, considering the strategic location of these islands. It was felt that presently the long winded channels of decision making and inadequate delegation of financial and administrative powers against quick decision making. Therefore, the islands need more powers to be delegated to the UT Administration for smooth administration in such an isolated area. A case study on raising of Dhanikhari Dam for augmenting supply of drinking water, given below sharply illustrates the above concerns.

The Administrator of A&N Islands is vested with financial powers as per the Delegation of Financial Rules, 1978. The Ministry of Home Affairs has from time to time re-delegated powers to the Administrator in those important items as necessary for the smooth functioning of the administration.

Raising of Dhanikhari Dam: Case Study of a Drinking Water Supply Scheme

- The DPR prepared by NHPC was submitted to Secretary Ministry of Water Resources, GOI by Chief Secretary, Andamans on 08.01.2004.
- The Director (State Plans) and Deputy Advisor (Water Resources), GOI visited Dhanikhari Dam Site on 31/01.2004 for first stand information of the proposal.
- Again the Secretary (PWD) took up the matter with Joint Secretary (UD), Ministry of Urban Development vide letter dated 24/03/2004.
- The Director WS & PG Ministry of Urban Development sought some clarification vide letter dated 27/04/2004.
- The reply was sent by Commissioner-cum-Secretary (PWD) vide D.O. letter dated 09/06/2004.
- Further clarification by Under Secretary MOUD was sought vide letter dated 22/07/2004.
- The reply was sent by Secretary (PWD) to Director (WS & PG) vide letter dated 25/08/2004.
- The Central Water Commission asked for additional eight volume of DPR vide letter dated 25/05/2005 which was sent vide our letter dated 07/06/2005.
- Chief Engineer, APWD informed Joint Secretary (MORWS) regarding submission of all quarries vide fax message dated 06/08/2005.
- Further technical clarification was sought by the Director (UT) vide letter dated 06/11/2006.
- The reply was sent by Superintending Engineer, PBCC vide letter dated 08/11/2006.
- On further request from Ministry the modified cost estimation amounting to Rs.19.43 crores was submitted to Director, Central Water Commission vide Superintending Engineer, PBCC letter dated 09/05/2007.
- Technical clearance was conveyed by Ministry of Urban Development vide letter dated 13/07/2007.
- Administrative approval was conveyed vide letter dated 08/08/2007 of Director, Water Supply, Ministry of Urban Development.
- SFC cleared the Expenditure Sanction vide Minutes dated 24/04/2008.
- MoU signed between Administration & NHPC on 25/09/2008.

Source: Presentation made by the A&N Administration during the visit of Commission to the Islands.

The Commission is of the view that there is urgent need to address this issue and ensure adequate administrative/financial powers to the Andaman & Nicobar Administration, which should be revised once in five years.

Recommendations

a) The Union Government should constitute an Advisory Council to the Administrator of Andaman & Nicobar Islands consisting of the local Member of Parliament, the Chief Secretary, Chairpersons of the Zila Parishad and Municipal Concil and senior representatives from the Ministries of Home Affairs, Tribal Affairs, Environment, Forests and Defence and the Planning Commission to advise him on all important matters of administration.

b) The Home Minister's Advisory Committee may be replaced by a Committee under the Chairmanship of the Home Secretary with officers of suitable seniority from the Ministries of Environment and Forests, Tribal Affairs, Finance, Defence, Shipping and Planning Commission to examine and give prima facie administrative approval to important proposals concerning this Territory.

c) The IDA may be replaced by a multi-disciplinary task force under the Chairmanship of the Deputy Chairman, Planning Commission. This body should be responsible for laying down guidelines for preparing medium and long term perspective plans for the overall development of the islands and monitoring its implementations.

d) Recommendations made by the Commission in its Report on Local Governance (Sixth Report) should be examined and implemented to the extent they are relevant to strengthening and empowering local government institutions in the Andaman & Nicobar Islands.

e) The Union Government should enhance financial powers of the UT administration. This should be revised once in five years. Within such delegated powers, the UT

Administration must be given full administrative and functional autonomy.

LAKSHADWEEP

The Union Territory of Lakshadweep is a group of 37 Islands with a total land area of 32 sq.km. Considering the lagoon area of 4,200 Sq.kms, 20,000 Sq.kms of territorial waters and about 4 lakhs Sq.kms. of economic zone, Lakshadweep is a fairly large territory. It consists of ten inhabited and 17 uninhabited islands, four newly formed islets and 5 submerged reefs. The inhabited islands are Kavaratti, Agatti, Amini, Kadmat, Kiltan, Chetlat, Bitra, Andrott, Kalpeni and Minicoy, popularly known as Laccadives. Its total population is 60,650 with an urban component of 44.47%. Its literacy rate is 86.7%. It consists of only one district which is a Lok Sabha Constituency too.

Administration in Lakshadweep: Need for an Apex Representative Structure for the UT

Formed as a Union Territory in 1956, it was named Lakshadweep in 1973. It was brought under the direct control of the Ministry of Home Affairs, in order to bring these Islands in the mainstream of development. Since then it is being administered by the Union Government through an Administrator appointed for this purpose. Comprising of a single district, it is the smallest UT in the Indian Union. The area is further divided into 4 tehsils and 5 community development blocks. The Panchayati Raj Institutions started functioning here in 1997 with a 2 tier system comprising of 10 Villages (Dweep) Panchayats and one District Panchayat. There are 79 Village Dweep Panchayat Wards, 22 District Panchayat Wards and one Lok Sabha seat. The Headquarters island of Lakshadweep is Kavaratti. Its distance by sea is 346 kms. from Khozikode, 404 kms. from Kochi and 352 kms. from Mangalore.

The Island has an Advisory Committee chaired by the Home Minister which has a mandate to review its socio economic development. The Committee consists of the Administrator of

Lakshadweep, the local Member of the Parliament and representatives of PRIs. An Island Development Authority constituted in 1986 is responsible for formulating policies and programmes for integrated development of Lakshadweep and the A&N Islands.

The Commission is of the view that the issues of governance in the Lakshadweep Islands are more or less similar to those of the A&N Islands, though in a smaller measure. There are strategic security concerns, preservation of natural resources, development, empowerment of local governments, involvement of local people in the administration, transport and connectivity. In order to meet the challenges of governance in these Islands, the Commission suggested a new institutional set up in the case of the A&N Islands, in an earlier Chapter. These suggestions would be applicable to Lakshadweep also with suitable modifications. Accordingly, an Advisory Council to the Administrator of Lakshadweep may be constituted consisting of the local Member of Parliament, Chairman of the Zila Parishad and representatives of the Ministries of Home Affairs, Tribal Affairs, Environment, Forests and Defence and the Planning Commission. The Home Minister's Advisory Committee for Lakshadweep may be replaced by a Committee under the Chairmanship of the Home Secretary with officers of suitable seniority from the Ministries of Environment and Forests, Tribal Affairs, Finance, Defence, Shipping and Planning Commission to examine and give prima facie approval to important proposals concerning the UT administration.

As suggested in the case of the A&N Islands, the IDA to be replaced by a multidisciplinary task force under the Deputy Chairman of the Planning Commission could also lay down guidelines for preparing and monitoring the medium and long term perspective plans for overall development of the Lakshadweep islands.

Local Government

Consequent to the 73rd Constitutional Amendment, the Lakshadweep Panchayats Regulation, 1994 was promulgated by the President of India on 23rd April, 1994 and the provisions of the Regulation were brought into force on 23rd May, 1995. The first village panchayats were constituted in December 1997 and the District Panchayat in January, 1998. In all, there are ten Village (Dweep) Panchayats falling under the District Panchayat. Sanitation, Public Health, Public Works, Planning and Development and Social Welfare are the major matters which fall within the jurisdiction of Village Panchayat; whereas the District Panchayat has been given 29 matters which cover the subjects listed under the 11th Schedule of the Constitution.

As mentioned earlier, the Union Territory of Lakshadweep is administered by the Union Government through a senior officer designated as the Administrator. PRIs are the elected institutions which give voice to the aspirations of local people and which involve them in the developmental process. Considering the unique topography of the UT, therefore, strengthening and empowering institutions of local governance is crucial in providing good governance to the citizens. Although steps have been taken to constitute and activate Panchayati Raj Institutions as per provisions of the Panchayat Regulation discussed above, the Commission during its visit, felt that they need to be further strengthened.

A closer examination of the Panchayats Regulation, 1994 indicates that major powers regarding control and supervision over the Panchayats lie with the Administrator. The Administrator has been given powers to issue directions, sanction projects, accord previous sanction before acquiring property, disqualify the members, powers to inspect etc. These powers are almost identical with those enjoyed by governments of the larges States in the country (vide State Panchayat Raj Acts of Bihar, U.P., M.P. etc.).

It is a well accepted principle that in order to make PRIs effective institutions of self governance, devolution of functions will have to be suitably matched by devolution of adequate funds and functionaries. The interactions of the Commission with the representatives of various Panchayats during its visit to

Lakshadweep indicated that the actual position in both these respects is not satisfactory. PRIs have not been provided with adequate staff to assist them in discharging various developmental functions entrusted to them.

As regards funds, PRIs in Lakshadweep are fully dependent on the grants and assistance provided by the UT administration. Though, they have been given powers to collect certain taxes and fees, their own resource generation is very meager. It was observed that the grants given to them by the Administration are not based on any rational criteria. For example, the Administration provides an untied developmental grant of Rs 20 lakhs to the District Panchayat and Rs 5 lakhs each to the Dweep Panchayats every year for the developmental schemes implemented by them. Such blanket and uniform grants without any analysis of the actual requirements of a particular Dweep Panchayat is not fair and needs to be based on some criteria and the needs of each Panchayat.

The Commission has considered all major issues pertaining to the strengthening and empowerment of PRIs in its Report on "Local Governance" and suggested a number of measures to increase their efficacy. The Ministry of Home Affairs may take immediate steps to implement these recommendations in Lakshadweep.

Financial and Administrative Delegation

As in the case of other Union Territories, the model financial delegation could be as under:

Proposed Financial Delegation in Respect of Lakshadweep Administration

Sl. No.	Items of Expenditure	Existing Financial Delegation	Proposed Financial Delegation
1.	Rule 18 of the DFR Expenditure on Schemes/ Projects (Plan)	5.00 Crore	10.00

(contd.)

2.	Rule 18 of the DFR Expenditure on Works (Plan)	2.40 Crore	5.00
3.	Rule 21 of the DFR Expenditure on indents/ Purchases	Same as above	5.00

The delegated powers should be revised once in five years. Within these powers, the UT Administration should be given full administrative and functional autonomy.

Recommendations

a) The Union Government should constitute an Advisory Council to the Administrator of Lakshadweep consisting of the local Member of Parliament, Chairman of the Zila Parishad and representatives of the Ministries of Home Affairs, Tribal Affairs, Environment and Forests and Defence and the Planning Commission to advise him on all important matters of administration.

b) The Home Minister's Advisory Committee as existing today may be replaced by a Committee under the Chairmanship of the Home Secretary with officers of suitable seniority from the Ministries of Environment and Forests, Tribal Affairs, Finance, Defence, Shipping and Planning Commission to examine and give prima facie approval to important proposals concerning this territory.

c) The multi-disciplinary task force under the Chairmanship of the Deputy Chairman, Planning Commission, recommended to be set up for the Andaman & Nicobar Islands in place of the Island Development Authority should also include the Lakshadweep Islands. This Committee would be responsible for laying down guidelines for preparing medium and long term perspective plans for the over all development of the Islands and for monitoring its implementation.

d) Recommendations made by the Commission in its Report on Local Governance (Sixth Report) should be examined and implemented to the extent they are relevant to strengthening and empowering local government institutions in Lakshadweep Islands.

e) The Union Government should enhance the financial powers of the UT administration by notifying the delegation proposed in the Table No. 4.15. This could be reviewed once in five years. Within such delegated powers, the UT Administration should be given full administrative and functional autonomy.

DAMAN & DIU AND DADRA & NAGAR HAVELI

Daman & Diu

Located on the Western Coast Daman & Diu is the second smallest Union Territory of India. Daman is situated near Surat while Diu is located close to Junagadh in the Saurashtra Peninsula of Gujarat. Till 1987, Daman & Diu were parts of the UT of Goa. When Goa became a fullfledged State, they were converted into a separate UT, consisting of 2 districts Daman & Diu. It has an area 112 Sq.Km. with a population of 1,58,204 and literacy rate 78.20%.

Dadra & Nagar Haveli

The UT of Dadra & Nagar Haveli with a population of 2,20,490 and literacy rate of 57.6% consists of two separate enclaves. Dadra is surrounded by the State of Gujarat, whereas Nagar Haveli lies on the borders between Maharashtra and Gujarat. Dadra consists of three villages and Nagar Haveli consists of a town named Silvassa and 68 villages with an area of 491 Sq.Km. The territory is inhabited by a number of ethnic groups, viz. the Varlis, Dublas, Dhodias and Koknans. Agriculture is the main occupation and the area produces rice, pulses and fruits. Dadra & Nagar Haveli came under Portuguese Rule between 1783 and 1785. It became a Union Territory in 1961. Silvassa, its capital is about 14 Kms, from Bhilad and Vapi.

Administration of the UT and Local Government

Daman & Diu

Prior to the 73rd Constitutional Amendment, the UT of Daman and Diu had Panchayats only at the village level. These Panchayats were regulated under the provisions of the Goa, Daman and Diu Village Panchayat Regulation, 1962. But they are now being governed by the Daman and Diu Village Panchayats (Amended) Regulations 1994, under which a two tier Panchayat consisting of District and Village Panchayats exists in the Territory. There are two District Panchayats, one at Daman and the other at Diu.

Consequent to the 73rd Constitutional Amendment and as provided under Article 243G of the Constitution of India, all 29 matters listed in the Eleventh Schedule of the Constitution have been transferred to District Panchayats through a notification in July 2006. However, the actual activity mapping has been done so far for only 18 subjects. As a result, the Panchayats play only a nominal role in the transferred functions. Unlike in other UTs, the Daman and Diu Village Panchayat (Amendment) Act 1994 provides specifically and statutorily that planning functions should be performed by Village and District Panchayats. Another unique feature of the 1994 Act is the provision for consultations by the Administrator with the president-cum-chief counsellor and the vice president-cumcounsellor who are elected office bearers of the District Panchayat, on any matter specified in its Fourth Schedule relating to Panchayats, training of Panchayat staff, administration and coordination of Panchayat activities, public distribution system, rural electrification, tax proposals and on any other matter on which the administration may like to consult. This provision is an important link between the Administration and the Panchayats.

In 1996, the UT Administration initiated steps to post adequate number of personnel to the District Panchayats, so that they could be enabled to exercise their functions and powers effectively. While the exercise was still underway to devolve activities relating to the 29 matters listed in the Eleventh Schedule, a detailed order was notified in September 2006, transferring the officials concerned from the departments of the government to the Panchayats.

The Ministry of Panchayati Raj, Government of India has closely examined the status of Panchayati Raj in all the States and Union Territories in its Report on "The State of Panchayats 2007-08: An Independent Assessment". For Daman and Diu, this paper makes the following important observations:

> "The Panchayats in Daman and Diu have been formally devolved powers and functions relating to the 29 matters listed in the Eleventh Schedule of the Constitution through incorporation in the PR Act. Activity mapping is claimed to have been carried out for 18 matters. Following the report of the First Finance commission and consequent to the approval of the Ministry of Home Affairs, activities and schemes have been transferred to the Panchayats in respect of these in 2001. An examination of these orders would show that most activities have been devolved to the District Panchayat. However, the District Panchayat has few executive powers and most continue with the Administrator. There are overlaps between the functional domain of the District and the Village Panchayats. Ambiguity in the functional domain has resulted in a lack of role clarity between departments and panchayats thereby enabling line departments to carry out their activities unhindered as before. It therefore appears that the devolution of functions has remained largely on paper and there is a long way to go before Panchayats actually are de facto empowered and elected Panchayat members clearly know the extent of power and responsibilities that have been entrusted to them. The Sarpanch and Village Panchayat members have very little information on the power devolved and they still view Panchayats as a medium to implement development schemes rather than to design and make their own plans for development. Even though

functionaries have been devolved on paper to the Panchayats, they continue to function under the supervision and control of the Collector's office and the Panchayats have no control over them."

A glance at the scheme of devolution reveals that the execution of only certain schemes has been given to the Panchayats. The responsibilities of the Panchayats remain vague. Even for schemes which stand transferred to the Panchayats, the allocations are woefully inadequate. The Commission feels that departments like education and health which account for the bulk of the functionaries as well as the budget can be transferred to Panchayats without much delay. Civic services such as provision of drinking water, sanitation, and street lighting could also be handed over to the Panchayats.

The delegation of financial powers to Panchayats too, is restricted. A Sarpanch is authorized to spend only Rs.500 in cash on a project. He can purchase materials upto Rs.5000 but only after obtaining prior approval of the Block Development Officer. The income from taxes and fees collected by the Village Panchayat is meager and needs to be increased substantially through better mobilization of tax revenues and supplemented by financial assistance from government. More powers need to be given to the Panchayats so that they can utilize their funds for the benefit of their areas. The institutional linkage between the two tiers of Panchayat as well as that between the Panchayats and the government departments are weak.

Dadra & Nagar Haveli

Panchayats came into existence in this part of the country in 1965 when the Dadra and Nagar Haveli Panchayat Regulation was enacted (1965) to establish local government in this territory. After the 73rd Constitutional Amendment, the Dadra and Nagar Haveli Village Panchayat (Amendment) Regulation, 1994 (amended in 2002) brought a two tier Panchayatiraj structure into existence.

Activity mapping for devolution of functions, functionaries and funds was completed in this Territory in 2004. Out of the 29 subjects mentioned for devolution in the Eleventh Schedule, 20 subjects have been transferred fully and seven subjects partially to Panchayats. All these functions have been transferred formally to the District Panchayat except Libraries which stand transferred to Gram Panchayats.

The functionaries of the 26 subjects listed in the Eleventh Schedule have been placed partially under the control of the Panchayats. But they draw their salary from the respective parent department. These transferred officials work under the administrative control of Panchayats. But major powers such as the power to take disciplinary action still lies with the respective line department. Panchayats also do not have their own staff, though some Village Panchayats have appointed peon and support staff like electricians and computer operators from the fund generated by tax collections.

The Ministry of Panchayati Raj, Government of India has examined the status of Panchayati Raj in the States and Union Territories of the country in its Report as "The State of Panchayats 2007-08: An Independent Assessment". For the Union Territory of Dadra and Nagar Haveli, this paper makes following important observations:-

> "Panchayats seem to be working well with devolution of many functions. Their effectiveness can be improved further by completely devolving functionaries and funds to them rather than transferring officials in diverted capacity and providing tied funds. The service rules for Panchayats may be framed for functioning of Panchayats more efficiently. These efforts would require suitable capacity building to achieve successful outcomes."

The Commission has examined all these issues in its Sixth Report on 'Local Governance' and has made a number of important recommendations covering devolution of functions, activity mapping, devolution of fund, resource generation by Panchayats, personnel management, issues of accountability etc. Some of these recommendations have also been summarized in Chapter 1 of this Report. The Commission reiterates that the implementation of these recommendations would go a long way in strengthening local government institutions in these Union Territories.

Financial Delegation

Under the "Delegation of Financial Powers Rules, 1978" the Government of India has been delegating financial powers under various categories to the Administrator of the Union Territories. Under Rule 13 of the DFR, the Administrator has been given full powers with respect to contingent and miscellaneous expenditure. But for sanction of a new scheme/ project (under Rule 18 of the DFR), the Administrator's power is limited only upto Rs.5 crores whereas, for expenditure on works, the Administrator's power goes upto Rs.2.4 crores. For speedier decision making and faster implementation of projects, these powers need to be enhanced.

Issue of Human Resources

In its interaction with the Commission, the Administration of Daman & Diu pointed out the difficulties being faced by it in implementing various projects and programmes of the government, due to inadequacy of staff at the operational levels.

In respect of Daman & Diu, following the creation of a separate Union Territory, the Government of India at different times, sanctioned a number of senior level posts to man the administration. These include the Chief Secretary-cum-Development Commissionercum- Inspector General of Police, Finance Secretary, Deputy Inspector General of Police and Law Officer and later, the ex-cadre posts of Administrator of Daman & Diu and Managing Director of the Omnibus Industrial Development Corporation. Two posts of Collector and two posts of Supdt. Of Police (for Daman & Diu) were also sanctioned. All these posts were filled up by officers of the All India Services. In addition, the UT also has 10 posts which are staffed by officers of the Daman & Diu and Andaman & Nicobar Civil Services (DANICS cadre) and two posts manned by the DANIPS of Daman & Diu and Andaman & Nicobar Police Service8. This has resulted in an administrative structure which is top heavy.

Over a period of time, there has been significant increase in the activities of the UT Administration because of rapid growth and establishment of business and industrial activity in the area with a consequent increase in the population.

This has necessitated strong presence in the departments dealing with commercial taxes, labour, employment and factories. Programmes dealing with primary education and health have also substantially increased. Unfortunately, there has not been a corresponding increase in the operational staff of the concerned departments. This inadequacy of staff has also affected activities relating to promotion of tourism and implementation of centrally Sponsored Schemes. The large coastal area, because of recent activities by terrorist organizations and other clandestine groups, has highlighted the need for much more extensive patrolling for which the police will also need to be appropriately strengthened.

The Commission feels that in the interests of good governance, there is need to have adequate staff at operational levels in the different departments in both the UTs. Any attempt to fix the number of government employees on the basis of a pre-conceived notion of right sizing will not be fair. There is need to rationalize the size of the governmental machinery by suitably adjusting the strength of the staff on the basis of functional requirements. The operating levels must be adequately manned. At the same time, the government needs to examine the issue of having so many senior level posts in Daman & Diu.

Recommendations

a) The recommendations made by the Commission in its Report on 'Local Governance' should be implemented on priority by the Union Government in Daman & Diu and Dadra & Nagar Haveli.

b) The Union Government should immediately enhance financial powers of the UT administration. This should be revised once in five years. Within such delegated powers, the UT Administration must be given full administrative and functional autonomy.

c) The Union Government should review the requirement of personnel at different levels in both the UTs. The operating levels should be adequately manned. At the same time, the Government should examine the issue of having so many senior level posts in Daman & Diu, which has resulted in a top-heavy administration.

5

Governance Issues in the North-Eastern States

INTRODUCTION

India's North Eastern Region consisting of Assam, Meghalaya, Tripura, Manipur, Nagaland, Mizoram, Arunachal Pradesh and Sikkim is a rich mosaic of diverse customs, practices, terrain, climate, ethnicity (over 140 major tribes out of 573 in the country), institutions, land systems, languages and cultural norms. The area is geographically divided into discrete plains and regions encompassed within hills, having a number of agro-climatic zones within them. Almost the whole of it is characterized by heavy precipitation (200 mm to 600 mm), rich bio-diversity, fragile hills, high seismicity, and a drainage system marked by extensive lateral valleys in the north and transverse valleys in the south. The terrain is dissected by perennial rivers and raging torrents and the relief varies from less than 50 metres to more than 5000 metres above the mean sea level. Communication in the area is difficult and expensive.

The region was in a better economic condition a century ago. The vast river systems and small rivulets were a means of livelihood for a majority of the population in the valleys and the plains. Global trade was conducted through the sea-route, a network of inland waterways, and land transportation through road and railways. In fact, the railway network between Dibrugarh and Chittagong constructed by the British in the late nineteenth

Map of North-Eastern States of India

century was one of their earliest projects in India. The natural transportation route through East Bengal not only reduced the physical distance but also provided emotional integration among people of this region. The rapid spread of tea plantation in India followed the establishment of the first tea garden in this region in 1835 and the export of the first consignment of tea to London in 1838. The discovery of oil in Makum and establishment of a refinery in Digboi in 1890 laid the foundation for the development of an undivided Assam.

The Partition in 1947 changed the socio-economic landscape of this region. It shared 4500 kms. of frontiers with 5 countries – the People's Republic of China, Myanmar, Bangladesh (earlier East Pakistan), Bhutan and Tibet, whereas its connection with the Indian mainland was through a slender 22 kms. Siliguri corridor, also called the Gateway to the Northeast. This alteration in the geo-political environment led to severe market disruption and socio-economic distancing for the whole of the North Eastern Region and resulted in economic distortions, which have still not been fully overcome.

The quest for ethnic and regional identity, nationalism, and ideological motivations formented a climate of insurgency in several parts of the Region. It has resulted in political fragmentation. This climate has found further support from a large number of factors such as, the slow pace of development, difficult terrain, dense forest cover, open borders with Myanmar and Bangladesh failure to adopt sustained measures of conflict resolution and the approach of 'one size fits all'.

The standard of living of the people in the region, as measured by the per capita Gross State Domestic Product (GSDP), has lagged significantly behind the rest of the country. At Rs. 18,027 in 2004-05, it was less than the all-State average of Rs. 25,968 by 31 per cent. Interestingly, available information shows that at the time of Independence per capita income in the undivided State of Assam was higher than the national average by 4 per cent. Thus, even under the British colonial rule the economic performance of the region was better than in many parts of the mainland and this shows its vast developmental potential. In the post Independence era, the economy of the region went on a path of decline and the growth rate of per capita GSDP started lagging behind the rest of the country and by the late 1960s, the per capita income in the region had dipped substantially. With the introduction of marketbased economic reforms, the difference in the growth rates increased still further. During the period 1990-91 to 2004-05, on an average, while the aggregate GSDP of all States at constant prices increased at the rate of 6 per cent per year, the corresponding growth for the region was 4.4 per cent. Similarly, the region's growth rate of per capita income (2.5 per cent) lagged behind the average growth rate of the country (4 per cent) during the period by 1.5 percentage points. Not surprisingly, the difference between the per capita income of the region and the all India coverage has steadily diverged. In 1990-91, the region's per capita income at current prices was lower than the national average by 20 per cent, a gap that widened to 31 per cent by 2004-05.

The aggregate picture presented above, however, hides the differences that exist between the urban and rural areas, between the hills and plains and among the States of the region. Except for Mizoram, Nagaland and Sikkim which recorded marginally higher growth rates than the national average, the per capita income levels in other States were low. Assam, the largest among the North Eastern States had the lowest per capita income at Rs. 15,661 which was lower than the national average by 40 per cent. Even in the three States with per capita income levels higher than the national average, much of the income generated was on account of government spending. In fact, the share of income generated by public administration at 10.6 per cent was significantly higher in the region than in the rest of the country (6.3 per cent). It was as high as 17 per cent in Arunachal Pradesh, Manipur and Sikkim. This underlines the overwhelming dependence of the population on the government for generating income, and a lack of productive economic activities in the primary, secondary and tertiary sectors of the economy.

The region lags behind the rest of the country not only in terms of per capita GSDP but in several other development indicators as well. People do not have access to basic services in adequate measure. The standard development indicators such as road length, access to healthcare, and power consumption in the region are below the national average.

The top-down module of development planning has not involved people in designing and implementing the programmes and, not surprisingly, the relationship between public spending and service delivery outcomes has been tenuous. Public projects in the region have not yielded commensurate benefits. Lack of people's involvement has robbed the system of a sense of belonging and led to inefficient and wasteful resource allocation on the one hand and a lack of social accountability on the other.

The situation is further compounded by the weak administrative capacity of the State institutions which have not been able to contain elements indulging in armed insurgency and extortion. The overall environment together with an adverse perception has been a major deterrent to private sector initiatives in economic activities in this part of the country.

Socio-economic and Cultural Features of the North-Eastern Region

Regional Peculiarities

- The hallmark of the eight political units is the diversity on account of terrain, climate, ethnicity, culture, institution, land system, language, food habits, and dresses and so on.
- These States have evolved in different time and function under different provisions of the Constitution of India.
- The regional identity of eight states as NER is a concept based on extreme intra-regional diversity.

Physiographic Profile

- The total area of NER is 2.62 lakh sq. km (7.98 % of India's total).
- Divided into discrete plains encompassed within hills (>70%).
- Hills are generally rugged and vast areas are inaccessible.
- Relief varies from less than 50 m to more than 5000 m above mean sea level (amsl) and falls in high seismic zone.
- Four physiographic divisions – Active Flood Plains, Flood-Free Plains and Valleys, Low Hill Areas (100 to 1000 m amsl) and High Hill Areas (>1000 m amsl).
- Soil mostly acidic which adversely affect both animal and crop productivity.
- Climate is characterized by heavy precipitation (226mm to 602mm) during the four monsoon months (June to September).
- Located in the threshold of sub-tropics and has six agro-climatic zones.

Social Composition

- Home of over 140 major tribes out of 573 in the country besides nontribal with diverse ethnic origin and cultural diversity (2001 Census).
- The ST population (2001 Census) is 12.41% of India's ST total. It is 26.93% of NER's total population.
- SC population is 1.49% of India's total. It is 6.40% of NER's total population.

Local Governance System

- The modern and traditional system of governance co-exist in the region.

(contd.)

- The age old traditional but unrecognized local bodies exist and functions (ex. Kebang among the Adis in Arunachal Pradesh, Mei among the Karbis of Assam, Khullakpa among the Kaboi in Manipur, Durbar Shong among the Khasis and Jaintias in Meghalaya etc.).
- PRI functions in Arunachal Pradesh (GP- 1747; PS- 150 and ZP -15) and Sikkim (GP- 159 and ZP -4) as on April, 2005.
- Both PRIs and Autonomous Council (AC) function in Assam (GP- 2489; PS- 203 and ZP -20 and AC- 5); Tripura (GP- 537; PS- 23 and ZP - 4 TTAADC - 1) in Manipur (GP- 166 and ZP -4 and AC- 4); as on April, 2005.
- Autonomous Council functions in entire Meghalaya (AC-3). In Mizoram, both Village Council (702) and AC (3) function while in Nagaland only Village Council (1029); as on April, 2005.

Land Tenure System

- Two broad types of land tenure systems operate in the region: (i) Revenue administration under government operates in the plains and valleys of Assam, Tripura, Manipur and in the hilly state of Sikkim and (ii) Customary land tenure system under Village level authority operates in the hilly states of Arunachal Pradesh, Meghalaya, Mizoram and Nagaland and in the hilly parts of Assam, Manipur and Tripura.
- Cadastral survey is not done in these areas.
- Land is held almost by all. Landless people are negligible in number. Marginal (<1 ha) and small farmers (1.0-2.0 ha) are the two dominant categories (78.92 %)
- Distribution is largely egalitarian rooted in the principle of community way of living and sharing.
- Operational availability of land is a small fraction of total availability in the hills.

Demographic Profile

- Total population is 388.58 lakh and is 3.79% of India's total (2001 Census).
- Mizoram is highly urbanized (49.63%) followed by Manipur (26.28%) and Sikkim is at the bottom (11.07%)
- The population density is 149 per sq. km as against 324 at all India level. The highest is in Assam (340) followed by Tripura (304). All the hill states have dispersed population with lowest density in Arunachal Pradesh (13).
- Sex ratio (2001 Census) is higher (937) as against all India level (933). It is highest in Manipur (978) followed by Meghalaya (975), Tripura

(contd.)

(950), Mizoram (938) and lower than all India average in Assam (932), Nagaland (909), Araunachal Pradesh (901) with lowest in Sikkim (875).

- The potential work force (15-59 years) constitutes 56.97% as against all India figure of 56.93%. It is highest in Manipur (59.45%) followed by Sikkim (59.34%), Mizoram (59.09%) Tripura (58.96%), Nagaland (58.62%) and lower than all India level in Assam (56.63%), Arunachal Pradesh (55.02%) and Meghalaya (52.90%).
- Literacy rate is marginally higher (65.83%) compared to all India level (64.80%).
- Female literacy is higher in all the states (56.03% in Assam to 86.13% in Mizoram) as against all India level (54.16%) except in Arunachal Pradesh (44.24%).

With an area of 2.62 lacs sq.kms (7.98% of the country's area) and a population of around 4 crores, the per capita cultivable land availability in the NER is limited. Over the years the land-man ratio has turned uneconomical. Except for the Imphal Valley in Manipur and some pockets in other States, the agricultural yield in the entire region is low, primarily because of soil acidity.

NATURAL RESOURCES AND CONSTRAINTS

Hydro Electric Power Potential

The region has the potential to generate 63257 MW of hydel power (42.54%), against an estimated 148701 MW for the whole country. Arunachal Pradesh alone can generate as much as about 50328 MW - around 80% of the total hydro-power potential of the NER and 34% of the total potential of the country. Despite this recognition, there is much to be done as hydro power generation requires mega investments. The Planning Commission has suggested an approach which has a two-pronged strategy; one is to have a focus on small/localized hydel and thermal stations for local needs and second to have high capacity hydel power units and thermal power projects with associated transmission lines for meeting the overall demands of the region and for selling the excess to the national Grid. Transmission, subtransmission and distribution system improvements have been identified as thrust areas for the Eleventh

Plan. It is also envisaged to prepare a composite master plan for power development of the entire region including appropriate funding mechanism.

Forest Resources

The forests of the North Eastern Region face unrelenting pressures from the increasing population and galloping development needs. It has resulted in alarming levels of degradation and deforestation. Over-exploitation due to the shortening cycle of shifting cultivation is one of the key factors behind it. The biodiversity of the region is in deep peril.

The statistics of NER forests reveal some contradictory trends. One set of data (forest survey) shows a steady reduction in forest cover at an annual rate of 0.15% during 1991–2001, whereas, the State-level data exhibits a marginal increase in almost all the States during the period 1997–2001. It has led to a perception that the biological potential for carbon finance in the forest sector of the NER is substantial. Planners suggest taking up large scale afforestation and reforestation in the entire region. This again needs huge investment, which the States are unable to meet from their own resources.

Natural Calamities

The entire North-East Region suffers heavily on account of floods and landslides. Damages caused by floods, which assume an alarming proportion, in the Brahamputra and Barak Valleys of Assam, exert considerable strain on the economy not only of Assam but also of other North Eastern States. Besides working on temporary measures such as construction of embankments and spurs, taking long term measures such as erection of multi-purpose storage dams is the need of the hour.

Primary Sector Development

The pattern of agricultural growth has been uneven across the region. The NER is a category of its own kind. With about

8% of the country's area geographically, its contribution to the country's foodgrain production is just 1.5%.

Agriculture, horticulture and related activities could be the prime movers of the region's economic growth and hence should be the focus of development planning for the whole of this area. The overall thrust of the Eleventh Plan, in the NER is on ensuring availability of critical inputs such as fertilizers, HYV seeds and institutional credit. The implementation of such a region-specific strategy will depend heavily on the performance of the State-level agencies.

Road Ahead

The Vision Document 2020 of the North Eastern Region prepared by the Ministry of DONER and North Eastern Council has identified 9 critical areas which need priority attention for bringing peace and prosperity in the region by the year 2020. These are:

a) Catching up with the rest of the country
b) Bringing structural transformation in the economies
c) Poverty alleviation
d) Maximising self-governance
e) Harnessing resources for the benefit of the people
f) Building capacity in people and institutions
g) Strengthening infrastructure
h) Creating a centre for trade and commerce
i) Effective governance : establishing peace and harmony

The strategy would be:

(a) empowering people for decentralized governance and participatory development
(b) ensuring gender sensitivity in governance

(c) accelerating agricultural growth, rural development and expanding non-farm employment

(d) developing sectors with comparative advantage

(e) capacity building of people and institutions

(f) strengthening infrastructure and connectivity and

(g) raising resources for development

An efficient governance system is a sine qua non for actualization of such an ambitious strategy

In the North-East, the ethnic diversity of the region and susceptibility to serious militancy and linguistic and communal violence have given rise to peculiar problems of governance. As such, the Commission deems it a special responsibility to look at the governance issues of this region in greater detail and suggest measures that need to be taken.

The polity and administration in this region are marked by certain special features and issues. They are:-

(a) Ethnic conflicts – in places, manifesting as territorial conflicts and violence.

(b) Existence of special Constitutional provisions under the Sixth Schedule of the Indian Constitution applicable to the administration of tribal areas in the States of Assam, Meghalaya, Tripura and Mizoram which provides for creation of Autonomous Councils.

(c) *Ad hoc* transfer of subjects/activities to the Autonomous Councils, leading to differences in devolution and impediments in the implementation of the transferred powers.

(d) Predominance of non-elected customary heads / bodies at the village level; issue of Village Self Governance in the Sixth Schedule Areas.

(e) Absence of linkage between the Sixth Schedule and the 73rd amendment.

(f) Special powers of the Governors with respect to Sixth Schedule areas.

(g) Special provisions in the Constitution under Articles 371A, 371B, 371C, 371F, 371G and 371H applicable to North-Eastern States; special responsibility given with respect to law and order to the Governors of Nagaland under Article 371A and Arunachal Pradesh under Article 371H.

(h) Creation of Special Autonomous Councils under State enactments in Assam and Manipur.

(i) Administration of tribal areas outside the purview of both the Sixth Schedule and the 73rd amendment.

(j) Lack of capacity-building in administration and personnel management. These are dealt with in the following sections.

ETHNIC CONFLICTS – in Places, Manifesting as Territorial Conflicts and Violence

(Problem of Insurgency and Law and Order)

The Vision 2020 document in respect of the North Eastern Region has aptly noted that:

> 'Insurgency and underdevelopment, especially unemployment, feed on each other. Poor governance, corruption and economic performance sustain conditions for insurgency and alienation.'

It has also come to the conclusion that

> '. . . insurgency continuously hampers the economic performance of the region, so rapid economic development will not be possible without a proper strategic and security policy by the Central Government'. It has also identified the minima required. '... free and unhindered mobility of goods and services (infrastructure) across the region as well as within the region; well-defined property rights; and law and order and security of life . . .'.

The document has further noted that

> 'not less than 40 armed groups function in seven States, although only a clutch are dominant and powerful enough to make a substantial impact. The smaller ones function often either as extortionist rings or as part of a network of informers and rent collectors for the bigger ones. . . .'
>
> 'Many of the armed groups are widely viewed in the NER as extortionists who have lost public support and have become, in the eyes of many, illegal enterprises which prey on fear and vulnerability and profit from extensive corruption, rent-seeking and poor governance'.

A good law and order situation is a necessary condition for a robust economic development. It is also necessary for good governance as insurgents seek to intimidate public servants and interfere in political processes. Public servants have been killed in the line of duty, and assassination attempts made on political figures. The Commission is aware that both, the Union and the State Governments have been taking necessary steps to deal with the situation arising out of insurgency and poor public order in the North East. However, since the situation is still far from satisfactory, several more measures need to be considered. On the basis of discussions held with the State Governments and with people well conversant with the region, the Commission would specifically like to recommend the following:-

i. **Need for continued political dialogue**: Political dialogue to address genuine and legitimate concerns will need to continue. The experience of Mizoram, where peace was established through negotiations after years of insurgency is an example of what is possible through sincere, wise and good faith dialogue. Any agreement arrived as a result of such dialogue, however, needs to be adhered to rigorously. At present there is an agreement between the Union Government and one of the major insurgent groups. But it has been brought to the notice of the Commission that these are being constantly flouted by the insurgent groups. For example, the agreement stipulates that insurgents must stay in designated camps and not venture out with arms. Notwithstanding this agreement, armed groups are reported to be active in Manipur and Arunachal Pradesh, thus flouting this important condition of the ceasefire. Laxity in adherence to agreements devalues the process of negotiations and it is, therefore, necessary to ensure that all parties to the agreement abide by their commitments.

ii. **The police must act to uphold the law.** The police is an instrument of the State Government and maintenance of law and order is the responsibility of the State Government. In its earlier Reports on Public Order and Conflict Resolution, the Commission had recommended that law and order problems must be handled by the State Police with the Armed Forces in the background. The Commission re-iterates these recommendations and again emphasizes that it would be necessary to upgrade the capacity and capability of the police forces through better training, better arms and, wherever required, more manpower. Since the State Governments lack adequate financial and training resources, the Union Government will need to make special provisions in respect of these States.

iii. **Diplomatic efforts**: Diplomatic efforts aimed at controlling cross border movement of insurgents have yielded good results in the past. For example, the denial of sanctuaries in Bhutan to insurgents in Assam contributed to improvement of law and order in that State. No doubt, similar efforts are ongoing between the Government of India and Governments of neighboring countries like Bangladesh and Myanmar, and these need to be pursued to bring about positive results.

Enhanced Role of the Union Government

The Commission is of the view that while the role of the State Governments in ensuring stability in their respective jurisdiction (region) is critical, in view of the extenuating circumstances which are listed below, the Union Government's active support and intervention, needs to be further strengthened:-

(a) Insurgency and cases of extortion have inter-state ramifications and the Ministry of Home Affairs would, therefore, have a special responsibility to ensure necessary coordination pertaining to intelligence, conducting joint operations etc.

(b) With the exception of Tripura and Sikkim, all the hill States abut Assam, as they were carved out of Assam. There are a number of boundary disputes which every now and then erupt into confrontation between people and between States. Boundary disputes cannot be left to the States to manage and the Union Government has a significant role in steering agreements. Boundary disputes often distract attention from more fundamental concerns like insurgency and should not be permitted to occupy centre-stage.

(c) The Vision 2020 documents have identified various measures that need to be taken for the human resource and economic development of the North Eastern Region. The main challenge, however, is timely implementation. The Commission, therefore, would suggest that the Union Government (Ministry of Home Affairs, Planning Commission and subject matter Ministry) along with State Governments specify specific targets within important parameters (for example infant mortality reduction, increased literacy, productivity in the primary sector, connectivity etc.) that should be set for achieving these in a definite time frame. Five year Plans and Annual Plans should flow from these targets.

(d) At present, the work pertaining to the North Eastern Region is primarily allocated to the Ministry of Home Affairs and the Ministry of Development of North Eastern Region. In its seventh Report, the Commission has recommended the winding up of the Ministry of DONER and suggested that the Home Ministry may be the nodal Ministry in respect of this region and that the North Eastern Council should be suitably strengthened and restructured. On further consideration, the Commission would like to suggest some additional measures at the Union Government level to deal with the North Eastern Region, as follows:

Ministry of Home Affairs

i) At present there is a North East Division in the Ministry of Home Affairs which is headed by a Joint Secretary. The Commission, however, feels that for handling the increased workload (with many issues of a sensitive nature), a separate Wing in the Ministry of Home Affairs under either a Special Secretary or an Additional Secretary familiar with the North East Region and with adequate manpower should be created.

ii) A Standing Committee of the National Development Council (NDC) with the responsibility of overseeing the formulation and implementation of the Plans for the region should be constituted. Since law and order and development are inter-related this Committee would also need to have security issues that impinge on development in its purview. The Standing Committee may be headed by a Cabinet Minister selected by the Prime Minister and should report twice a year to the Chairman, NDC.

Recommendations

a) In order to address the genuine and legitimate concerns of the local people, there is need to continue political dialogue among various stakeholders. Steps should be taken to upgrade the capacity and capability of the police forces of the States so that they are able to uphold the law. In order to control cross border movement of insurgents, in addition to other measures, diplomatic efforts should be stepped up.

b) The North-East Division of the Ministry of Home Affairs should be upgraded to a separate wing and put under the charge of an Additional/ Special Secretary to handle the increased and complex workload pertaining to the region.

c) To oversee the formulation and implementation of the plans for this region, a Standing Committee of the National Development Council should be constituted and may be headed by a Cabinet Minister. The Committee should report to the Chairman, NDC twice a year to ensure both speedy resolution of any differences and coordinated action regarding development of the region.

PROVISIONS OF THE SIXTH SCHEDULE OF THE CONSTITUTION WITH RESPECT TO ASSAM, MEGHALAYA, TRIPURA AND MIZORAM

One of the most important features of administration in the north-east is the Sixth Schedule of the Constitution which provides for the setting up of Autonomous Regional/ District Councils in the four States of Assam, Tripura, Meghalaya and Mizoram. These provisions have been made in exercise of the enabling provisions given in Article 244(2) and 275(1) of the Constitution. Currently, the following ten Autonomous Councils are functioning in these States.

Assam

1. The North Cachar Hills District Autonomous Council (NCHAC)
2. The Karbi Anglog District Autonomous Council (KAAC)
3. Bodoland Territorial Council (BTC)

Meghalaya

4. Khasi Hills District Autonomous Council (KHAC)
5. Jaintia Hills District Autonomous Council (JHAC)
6. The Garo Hills District Autonomous Council (GHAC)

Tripura

7. Tripura Tribal Areas District Autonomous Council (TTADC)

Mizoram

8. The Chakma District Autonomous Council
9. The Mara District Autonomous Council
10. The Lai District Autonomous Council

The philosophy behind the Sixth Schedule of the Constitution is to protecttribes, their population and their interests by constitutionally mandating a special kind of autonomous governance structure. The Schedule endows these Councils with extensive, legislative, judicial, executive and financial powers, the details of which are as follows:-

Legislative Powers of District and Regional Councils

Under Para 3, District and Regional Councils are empowered with the assent of the Governor, to make laws with respect to:

(a) The allotment, occupation or use, or the setting apart, of land, other than any land which is a reserved forest for the purposes of agriculture or grazing or for residential or other non-agricultural purposes or for any other purpose likely to promote the interests of the inhabitants of any village or town;

(b) The management of any forest not being a reserved forest;

(c) The use of any canal or water-course for the purpose of agriculture;

(d) The regulation of the practice of jhum or other forms of shifting cultivation;

(e) The establishment of village or town committees or councils and their powers;

(f) Any other matter relating to village or town administration, including village or town police and public health and sanitation;

(g) The appointment or succession of Chiefs or Headmen;

(h) Inheritance of property;

(i) Marriage and divorce; and

(j) Social customs.

Under Paragraph 2(7), the District or the Regional Council is empowered to make rules inter alia, regarding formation of subordinate local Councils or Boards and their procedure and the conduct of their business, with the approval of the Governor. In addition, Paragraph 10 empowers District Councils to make regulations for the control of money-lending and trading by non-tribals.

Judicial Powers of District and Regional Councils

Paragraph 4 provides for Regional and District Councils to constitute Village Councils or Courts to the exclusion of any Court in the State for the trial of suits and cases between Scheduled Tribes within such areas, with certain exceptions. The Regional or District Council can appoint members and presiding officers of such Village Councils The Regional and District Council are also empowered to act as, or constitute separate Courts of Appeal.

Executive Functions of District Councils

The range of executive functions of District and Regional Councils vary from Council to Council, based on several amendments made to the Sixth Schedule. The common range of executive functions are laid down in Paragraph 6, under which

District and Regional Councils are empowered to establish, construct, or manage primary schools, dispensaries, markets, cattle pounds, ferries, fisheries, roads, road transport and waterways in the district and may make regulations for their regulation and control. It is also specifically empowered to prescribe the language and the manner in which primary education shall be imparted in the primary schools in the district. Functions relating to agriculture, animal husbandry, community projects, co-operative societies, social welfare, village planning or any other matter to which the executive power of the State extends can also be entrusted to Councils.

Financial Powers of District and Regional Councils

Constitution of District and Regional Funds: Para 7 provides for each autonomous district, a District Fund and for each autonomous region, a Regional Fund to which shall be credited all moneys received respectively by the said District and Regional Councils. The accounts of the District and Regional Councils are to be maintained as prescribed by the Comptroller and Auditor-General of India, who is also entrusted with their audit.

Powers to Collect Taxes and Fees: Para 8 gives powers to Regional and District councils to assess and collect land revenue and to impose taxes within their jurisdictions such as on lands and buildings, on professions, trades, callings and employments, animals, vehicles and boats, on the entry of goods into a market, tolls on passengers and goods carried in ferries and for the maintenance of schools, dispensaries or roads.

Entitlement to Royalties: Para 9 entitles the District Council to receive a share of the royalties accruing each year from licences or leases for the purpose of prospecting for, or the extraction of, minerals granted by the State Government in respect of any area within an autonomous district as agreed upon with the Government. Disputes in this regard are to be referred to the Governor for settlement.

Indication of resources to be credited to Councils: Under Paragraph 13, estimated receipts and expenditure pertaining to autonomous districts which are to be credited to, or is to be made from the State Consolidated Fund shall be first placed before the District Council for discussion and then shown separately in the annual financial statement of the State to be laid before the Legislature of the State under Article 202.

Need for Redrafting Some Provisions of the Sixth Schedule

Over the years, the Sixth Schedule has undergone more than ten amendments. The amended provisions have been 'anchored' rather disjointedly in the text of the Schedule making their reading and comprehension a rather cumbersome exercise. There is need to bring clarity. The Commission is of the view that an exercise can be undertaken to incorporate provisions which currently occur as footnotes, in the main text of the Schedule. This will make the Schedule more accessible to members of the public.

Recommendation

a) The Government may undertake an exercise to incorporate provisions which currently occur as footnotes, in the main text of the Sixth Schedule. This will make the Schedule more accessible to members of the public.

Ad hoc Transfer of Subjects/Activities to the Autonomous Councils

Sixth Schedule Councils in Assam, Meghalaya, Tripura and Mizoram have been given legislative powers with respect to the subjects listed in para 3 of the Schedule. In addition, these Councils have also been given powers to legislate on few additional subjects under para 3A and 3B of the Schedule; 3A with respect to NCHAC and KAAC and 3B for BTC. The legislation under 3A and 3B, however, needs prior assent of the President. Alongwith the legislative powers, some explicit executive and regulatory functions have also been entrusted to the Councils.

These are;

(i) To establish Primary Schools, Dispensaries and similar public utilities; (Paragraph 6)

(ii) Power to levy, assess and collect land revenue; professions tax; taxes on animal boat and ferry; market and toll taxes; and taxes for maintenance of schools dispensaries and roads. (Paragraph-8)

(iii) Power to control money lending by non tribals and to grant licenses to non tribal money-lenders in Assam and Meghalya, and power to control and regulate money lending by tribals and non tribals alike in Tripura and Mizoram; (Paragraph 10).

Due to historical reasons and also on account of lack of proper understanding of the Constitutional scheme, a notion prevails that the role of the Autonomous Councils is confined to passing laws, establishing and administering justice through local courts and generally taking up a few regulatory functions. They are not expected to have any role in development matters. Even though some subjects stand formally transferred to the Councils under the Sixth Schedule, the State Governments have been slow in transferring related executive powers and control over the corresponding departments to them. The State Governments have continued to retain parallel development and administrative apparatus under their own command. This has led to functional overlap and conflicts between the States and the District Councils. The spirit and pattern of the Sixth Schedule clearly imply that the Autonomous Councils should have their own role in matters concerning local development.

The Indian Constitution does not specifically prescribe any separate division of executive powers between the States and the Union Government. Article-73 (1) provides that the executive power of the Union extends "to matters with respect to which Parliament has power to make laws;" Article 162 mutatis mutandis applies the same principle to the States. In other words, the executive powers of the Union and those of the States co-exist with their respective legislative powers. The powers given to Autonomous Councils under Schedule 6 also need to be interpreted in the same light: the legislative powers of the Sixth Schedule Councils in Paragraphs 3, 3A and 3B are to be taken as their executive powers.

Hence, the Commission is of the view that there is need to ensure devolution of activities relating to subjects mentioned in Para 3, 3A and 3B of the Schedule to the Autonomous Councils. While devolving activities the functions and responsibilities should be clearly delineated between different levels of administrative structures based on the principal of subsidiarity. In this context, it would be useful to refer to and adopt principles enunciated by the Commission for local bodies in its Report on 'Local Governance' (Sixth Report - Para 4.2.3.10). This will necessitate full transfer of field offices and institutions dealing with transferred functions and activities to the control of the Councils. The concerned State Governments may set up a Task Force to complete this work within a time bound manner (one year). A similar excercise will need to be carried out by the Union Government in respect of the Centrally Sponsored Schemes which are being implemented in these areas.

Recommendations

a) The power of the Councils to make laws, as permitted by the Schedule, should be respected in its true spirit and draft legislations should not be stalled at the State level for years, while ensuring that they are not inconsistent with the provisions of the Constitution and relevant Union and State Laws.

b) The States should undertake comprehensive activity mapping with regard to all the subjects mentioned in Para 3, 3A and 3B of the Sixth Schedule. This mapping should cover all aspects of the subjects viz planning, budgeting and provisioning of finances. This will necessitate full transfer of all government offices and institutions dealing with these activities to the control of the Councils. The State Government should set-up a Task Force to complete this work in a time span of one year.

c) The Union Government should also take similar action with regard to Centrally Sponsored Schemes being implemented in these areas.

PREDOMINANCE OF NON-ELECTED CUSTOMARY HEADS / BODIES AT THE VILLAGE LEVEL; ISSUE OF VILLAGE SELF GOVERNANCE IN THE SIXTH SCHEDULE AREAS

When the Sixth Schedule arrangements were formulated in the North-East, tribal customs reigned supreme in these areas. During the early years of the Constitution, there was no thought of elections at the village or district level and hence there was nothing unusual in the Sixth Schedule not paying attention to the democratic aspect of village self governance. The idea of a two / three tier elected panchayat structure germinated only with the Balwant Rai Mehta Committee Report in 1957. With various rural development schemes and programmes becoming village centric and with Panchayats (in non scheduled areas) increasingly becoming involved in implementation of such programmes, the issue of village governance in scheduled areas came to the fore.

The Expert Committee on Planning for the Sixth Schedule Areas recommended that "representative bodies for Village Development in whatever manner named, need to be constituted through legislation enacted by the Councils themselves. The fears and apprehensions that such councils may transgress into the powers of the Traditional Village level bodies are overstated. The system in Assam can be patterned as existent in Nagaland, where the traditional Council and the development body coexist. The communitisation of public services in Nagaland through Village Development Boards in Nagaland can be kept in mind when framing rules for village councils."

The Committee further observed that "the size and extent of such grassroot level bodies can vary depending upon the local terrain and habitation pattern. For instance, in NCHAC areas, clustering of scattered habitations for the formation of village councils could be envisaged. Since the councils would use their own legislative powers to constitute such bodies, their scope and ambit could easily be harmonized with the Traditional village level councils. This way, the apprehension of the traditional Chiefs that Panchayati Raj is being imposed on them, can be allayed. There is a need to highlight success stories of village level peoples' mobilization through NGO projects such as those operated by the IFAD, to stress the benefits that such arrangements carry for development. Arrangements adopted for village level planning and implementation for NREGA may be adopted for planning and implementation of other programmes also."

The Commission also examined this issue in its Report on Capacity Building for Conflict Resolution (7th Report) while dealing with conflicts in the North East and came to the conclusion that:

a. Measures should be taken to ensure that all the Autonomous Councils pass suitable legislation for establishing of village level bodies with well defined powers and a transparent system of allocation of resources.
b. Stipulation may be made in the rules relating to release of grants to the Autonomous Councils to the effect that passage of appropriate legislation for elected village level bodies and its implementation, will entitle the Councils to additional funding.
c. It is imperative that in all States where village bodies administer justice under customary laws by virtue of the Sixth Schedule or other laws, such laws are duly codified.

The Commission reiterates the above views. As is envisaged the village level Councils will need to be constituted by law to be passed by the respective Autonomous Councils. It may be worth while to briefly enunciate certain general principals that may be followed by the Councils while constituting village level Councils within their jurisdiction. Apart from the elected members, the traditional village functionaries will also need to be included in these Village Councils as ex-officio members. However, it needs to be ensured that the majority of the members are elected. The Village Councils so constituted should be involved and made responsible for implementation of development schemes at the village level including planning, site selection, monitoring of implementation and selection of beneficiaries. Their role could be equated with Village Panchayats in implementation of schemes meant to be implemented through the PRIs. At the same time the Commission feels that the appropriate District Council legislation may, if considered advisable, provide for different arrangements for administration of justice and prevention of crimes.

Recommendations

a) Autonomous Councils should be encouraged to pass suitable legislation for establishment of elected bodies at the village level with well defined powers and a transparent system of allocation of resources.

b) Suitable stipulations may be made in the procedure for release of grants to the Councils that a certain portion thereof will be disbursed only in the event of a Council passing and implementing the legislation referred at (a) above.

While an Autonomous District Council should be free to lay down a suitable framework for Village Councils under its jurisdiction, this freedom should be subject to certain general principles such as, the number of ex officio members/ traditional village functionaries should not be in a majority and the Village Council should be responsible for implementation of development schemes at the village level (including planning, monitoring and selection of beneficiaries).

ABSENCE OF LINKAGE BETWEEN THE SIXTH SCHEDULE AND THE 73RD AMENDMENT

Article 243M (1) expressly keeps the Sixth Schedule areas out of the purview of Part IX of the Constitution (inserted through the 73rd amendment) as the organizational paradigm in this part is at radical variance with the system prevailing in the rest of the country. Their standalone existence puts them perpetually at the mercy of the State Governments for budgetary support. They find themselves at a distance from Constitutional bodies such as the State Finance Commission or the State Election Commission. There is a view that the 'supportive provisions' of Chapter IX, the State Finance Commission and the State Election Commission (Articles 243-I and 245K respectively) could be beneficial to the District/ Regional Councils. Adequate objectivity and transparency would be needed in transfer of resources from the State Government to these bodies. Similarly, there are definite advantages if an independent body oversees preparation and conduct of elections to the Councils/ Village Councils. In Tripura, the State Election Commission has already been involved in conduct of elections for the Tripura Tribal Areas Autonomous District.

While examining various characteristics of conflicts in the North East in its Seventh Report, (dealing with Conflict Resolution) the Commission observed that, "another emerging area of conflict is the rising disparity between the autonomous Councils and the local bodies established in pursuance of the Seventy-third Amendment as the latter are being more liberally funded through the State Finance Commissions. This disparity is likely to become particularly important in Assam and Tripura where both categories of local bodies co-exist. Similarly, there is a feeling of discontent in the two older Councils of Assam over what is perceived as preferential treatment to the new autonomous Council viz the Bodoland Territorial Council, in the matter of procedures relating to release of funds as well as the basis of budget allocations etc. While Article 243 M (1) expressly exempts areas under the Sixth Schedule from operation of the Seventy-third Amendment, there is no bar on some of the arrangements introduced by it to be engrafted in that Schedule."

Recommendation

Autonomous Districts/Councils in Sixth Schedule Areas should also be covered by the State Finance Commission and the State Election Commission.

SPECIAL POWERS OF THE GOVERNORS OF ASSAM, MEGHALAYA, TRIPURA AND MIZORAM WITH RESPECT TO SCHEDULE 6 AREAS

The Sixth Schedule has vested the Governor of Assam, Meghalaya, Tripura and Mizoram with considerable special powers for administration of autonomous districts and regional councils.

The empowerment of the Governor in a large number of provisions of the Sixth Schedule emphatically indicates that the role of the Governor is very special in these areas in the context of District and Regional Councils and the welfare of the concerned tribes. There is a need for the Governors to be proactive in order to empower tribal people and promote and facilitate local participative planning in Sixth Schedule areas. The spirit of the Sixth Schedule is that the Governors should function as custodians of tribal autonomy.

While Analyzing the Role of the Governor in Sixth Schedule Areas, Two Sets of Provisions of this Schedule are of Particular Importance

Provisions under paragraphs 12, 12A, 12AA and 12B

These paragraphs deal with the application of Acts of Parliament and of the Legislature of the States of Assam, Meghalaya, Tripura and Mizoram to their autonomous districts and autonomous regions.

12. Application of Acts of Parliament and of the Legislature of the State of Assam to autonomous districts and autonomous regions in the State of Assam:

"(1) Notwithstanding anything in this Constitution:-

(a) no Act of the 3[Legislature of the State of Assam] in respect of any of the matters specified in paragraph 3 of this Schedule as matters with respect to which a District Council or a Regional Council may make laws, and no Act of the [Legislature of the State of Assam] prohibiting or restricting the consumption of any non-distilled alcoholic liquor shall apply to any autonomous district or autonomous region [in that State]unless in either case the District Council for such district or having jurisdiction over such region by public notification so directs, and the District Council in giving such direction with respect to any Act may direct that the Act shall in its application to such district or region or any part thereof have effect subject to such exceptions or modifications as it thinks fit;

(b) the Governor may, by public notification, direct that any Act of Parliament or of the [Legislature of the State of Assam] to which theprovisions of clause (a) of this sub-paragraph do not apply shall not apply to an autonomous district or an autonomous region [in that State], or shall apply to such district or region or any part thereof subject to such exceptions or modifications as he may specify in the notification.

(2) Any direction given under sub-paragraph (1) of this paragraph may be given so as to have retrospective effect."

12A. Application of Acts of Parliament and of the Legislature of the State of Meghalaya to autonomous districts and autonomous regions in the State of Meghalaya

"Notwithstanding anything in this Constitution,–

(a) if any provision of a law made by a District or Regional

Council in the State of Meghalaya with respect to any matter specified in sub paragraph (1) of paragraph 3 of this Schedule or if any provision of any regulation made by a District Council or a Regional Council in that State under paragraph 8 or paragraph 10 of this Schedule, is repugnant to any provision of a law made by the Legislature of the State of Meghalaya with respect to that matter, then, the law or regulation made by the District Council or, as the case may be, the Regional Council whether made before or after the law made by the Legislature of the State of Meghalaya, shall, to the extent of repugnancy, be void and the law made by the Legislature of the State of Meghalaya shall prevail;

(b) the President may, with respect to any Act of Parliament, by notification, direct that it shall not apply to an autonomous district or an autonomous region in the State of Meghalaya, or shall apply to such district or region or any part thereof subject to such exceptions or modifications as he may specify in the notification and any such direction may be given so as to have retrospective effect."

12AA. Application of Acts of Parliament and of the Legislature of the State of Tripura to the autonomous district and autonomous regions in the State of Tripura

"Notwithstanding anything in this Constitution,—

(a) no Act of the Legislature of the State of Tripura in respect of any of the matters specified in paragraph 3 of this Schedule as matters with respect to which a District Council or a Regional Council may make laws, and no Act of the Legislature of the State of Tripura prohibiting or restricting the consumption of any non-distilled alcoholic liquor shall apply to the autonomous district or autonomous region in that State unless, in either case, the District Council for that district or having jurisdiction over such region by public notification so directs, and the

District Council in giving such direction with respect to any Act may direct that the Act shall, in its application to that district or such region or any part thereof, have effect subject to such exceptions or modifications as it thinks fit;

(b) the Governor may, by public notification, direct that any Act of the Legislature of the State of Tripura to which the provisions of clause (a) of this sub-paragraph do not apply, shall not apply to the autonomous district or an autonomous region in that State, or shall apply to that district or such region, or any part thereof, subject to such exceptions or modifications, as he may specify in the notification; (c) the President may, with respect to any Act of Parliament, by notification, direct that it shall not apply to the autonomous district or an autonomous region in the State of Tripura, or shall apply to such district or region or any part thereof, subject to such exceptions or modifications as he may specify in the notification and any such direction may be given so as to have retrospective effect."

12B. Application of Acts of Parliament and of the Legislature of the State of Mizoram to autonomous districts and autonomous regions in the State of Mizoram

"Notwithstanding anything in this Constitution,—

(a) no Act of the Legislature of the State of Mizoram in respect of any of the matters specified in paragraph 3 of this Schedule as matters with respect to which a District Council or a Regional Council may make laws, and no Act of the Legislature of the State of Mizoram prohibiting or restricting the consumption of any non-distilled alcoholic liquor shall apply to any autonomous district or autonomous region in that State unless, in either case, the District Council for such district or having jurisdiction over such region, by public notification, so directs, and the District Council, in giving such direction with respect to any Act, may direct that the Act shall, in its application to such district or region or any part thereof, have effect subject to such exceptions or modifications as it thinks fit;

(b) the Governor may, by public notification, direct that any Act of the Legislature of the State of Mizoram to which the provisions of clause (a) of this sub-paragraph do not apply, shall not apply to an autonomous district or an autonomous region in that State, or shall apply to such district or region, or any part thereof, subject to such exceptions or modifications, as he may specify in the notification;

(c) the President may, with respect to any Act of Parliament, by notification, direct that it shall not apply to an autonomous district or an autonomous region in the State of Mizoram, or shall apply to such district or region or any part thereof, subject to such exceptions or modifications as he may specify in the notification and any such direction may be given so as to have retrospective effect."

The provisions contained in paragraphs 12, 12A, 12AA and 12B provide for different schemes with respect to:

a) Laws of the State Legislature on the subjects mentioned in paragraphs 3, 3A and 3B.
b) Laws of the State Legislature on the subjects other than those mentioned in para 3, 3A and 3B.
c) Laws of the State Legislature on subjects mentioned in paragraphs 8 and 10
d) Laws of the State Legislature prohibiting or restricting the consumption of any non-distilled alcoholic liquor; and
e) Laws made by Parliament.

The issue of giving more discretionary powers to the Governors in the Sixth Schedule areas in general was also taken up by the Commission in its Report on Conflict Resolution. The Commission observed that,

"During the Commission's visit to Assam and Meghalaya, representatives of the Councils expressed dissatisfaction about their inter-face with the State Governments concerned – there was a feeling that these autonomous bodies are treated as extensions of the Government. While the various provisions of the Schedule create an impression that the Governor under that Schedule is to act at his discretion, the present position is that in almost all matters the Governor acts on the aid and advice of the Council of Ministers. This is an important issue. There are provisions in the Schedule which envisage a role for the State Government. Paragraph 14(3), for instance, requires that one of the Ministers of the Government be put in charge with the subject of autonomous districts. Sub-paragraph (2) of the same provision requires that the report of Commission for inquiring into the affairs of autonomous Districts and creation of new Districts etc will be laid before the State legislature. Similarly, paragraph 15 dealing with annulment of resolutions and suspension of Councils, and paragraph 16 which enables their dissolution are subject respectively to the powers of revocation and approval of the State legislature. For matters requiring approval or ratification of the Assembly, it is obvious that the Governor would be acting on the 'aid and advice' within the meaning of Article 163 (1) of the Constitution and not on his discretion. There are other provisions, however, where there is scope for the Governor to act in his judgment after obtaining inputs from suitable sources including the State Government. Some of these provisions would appear to be conferment of powers on the Councils under the Code of Civil Procedure (CPC) and the CrPC (para 5); powers to approve Council legislations and regulations (paragraphs 3 and 8); resolving disputes about mining licences and leases (para 9) etc. The Commission is of the view that having regard to the spirit of the wide autonomy that underlines the Sixth Schedule, this aspect needs to be examined by the Ministry of Home Affairs."

Accordingly, the following recommendation was made:-

"Ministry of Home Affairs may, in consultation with the concerned State Governments and the Autonomous Councils, identify powers under the Sixth Schedule that Governors may exercise at their discretion without having to act on the 'aid and advice' of the Council of Ministers as envisaged in Article 163 (1) of the Constitution."

While reiterating, the above recommendation, the Commission would like to go a step further in the present Report and examine the issue of discretionary powers which have been given to the Governor by the provisions of paragraphs 20 BA and BB of the Sixth Schedule.

Provisions of Paragraph 20BA and 20 BB

Paragraph 20BA (inserted by the Constitutional Amendment of 1995) -

Applicable to Assam - Exercise of discretionary powers by the Governor in the discharge of his functions

> "The Governor in the discharge of his functions under sub-paragraphs (2) and (3) of paragraph 1, subparagraphs (1), (6), sub-paragraph (6A) excluding the first proviso and sub-paragraph (7) of paragraph 2, sub-paragraph (3) of paragraph 3, sub-paragraph (4) of paragraph 4, paragraph 5, sub-paragraph (1) of paragraph 6, sub-paragraph (2) of paragraph 7, sub-paragraph (4) of paragraph 8, sub-paragraph (3) of paragraph 9, sub-paragraph (3) of paragraph 10, sub-paragraph (1) of paragraph 14, subparagraph (1) of paragraph 15 and sub-paragraphs (1) and (2) of paragraph 16 of this Schedule, shall, after consulting the Council of Ministers and the North Cachar Hills Autonomous Council or the Karbi Anglong Autonomous Council, as the case may be, take such action as he considers necessary in his discretion."

After Paragraph 20B, the following paragraph has been inserted in its application to the States of Tripura and Mizoram, by the Sixth Schedule to the Constitution (Amendment) Act, 1988 (67 of 1988):

Paragraph 20BB - Applicable to Tripura and Mizoram - Exercise of discretionary powers by the Governor in the discharge of his functions:

"The Governor, in the discharge of his functions under sub-paragraphs (2) and (3) of paragraph 1, subparagraphs (1) and (7) of paragraph 2, sub-paragraph (3) of paragraph 3, sub-paragraph (4) of paragraph 4, paragraph 5, sub-paragraph (1) of paragraph 6, sub-paragraph (2) of paragraph 7, subparagraph (3) of paragraph 9, sub-paragraph (1) of paragraph 14, sub-paragraph (1) of paragraph 15 and sub-paragraphs (1) and (2) of paragraph 16 of this Schedule, shall, after consulting the Council of Ministers, and if he thinks it necessary, the District Council or the Regional Council concerned, take such action as he considers necessary in his discretion."

On a plain reading of the above provisions a view may be formed that these provisions have been inserted in the Sixth Schedule to give complete discretionary powers to the Governors of Assam, Tripura and Mizoram in the transferred subjects. But no such powers are available to the Governor of Meghalaya. In the exercise of these powers the Governor is only obliged to consult the Council of Ministers and if necessary to consult the District or Regional Council before taking appropriate action.

There have been conflicting views on whether the Governor is entitled to exercise such powers on the basis of his individual discretion or on advice of the Council of Ministers of the State concerned under provisions of Article 163 of the Constitution. One view expressed by Justice Hidayathullah in his Anundoram Barooah Law lecture Guwahati (1978) was that the Governor had historically been directly controlling the administration of these areas:

". . . it is not compulsory for the Governor to consult the Council of Ministers. He may do so, but he is not bound to do so, nor is he bound to accept their advice. The entire history of these areas, the thought that went into the enactment of the Sixth Schedule as a Constitution independent of the rest of the Constitution clearly establishes this"

He also refers to his dissenting judgement in Edwingson Bareh v. State of Assam, AIR 1966 SC 1120: (1966) 2 SCR 770 and stated that he still felt that he was right. Hidayatullah, CJ in the aforesaid lecture mentioned the following points to arrive at the conclusion:

1. Historically the administration of these areas was under the direct control of the Governor General of the Council, Chief Commissioner of Assam and the Governor.
2. The tribal areas are to be administered as per the provisions of the Sixth Schedule only, as stated in Article 244, which is in Part X of the Constitution. So, provisions in the other parts of the Constitution- be it in Part VI or in any other Part can have no connection with the administration of these areas. This aspect was emphasized by stating that both the Fifth and Sixth Schedules can be adequately described as "Constitution, within a Constitution," or in other words as 'miniature Constitutions for certain scheduled areas of India".
3. The Fifth Schedule contemplates not only administration but also control whereas the Sixth Schedule refers to administration only.

Justice Hansaria however disagreed with Hidayatullah CJ and expressed his views as follows:

"The Governor has to act in his discretion as regards those matters only which specifically require him to do so; in others "seen, thanks" should be enough. Such view would also be in harmony with the ethos which pervades the

Constitution which has to be viewed and interpreted as one organic document."

Justice Hansaria gives the following reasons for arriving at the conclusion that the Governor is required to act on the aid and advice of the Council of Minister except where otherwise specifically provided:

- Historically, the Governor was not exercising powers in his discretion for the entire tribal areas in as much as under the scheme of the Government of India Act, 1935, the 'excluded areas' were to be administered by the Governor acting in his discretion; and for the 'partially excluded areas' he had a special responsibility implying the power to over-ride the advice of the Ministers in his individual judgment, but normally the Governor would act on the advise of his ministers. A reference to the Government of India (Excluded and Partially Excluded Areas) Order, 1936, would show that all the areas covered by the Sixth Schedule were not included in the excluded area.
- The provisions of the Sixth Schedule cannot be interpreted by forgetting the texture on which the Constitution has been woven. The Sixth Schedule cannot be completely insulated from the rest of the Constitution and it is as much part of the Constitution as any other Schedule or provision.

This view was taken by Justice Hansaria, on the ground that the debates in the Constituent Assembly when the Sixth Schedule was being passed would indicate that the intention was to depart from the earlier pattern.

In the case of Pu Myllai Hlychho vs State of Assam 2003 (3) GLT 50 (55-56) judgement date 11.1.2005, the Supreme Court passed the following judgement:

"Relying on the object and reasons of the Amendment Act, the Counsel for the appellant contended that the Governor had used discretionary powers to nominate the members to the Council and the facts disclosed that he nominated members with the aid and advice of the Council of Ministers and this was not in accordance with the provisions of Paragraph 20BB and the autonomy envisaged under the provisions of the Sixth Schedule is not given its true and meaningful importance. The contention of the appellants is that by inserting Paragraph20-BB to the Sixth Schedule Governor is given more discretionary powers to protect the autonomy of the tribal areas and if Governor acts on the aid and advice of the Council of Ministers and does not act independently, the purpose of this legislation, is not achieved. Except for the feet that the file for nominating new members initiated from the Council of Ministers, there is nothing on record to show that the Governor failed to exercise the discretionary power vested in him. The Governor exercised his discretion after making proper consultations, as envisaged under Paragraph 20BB of the Sixth Schedule and the nomination of the four members had been validly made.

In the result, we hold that the Governor was bound by the aid and advice of the Council of Minsters and the termination of the four members from the MADC by order of the Governor on 5.12.2001 was perfectly in accordance with the Constitutional provisions and the Sixth Schedule to the Constitution. The nomination of the four members to the Council by order dated 6.12.2001 was legal and the Governor acted by virtue of the discretionary power vested in him. The Governor was justified in making consultation wih the Coucil of Ministers and the Governor making such incidental consultation with the Council of Ministers did not in any way affect his discretionary power. No other authority interfered with the independent exercise of the Governor's discretion in nominating the four members to the MADC and the Notification issued by the Governor on 6.12.2001 was validly made and the decisions of the Division Bench of Gauhati High Court does not call for any interference".

The Commission is of the view that the spirit of the Constitution and the amending Acts which introduced paragraphs 20BA and 20BB in the Sixth Schedule was to protect the autonomy of the tribal areas and to save them from the decisions of the overwhelming majority. The Governor enjoys these special powers as a custodian of tribal interests and hence he needs to be adequately empowered to do so. Any attempt to impose the views of the State Council of Ministers on the Governor may defeat the very purpose for which these paragraphs were introduced in the Sixth Schedule. As such the Commission feels that to put matters beyond doubt the Governors of Assam, Tripura and Mizoram may be empowered to exercise discretionary powers in respect of the provisions pertaining to Autonomous Councils under the Sixth Schedule in consultation with the Council of Ministers and if necessary, in consultation with these Councils. A Constitutional amendment will be required for this purpose.

Constitution of a Commission to submit a report on the administration of autonomous districts and autonomous regions: (Paragraph 14 of the Sixth Schedule)

This issue has also been dealt with by the Commission in its seventh Report. The observation of the Commission is;

> "At the commencement of the Constitution and for more than two decades thereafter, all the Autonomous Districts were located within the State of Assam. It was therefore quite in order in that State for the Governor to appoint a Commission to inquire into the state of administration in such districts and to examine other matters mentioned in paragraph 14. With four States now having such districts, this arrangement deserves reconsideration. Besides, in the last two decades this provision has not been invoked at all resulting in lower standards of governance in these sensitive areas. In the opinion of the Commission, there is a case for a common Commission for all Autonomous Districts under the Schedule by the Union Government and for providing

appointment of such a Commission at fixed intervals. The Commission also notes that a similar recommendation has been made by the Expert Committee of the Ministry of Panchayati Raj headed by one of its members (Shri V. Ramachandran)."

It was accordingly recommended that:

"Paragraph 14 of the Sixth Schedule may be suitably amended to enable the Union Government to appoint a common Commission for all autonomous districts for assessing their state of administration and making other recommendations envisaged in that paragraph. A periodicity may also be provided for the Commission."

The Commission would like to reiterate these recommendations.

Constitution of a High Level Review Committee headed by the Governor

In order to examine the functioning of these bodies, and to assess the problems that arise in their day to day operations in each Sixth Schedule State, the Governor himself should lead a high level review committee consisting of representatives from the State Government as well as the District/Autonomous Councils. This will help him make appropriate suggestions to the Union Government on Sixth Schedule issues.

Recommendations

a) The Governors of Assam, Tripura and Mizoram should be empowered to exercise discretionary powers in respect of all the provisions pertaining to the Autonomous Councils under the Sixth Schedule in consultation with the Council of Ministers and if necessary, in consultation with these Councils. A Constitutional amendment will be required for this purpose.

b) Paragraph 14 of the Sixth Schedule should be suitably amended to enable the Union Government to appoint a common Commission to review the working of all autonomous districts of the North-East and to make recommendations as envisaged therein. A periodicity may also be provided for the Commission.

c) A high-level Review Committee headed by the Governor and consisting of representatives of both the State Government and the District Councils should be formed in each State to review the functioning of these bodies. This Committee should submit its report to the Union Government.

SPECIAL PROVISIONS IN THE CONSTITUTION UNDER ARTICLES 371A, 371B, 371C, 371F, 371G & 371H APPLICABLE TO NORTH-EASTERN STATES

Article 371A (a) states that "no Act of Parliament in respect of –

i. Religious or social practices of the Nagas,

ii. Naga customary law and procedure,

iii. Administration of civil and criminal justice involving decisions according to Naga customary law;

iv. Ownership and transfer of land and its resources,

shall apply to the State of Nagaland unless the Legislative Assembly of Nagaland by a Resolution decides.

In terms of Article 371A(b),

"the Governor of Nagaland shall have special responsibility with respect to law and order in the State of Nagaland for so long as in his opinion internal disturbances occurring in the Naga-Hills Tuensang Area immediately before the formation of that State continue therein or in any part thereof and in the discharge of his functions in relation thereto the Governor shall, after consulting the Council of Ministers, exercise his individual judgment as to the action to be taken."

Further, the Articles provide that in making his recommendation with respect to any demand for a grant, the

Governor of Nagaland shall ensure that any money provided by the Government of India out of the Consolidated Fund of India for any specific service or purpose is included in the demand for a grant relating to that service or purpose and not in any other demand.

Article 371B states that—

"notwithstanding anything in this Constitution, the President may, by order made with respect to the State of Assam, provide for the constitution and functions of a committee of the Legislative Assembly of the State consisting of members of that Assembly elected from the tribal areas specified in [Part I] of the table appended to paragraph 20 of the Sixth Schedule and such number of other members of that Assembly as may be specified in the order and for the modifications to be made in the rules of procedure of that Assembly for the constitution and proper functioning of such committee."

Article 371C states that—

"(1) "notwithstanding anything in this Constitution, the President may, by order made with respect to the State of Manipur, provide for the constitution and functions of a committee of the Legislative Assembly of the State consisting of members of that Assembly elected from the Hill Areas of that State, for the modifications to be made in the rules of business of the Government and in the rules of procedure of the Legislative Assembly of the State and for any special responsibility of the Governor in order to secure the proper functioning of this committee. (2) The Governor shall annually, or whenever so required by the President, makes a report to the President regarding the administration of the Hill Areas in the State of Manipur and the executive power of the Union shall extend to the giving of directions to the State as to the administration of the said areas."

Article 371 F (g) confers special responsibility on the Governor of Sikkim. It states that,

> "the Governor of Sikkim shall have special responsibility for peace and for an equitable arrangement for ensuring the social and economic advancement of different sections of the population of Sikkim and in the discharge of his special responsibility under this clause, the Governor of Sikkim shall, subject to such directions as the President may, from time to time, deem fit to issue, act in his discretion."

A special provision in respect of Mizoram has been provided under Article 371 G which reads as, "no Act of Parliament in respect of—

(i) religious or social practices of the Mizos,

(ii) Mizo customary law and procedure,

(iii) administration of civil and criminal justice involving decisions according to Mizo customary law,

(iv) ownership and transfer of land,

shall apply to the State of Mizoram unless the Legislative Assembly of the State of Mizoram by a resolution so decides."

Article 371H contains special provision with respect to the State of Arunanchal Pradesh as follows,

"Notwithstanding anything in this Constitution,–

(a) the Governor of Arunachal Pradesh shall have special responsibility with respect to law and order in the State of Arunachal Pradesh and in the discharge of his functions in relation thereto, the Governor shall, after consulting the Council of Ministers, exercise his individual judgment as to the action to be taken.

Provided that if any question arises whether any matter is or is not a matter as respects which the Governor is under this clause required to act in the exercise of his individual judgment, the decision of the Governor in his discretion shall be final, and the validity of anything done by the Governor shall not be called in question on the ground that he ought or ought not to have acted in the exercise of his individual judgment."

SPECIAL AUTONOMOUS COUNCILS CREATED BY STATE ENACTMENTS (IN ASSAM AND MANIPUR)

In addition to the Autonomous Councils created under the provisions of the Sixth Schedule some tribe specific special Autonomous Councils have also been created through the State enactments in Assam and Manipur. These special Councils have been broadly patterned on the Sixth Schedule Councils but their powers and responsibilities are muchless. Issues concerning these special Councils have been dealt in detail following pages in this chapter.

ISSUES OF TRIBAL AREAS LYING OUTSIDE THE SIXTH SCHEDULE

With the States of Arunachal Pradesh and Sikkim being brought under the Seventy- Third Amendment and almost the whole of 'tribal Assam' covered by the Sixth Schedule, the areas falling under this classification are the State of Nagaland and the Hill Districts of Manipur.

Nagaland has made significant progress in empowering the village community. The village community participates in grass root level development programmes in close association with the traditional village chief. Communitization is an effective instrument to ensure that the institutions and services set up for their benefit operate efficiently and are accountable to the beneficiaries. Care is needed to ensure that communitization and village development boards do not become mutually antithetical. The decision of the State Government to declare each Village authority a 'local authority' within the meaning of the Communitization Act is a step in the right direction, It can be said that Nagaland is the only State in the North East where local empowerment has been more impressive at the village than at the higher levels – evidently an offshoot of the State not being covered by the Sixth Schedule (with emphasis on empowerment of autonomous Districts). A scheme of Autonomous Area Councils- tribe specific bodies conforming to the then existing districts was tried in 1970s but it turned out to be a short-lived affair. While it may not be desirable to lay down any formulation for the State from outside, its long term development will be better served if the process of decentralized self governance is carried forward to the supra village level.

In Manipur, on the other hand, there are no village level elected bodies. The Village Development Committees are purely nominated bodies, often the nominees of the traditional village leaders. The Hill District Councils are moribund for the last seventeen years, elections having been held as far back as in 1985. The persistent demand for declaration of the Hill Areas in the Sixth Schedule has caused a stalemate. The case against acceptance of this demand appears to be based on apprehensions about 'integrity of the State' and 'exacerbation of existing tensions'. It is not for the Commission to express any view as to the merits of the rival claims, but it has been observed that with the implementation of the Seventy-Third Amendment in the valley districts, there has been a significant improvement in various growth indices such as poverty ratio, literacy percentages and rural connectivity.

The Commission believes that for tribal areas which lie outside the Sixth Schedule as well as the Seventy-Third Amendment, the Ministries of Rural Development and Panchayat Raj and the Planning Commission should provide special incentives to the States concerned to devise ways and means of managing their District Rural Development Agencies in such a way that the DRDA function as bodies accountable to District Level Institutions which could be a mix of elected and traditionally selected members. This process could be taken further after assessing its initial impact.

Recommendations

a) For tribal areas which lie outside the Sixth Schedule as well as the Seventy Third Constitutional Amendment the State Government should take steps to create specially at the district level bodies which should consist of both elected as well as traditionally selected representatives. The States which show initiative and take a lead in this matter should be given incentives.

b) The District Rural Development Authority of the district should work as a body accountable to this District Level Body.

PERSONNEL MANAGEMENT AND CAPACITY BUILDING OF ADMINISTRATION

After Independence a special administrative service - the Indian Frontier Administrative Service (IFAS) was created to manage the administration of the frontier territories. The Constitution brought in special provisions from the Sixth Schedule to give enhanced attention to the predominantly tribal areas of the North East. One significant feature of this enactment was to introduce the concept of Autonomous Districts as a distinct tier of governance. Areas falling under Naga Hills, Lushai Hills, The United Khasi & Jaintia Hills, Garo Hills, North Cachar Hills and the Mikir Hills Districts of Assam were brought under its purview with elected District Councils exercising executive, judicial and legislative powers as detailed earlier. The remaining tribal areas outside the then 'Part C' states of Manipur and Tripura were held to be not yet ready to benefit from the autonomous District approach. These areas (called Part B areas in the Sixth Schedule) were the five 'frontier' tracts comprising the North East Frontier Agency (NEFA) including the 'Naga tribal areas' which later became the Mon and Teunsang Districts of the State of Nagland. Further, the Governor of Assam was designated as the 'agent' of the President to administer the affairs of NEFA. In discharge of these responsibilities the Governor was not responsible to the Government of Assam.

The IFAS personnel were initially deployed in Part B areas, for political administration. The Service underwent significant expansion from 1954 onwards, with new entrants being drawn from backgrounds as diverse as academics, agriculture, accountancy, civil service, police and scientific research etc. This diversified cadre – members of service spent long years in the region, was in a position to understand and deal with local and developmental issues of the tribal areas. In 1955 a formal secretariat for NEFA was established at Shillong and the tradition of formal, development oriented governance was laid. The deployment of the IFAS was later extended to the Part C states of Manipur and Tripura (designated as Union Territories in 1960). Exceptions involving a few young educated tribals apart, there was no direct recruitment to the IFAS; most of the 'inductees' had previous professional experience.

Subject to the pre-eminent authority of the Autonomous District Councils, the general administration of the Sixth Schedule areas remained with the Government of Assam. Posts of Deputy Commissioners and Superintendents of Police were manned by the members of the All India Services. With the formation of the Union Territories Cadre of the Indian Administrative Service in 1962 and of the Indian Police Service a little later, the number of positions available to the members of the IFAS in Manipur and Tripura became limited. With effect from 1.1.1968 all members of that service exercising an option in that behalf were transferred to the Indian Administrative Service and accommodated within the Union Territories cadre. With the formation of the States of Himachal Pradesh, Manipur and Tripura in 1971-72 some of the officers were accommodated in these cadres as well.

Sikkim is a sui generis case as its administration descends from a princely protectorate. Due to paucity of resources there were very few organised departments or agencies. But after the merger, the overall administrative structure of the State is on the pattern followed in West Bengal.

The Commission has suggested a large number of measures for improvement of personnel management in the North-Eastern States in its Seventh and Tenth Reports. They need to be implemented.

Training of Government Personnel

Professional competence of personnel is an essential feature of a public administration system. This is particularly true for the States of the North East where the challenges of governance are far more complicated than those in other parts of the country. Except for the induction level training which is given to directly recruited Grade B officials of civil administration, police and forest departments, very few other capacity building measures are visible in the administration of these states.

Leaving aside, the degree-awarding Universities and Technical Institutions located in these States such as NEHU and IIM in Meghalaya and IIT in Assam, there are eight major training institutions which have been established for capacity building of government employees of the North Eastern States. They are –

- (i) State Institute of Public Administrative & Rural Development (SIPARD), Agartala.
- (ii) Administrative Training Institute, Shillong
- (iii) State Academy of Training, Imphal.
- (iv) Administrative Training Institute, Arunachal Pradesh.
- (v) Administrative Training Institute, Gangtok.
- (vi) Assam Administrative Staff College, Guwahati
- (vii) Administrative Training School, Aizawl
- (viii) Administrative Training Institute, Kohima

Then there is the North East Police Academy NEPA at Shillong under the Ministry of Home Affairs which runs specialized courses for police officers of this region.

Many of these institutions are not functioning effectively. The main reasons are:

(i) the issue of capacity building and training of government personnel is not high on the agenda of the State Governments;

(ii) inadequate funding of the institutions; and

(iii) paucity of faculty.

The Commission is of the view that the training needs of government personnel should be addressed on a priority basis, (i) Every government employee should undergo a long duration induction training when he joins service, (ii) There should be provision for mid career training, and (iii) Officials should be encouraged to acquire higher professional qualifications and skills in their respective branches and also in subjects such as – Public Administration, Policy, Trade laws, project investment, appraisal, management and information technology applications. Recruitment/Promotion Rules for senior officers need to be amended to give adequate importance and weightage to mid career capability acquisitions. The Commission is also of the view that since the States of the region are small, setting up a centre of excellence in each of them does not seem to be a viable proposition; there is need to have a properly equipped central institution catering to the training needs of all the eight States.

While dealing with the 'Conflicts in the North East" in its seventh Report, the Commission recommended that "Regional training institutions for various branches of administration, including the technical services may be operated by the North Eastern Council." Taking it further, the Commission feels that the NEC should establish an apex Regional Academy for Human Resource Development, as an autonomous body with academic and executive flexibility. The mandate of the Academy may extend to the entire range of services under the government. Besides running 'flagship training programmes' for all the NE States, the Academy should give emphasis to overall planning and implementation of human resource development, preparation of Regional handbooks and manuals for various sectors and designing applied and action research professional courses in coordination with various Universities and institutions in the country.

Strengthening pre recruitment facilities

The exact data on the number of candidates selected from the North Eastern States to various All India and Central Services is not available. However, on the basis of the available information, the number of candidates belonging to Scheduled Tribes selected to the All India Services from this region on a decadal basis may be summarized as follows:

Representation of ST Candidates from North-Eastern Region in All India Services

Decade	IAS		IPS	IFS
	ST	Gen		
1970s	35	06	09	18
1980s	28	07	10	83
1990s	14	04	12	39

Source: Executive Record Sheets

Even assuming a reduction in the annual intake of candidates for many of these services, the declining trend is significant. The point is brought home more forcefully if the percentage share of members of the Scheduled Tribes from the North East in the overall appointments from that category is analyzed. Collation of information gathered from the relevant civil lists in respect of direct recruitment to the IAS reveals the following table.

The representation of the tribal population of the North East in the civil services shows a downword trend. This issue needs to be addressed on priority. Adequate local representation in the mainstream administration will help in addressing the issue of perceived alienation.

Percentage Share of ST Candidates from the North-Eastern Region in Overall appointment from ST Category

Decade	No. of Appointees (ST)		% of Appointees (ST) from NE
	North East	All India	
1970s	35	73	48
1980s	28	99	27
1990s	14	79	18

The Commission feels that since private sector growth has not occurred in the region adequately, there is little scope for employment of qualified personnel in this area. Steps are necessary to improve their chances of selection into civil services and other competitive examinations including recruitment to the Armed Forces etc. Measure taken in this direction by the Ministries of Social Justice and Empowerment and Tribal Affairs have not yielded the desired results. Therefore, efforts are needed to involve educational institutions, particularly the Universities of the region in running Orientation and Coaching programmes. The NEC can coordinate these efforts.

Recommendation

The North Eastern Council, in consultation with the Universities and other educational institutions of the region, should draw up programmes for coaching students for the Civil Services, and other competitive tests such as the Combined Defence Services Examination and the Engineering/ Medical Examinations.

ISSUES OF RECRUITMENT IN THE SIXTH SCHEDULE AREAS

Autonomous Councils have frequently pleaded for separation of cadres of 'Line Departments' whose functions figure in the list of responsibilities assigned to these bodies under Paragraph 3, or 3A (the two older Assam Councils) or 3B (the BTC). Such proposals have varied from having a 'composite cadre' for the

Scheduled Districts to District specific outfits. In Assam, the recruitment of medical officers in the BTC areas was delegated to the Bodo Tribal Council. This approach is likely to cause problems in retaining qualified training personnel. The prospect of spending an entire career in a Scheduled District or in the Sixth Schedule areas deters them from joining the service. The Commission feels that there is need to adopt a procedure which would lead to retention of technical and professional expertise in these areas. Thus, in these areas while steps are necessary to ensure that technical and other personnel remain in position in Sixth Schedule and other tribal areas, creating separate cadres for overall administration does not appear to be a viable proposition. While it is advisable to constitute District cadres for Group C and D posts, recruitments to the higher levels should be left to the State Governments. The State Government and the Councils should jointly devise a way so that the requirement of tribal areas gets precedence over that of the other areas. Officers should have a fixed tenure in the tribal areas (unless they voluntarily desire to continue) and thereafter as far as possible they should get a posting of their choice. Other incentives such as deputation to training programmes both within the country and abroad and some weightage in departmental promotions could be considered. These steps may however need State specific adaptation and modifications.

Recommendations

a) Immediate steps should be taken to constitute District cadres for all Groups 'C' and 'D' posts (Classes III and IV) for performance of all 'transferred functions' wherever such action has not been taken.

b) Recruitment to Groups 'A' and 'B' posts (Classes I and II) by the Autonomous District Councils or analogous bodies particularly to positions requiring technical/ professional qualifications should ordinarily be left to the State level.

c) State Governments and the Autonomous District Councils should jointly draw up norms for arriving at the number of technical and professional posts required in the tribal areas. Personnel for such posts should be made available on priority basis.

d) Postings to the tribal areas should be for a fixed tenure and must be followed by, as far as practicable, to a posting at a place of the officer's choice.

e) On satisfactory completion of tenure in such areas the incumbent should be entitled to benefits like deputation for higher professional qualifications, training abroad and higher weightage in Departmental promotions.

REGIONAL INSTITUTES

In pursuance of a planned strategy for the regional development of the North Eastern States, over the years, a large number of regional Institutes were set up in various fields including science and technology, water and land management, agriculture, health/medical, education, power, cane and bamboo technology, training institutes for police, etc. Many of these Institutes were initially set up under the auspices of the North-Eastern Council and later transferred to Union Ministries; for example, the North Eastern Police Academy which is now with the Home Ministsry and the North-Eastern Energy and Power Corporation, now with the Ministry of Power. Others were directly set up by the concerned Ministries and continue to be with them; for example, North Eastern Indira Gandhi Regional Institute of Medical Sciences, Shillong under the Ministry of Health, North-Eastern Institute of Bank Management with the Ministry of Finance etc.

During its visit to the North-Eastern States the Commission was informed that the effective performance of the Institutes greatly varied with some of them functioning well and playing a major role in the regional development in their areas of expertise. However, a number of other Institutes became ineffective either because of lack of funds and technical resources, non-availability of competent professionals to head the Institutes, etc. Since a great deal of effort, resources, planning and expectations were involved in setting up these Institutes it would be essential to review their working, identify the shortcomings and take necessary action within a stipulated time frame to make them functionally effective institutions of excellence in the Region.

Keeping in view the fact that the North-Eastern Council is the strategic planning body for the region and the nodal agency for its socio- economic development it should be given the responsibility to undertake a review of these Institutes and come up with suitable recommendations for their improvement wherever required. One of the Members of the NEC could head this Committee with representatives from the region as well as from the Government of India. In addition, it would be useful if the Secretary/Member(s) of the NEC is represented on the governing body of those Institutes which are no longer under its administrative supervision/ control. Permanent arrangements for monitoring the evaluation of these Institutes would also be necessary which could be based within the NEC.

The Commission in its Seventh Report has recommended suitable strengthening of the NEC. Once this is done it should be possible for the NEC to undertake these additional and important responsibilities.

The Commission is of the view that the North Eastern Hill University (NEHU) could provide the academic foundation for policy research on issues impinging on the entire region and which need to be addressed by State action.

Recommendations

a) For improving delivery systems and development processes, emphasis ought to be given to capacity building of personnel and it should be a priority activity of the government.

b) There should be comprehensive training programmes for all government employees working in the North-Eastern States. The programmes should consist of (i) a long duration induction module when he joins service, (ii) mid career training opportunities and (iii) officials should be encouraged to acquire higher professional qualifications/ skill sets in their respective branches and also in subjects such as Public Administration, Trade laws, project investment/ appraisal/ management and information technology applications.

c) The North Eastern Council (NEC) should establish an apex Regional Academy for Human Resource Development as an autonomous body with academic and executive flexibility. The mandate of the Academy may extend to the entire range of services under the government.

d) The North-Eastern Council should be given the responsibility to undertake a review of various regional institutes under the Union Government/ Ministries and come up with suitable recommendations for bringing improvements in their functioning whenever required. An officer/ member of the NEC should be placed on the governing body of these institutions.

e) The NEC should take up monitoring and evaluation of these Institutes. The Commission in its Seventh Report has already recommended that the NEC should be suitably strengthened. Once this is done, it should be possible for the NEC to undertake these additional and important responsibilities.

f) The North Eastern Hill University (NEHU) could provide the academic foundation for policy research on issues impinging on the entire region and which need to be addressed by State action.

STATE SPECIFIC ISSUES

Apart from the common issues dealt with above, the States of the NE Region also have someState specific problems which need attention. These are being discussed in the subsequent sections of this Report.

Assam

Assam accounts for around 30% of the area and 68% population of the North East (including Sikkim). At the commencement of the Constitution (1950) 'area domination' of the State was of the order of 53% as the present states of Meghalya, Mizoram and Nagaland formed its four Districts. The reduction in area of the State has had important geo-political implications. Even demographically, Assam displays certain anomalies- its population more than doubled in the first half of the last century largely due to migrations. Factors such as availability of large tracts of fallow land, demand for labour in plantations and overpopulation in adjoining Districts of Bengal with consequent landlessness have all been implicated for this phenomenon. These factors, have also contributed to frequent conflicts and unrest within the State with deleterious effects within the region. The dependence of the State on agriculture and allied sectors is evident from the fact that despite its relative proximity to the rest of the country, Assam has the lowest share of urban population at 12.90% as against 15.66% for the North East as a whole.

Assam also has the lowest share of Scheduled Tribe population in the region (13%). Yet, with six districts in the Sixth Schedule and the whole or parts of another twelve being under Tribe specific Autonomous Councils, there is a great deal of complexity in the administration of the State. The clash of interests between one tribal group and the other and that between a tribal group and non-tribals creates enormous challenges for governance in the State. The situation is further compounded by a significant presence of religious and linguistic minorities, approximately 18% and 30% respectively. It is interesting to note that a large section of population qualifies, concurrently for both the categories. In short, the State of Assam faces problems which emerge out of conflicts as well as the development needs of the people.

Sixth Schedule District Councils

The Constitution provides a framework for participatory district level government for the major tribal communities of the State in the form of the Sixth Schedule autonomous District Councils. For reasons too well known to recount, these arrangements were primarily intended to meet the political aspirations of the then Naga Hills District. But the strong reservations of the Nagas did not allow it. Five Autonomous Councils were established for other major tribes. Following the reorganization of the North Eastern Region in 1972, three of the Council Districts ceased to be part of Assam and the State was left with two such Councils. Following the Bodoland Accord in 2003, another Sixth Schedule Council- the multi-District Bodoland Territorial Council- was also established. At present, therefore, there are three such Councils in Assam- two in existence since the introduction of the Schedule and the third established in 2003.They are:-

(i) Karbi Anglong Autonomous Council (KAAC)

(ii) North Cachar Hills Autonomous Council (NHAC)

(iii) Bodoland Territorial Areas District / Bodoland Territorial Council (BTC).

While the Karbi Anglong and North Cachar Councils have identical roles in terms of Paragraphs 3 and 3A of the Schedule- they exercise similar judicial and limited executive powers involving a limited range of subjects in List-II of the Seventh Schedulethe Bodoland Council differs in certain respects from the other Councils.

NCHAC and KAAC were given additional powers to make laws with respect to the following subjects vide paragraph 3A of the Sixth Schedule inserted by the Constitutional (Amendment) Act, 1995:-

1. Industries
2. Communications
3. Alienation of land
4. Flood control
5. Agriculture
6. Fisheries
7. Animal husbandry
8. Minor irrigation
9. Social security and social insurance
10. Theatre and dramatic performances
11. Primary and secondary education
12. Entertainments and amusements
13. Public health and sanitation
14. Hospitals and dispensaries
15. Water
16. Sports
17. Libraries
18. Museums
19. Ancient and historical monuments
20. Trade and commerce in, and the production supply and distribution of, foodstuffs, cattle fodder, raw cotton and raw jute

In order to exercise executive functions with respect to the subjects mentioned in Paragraph 3 and 3A of the Schedule, the following departments are to be 'transferred' to the KAAC and NCHAC :

1. Industry
2. Animal Husbandry & Veterinary

3. Forest
4. Agriculture
5. Public Works Department
6. Sericulture
7. Education
8. Cultural Affairs
9. Soil Conservation
10. Co-operation
11. Fisheries
12. Panchayat and Rural Development including DRDA
13. Handloom and textiles
14. Health & Family Welfare
15. Public Health Engineering
16. Irrigation
17. Social Welfare
18. Flood Control
19. Sports and youth welfare
20. Weights and Measures
21. Food and Civil supplies
22. Town and Country Planning
23. College Education
24. Land Reforms
25. Publicity and Public Relations
26. Printing & Stationery
27. Tourism
28. Transport
29. Excise
30. Finance including sales tax etc

All residents of the relevant 'Council area' above 25 years of age are eligible to contest elections. Elections are conducted by the State Government and not by the State Election Commission. The State Government also exercises all the supervisory powers nominally given to the Governor except the power to arbitrate in a dispute between the Council and the Government over Royalty of minerals; in such cases the Governor acts in his discretion. The powers of the State Government also extend to approving the legislations passed by the Councils. As grants are released to the Councils from the consolidated fund of the State, the Councils are amenable to the jurisdiction of the Committees of the State legislature. The Councils are responsible for implementation of rural development and poverty alleviation programmes as they come within the ambit of "transferred subjects".

The related field offices of the "Line Departments" and the DRDA are also controlled by these bodies. Traditional village level institutions mostly consisting of heriditory pradhans survive in the rural areas. By virtue of Article 243M (1) of the Constitution, the provisions of Seventy-third Amendment do not apply to the areas under the jurisdiction of these Councils.

Bodoland Territorial Council (BTC) - Distinctive Features

BTC was initially established in 1993 as a "Tribe Specific" Council under a State legislation. Following the Bodoland Accord of 2003 it was raised to the status of an Autonomous Council under the Sixth Schedule. It enjoys powers which far exceed those given to the earlier two autonomous Councils (KAAC and NHAC). It has been entrusted with a majority of List-II (State) and List-III (Concurrent) functions.

In order to enable it to carry out executive functions, more than 40 departments have been attached to the BTC as shown below:

1. Industry
2. Co-operation
3. Forest

4. Agriculture
5. Fisheries
6. Sericulture
7. Education
8. Irrigation
9. Soil Conservation
10. Animal Husbandry & Veterinary
11. Public Works Department
12. Public Health Engineering
13. Handloom and textiles
14. Health & Family Welfare
15. Social Welfare
16. Cultural Affairs
17. Library services
18. Tribal research Institute
19. College Education
20. Weights and Measures
21. Lotteries, Theatres, Dramatic performance and Cinemas
22. Municipal Corporation. Improvement trust, district boards and other local authorities
23. Urban development Town and country planning
24. Panchayat and Rural Development including DRDA
25. Land revenue
26. Publicity and Public Relations
27. Printing & Stationery
28. Markets and fairs
29. Food and Civil supplies
30. Town and Country Planning
31. Sports and youth welfare
32. Planning and development

33. Tourism
34. Flood Control
35. Statistics
36. Transport
37. Intoxicating liquors, opium and derivatives
38. Welfare of plain tribes and backward classes
39. Relief and Rehabilitation
40. Registration of Births and Deaths
41. Land Reforms
42. Museum & Archaeology
43. Labour and employment
44. Food and Civil supplies

Funds and Budget of the Council

The State Government provides funds to the BTC on the basis of its population. This is in addition to the Government of India's grant of Rs 500 crores. The allocation is released by the State Government in two equal half yearly installments; first in April / May and the second in September / October of the year. This fund is totally untied. Thereafter the BTC makes district wise allocations.

- It is the only Council with a few seats exclusively reserved for non-tribals.
- Again, with its jurisdiction extending over four districts, the "Divisional Cadres" of line departments have also been transferred to the Council.
- But, the BTC is the only 'Sixth Schedule Council' which does not have judicial powers. The judiciary as existent in other parts of the country was fully functional in these areas by the time the BTC was born.
- Compared to other two Sixth Schedule Councils of Assam, the size of fund at the disposal of the BTC is much larger.

It is obvious that the BTC has been given greater administrative and financial powers and is treated on a different footing as compared to the Karbi Anglong Autonomous Council (KAAC) and the North Cachar Hills Autonomous Council (NHAC). This disparity has been a cause of resentment among the people of the latter two Councils. There is a growing demand that there should be full parity among the three Councils in terms of legislative and executive powers and functions. The Commission is of the view that in order to avoid conflicts, priority steps are needed in this direction.

The Councils can exercise executive powers under Paragraph-3 (Paragraphs 3A and 3B in case of the KAAC & NHAC and the BTC respectively) on all subjects on which they have power to legislate. So far the Councils have generally exercised very limited exeuctive powers mainly due to paucity of resources. There is need to normatively assess their financial requirements (with reference to factors such as minimum standards of services, local resource mobilization potential and the ambit of prescribed responsibility).

It goes without saying that this approach would entail considerably larger subventions from the State Governments. But the net additional burden on the State on this account is, however, liable to be taken care of by the Central Finance Commission in due course. The Commission feels that in order to enable the Autonomous Councils to discharge their responsibilities satisfactorily, it is imperative that the requirement of funds by these bodies is worked out normatively with reference to the minimum standards of service to be provided and assessed capacity to raise local resources. Such exercise could be undertaken by the State Finance Commission.

Apart from making adequate resources available, it is equally important to ensure smooth and timely flow of funds to the Councils. As per the existing arrangements, the funds are to be transferred to the Councils in two equal installments. This needs to be strictly adhered to by the State Government. In the case of BTC, the funds are released by various departments of the Assam Government in favour of the BTC Department. The BTC Department of the State Government then acts as a single window for release of funds to the BTC. There are some exceptions; the Union Ministry of Tribal Affairs routes its allocation through the State Tribal Welfare Department.

The advantage of a single window system is that the Council is broadly aware of the likely size of the funds they would be getting from each department. This system needs to be further fine tuned to make it more effective and hassle free. Such a hassle free system needs to be adopted for the other two Councils of this State (KAAC and NCHAC) also with adequate delegation of financial powers.

Recommendations

a) All the three Sixth Schedule Autonomous Councils of Assam should be given parity with regard to legislative and executive powers.

b) Adequate resources should be provided to the Autonomous Councils so that they are able to carry out their assigned responsibilities effectively. The allocation of funds to these bodies should be based on pre-settled norms (with reference to the minimum standards of service to be provided and their capacity to raise local resources). This exercise could be undertaken by the State Finance Commission.

c) The system of release of funds to the BTC through a single window system should be further fine tuned to make it more effective and hassle free. Such a hassle free system of fund release should be adopted for the other two Councils also with adequate delegation of financial powers.

Tribe Specific Councils (created under State enactment)

Assam has a significant tribal population living outside the Sixth Schedule areas. These tribes too have been demanding special powers and budgetary allocations on the pattern of those given to Sixth Schedule Autonomous Councils. During a period of ten years from 1995-2005, the Government of Assam entered into a Memorandum of Understanding with a large number of such tribes to establish exclusive Autonomous Councils for them. The Government legislated to create six 'Tribe Specific' Autonomous Councils (with Village Councils under them) in different parts of the States. But these Councils are not compact geographical territories. Since members of a specific tribe may be residing in pockets located in more than one district, the jurisdiction of a Council often extends to several districts.

The Tribal Council may have a smaller Council under it consisting of pockets which are dispersed over a large area and cover a block of several revenue villages. The population of such a 'block' varies with the tribe e.g. it is 6000-8000 in case of Rabha Hasing and Mising and Tiwa Councils; 3000-5000 in Deori and Thengal Kahari Councils. These smaller Councils (often called a village Council) work under the overall control and supervision of the concerned autonomous tribal council.

In order to cover the largest possible numbers of the relevant tribe, a further 'innovation' has been made to identify satellite areas i.e. isolated pockets with significant population of the target group. Such areas are kept within the purview of the Council despite the fact that they are cut off from the core areas i.e. geographically contiguous areas predominated by the tribe concerned. In short, such Councils also contain isolated pockets at sporadic locations over a number of Districts. The complexity is confounded by the fact that the Districts concerned are under the purview of the 73rd Constitutional amendment with the regular Panchayat institutions operating in such areas. Each Tribe specific Council exists along with several Zila Parishads while tribal Village Councils and Village Panchayats also co-exist though their jurisdictions are not co-terminus.

In view of the lack of spatial cohesion of these bodies- interspersed as the tribe specific Councils are over scattered pockets with concentration of the tribe concerned over a number of Districts- their programmes in spheres like rural roads, minor irrigation, control of soil erosion and village and cottage industries are difficult to implement over 'disjointed' areas. In fact, the funding of these bodies is exclusively dependant on allocations from the tribal sub-plan and the outlays available from this source are by no means adequate to meet the requirements sought to be met by the Councils. The Commission appreciates that compelling socio-political reasons had weighed with the State Government in establishing these bodies. Aspirations of tribes not dominating a geographically discrete area could arguably be made perfect only through imperfect solutions. The arrangement, however, gives cause for concern as to its potential for conflict and viability as also to meet the aspirations in an effective manner.

It is clear that efforts must be made to ensure that as far as possible the role to be performed by tribe-specific bodies does not overlap with Panchayati institutions. It must be borne in mind that in areas of mixed ethnic composition existence of bodies with overlapping jurisdiction should not be allowed to exacerbate communal conflicts and tensions. It would appear that such objectives can best be achieved if the functional responsibilities of the two streams are kept as distinct as possible. This is particularly so in a situation where successful and effective implementation of the programmes implemented through the Panchayati institutions will benefit tribals and non tribals alike.

The Expert Committee on Planning for the Sixth Schedule Areas formed by the Ministry of Panchayati Raj under the Chairmanship of Shri V. Ramachandran made the following important observations in this regard:-

"An examination of the functioning of these councils shows a picture of confusion. The Panchayati Raj system continues to exist in these areas, as there is no constitutional basis for their removal. These areas are not exempt from Panchayati Raj in the same manner as other areas such as Nagaland and hill areas of Manipur have been exempted. The problems of institutional overlap in such areas are thus further compounded by the formation of these councils. There are three authorities operating in parallel in these areas, namely, the Council, the State departmental system and the Panchayati Raj system. These issues must be urgently solved so that there is only one single authority. The Committee is of the view that the Constitutional pattern will need to be respected and Panchayati Raj be strengthened in these areas, rather than to create councils on the basis of ethnic identity alone, without any geographical jurisdiction. Such bodies are inherently incapable of functioning as local self governments and at best, can function as group focused development authorities, say, in the same manner as SC and Tribal and OBC Development Corporations."

The Commission also examined this issue in its Report on Capacity Building for Conflict Resolution. It again reiterates its earlier recommendations.

Recommendations

a) The Government of Assam should apportion functions between the tribe specific Councils/Village Councils and the Panchayati Raj Institutions in a manner that schemes involving individual tribal beneficiaries may be assigned to the 'Tribe Specific Councils' while area development schemes are assigned to the latter.

b) The State Government should initiate a system of meeting at least the establishment costs of the 'Tribe Specific Councils' from sources outside the tribal sub plan and build in these requirements in their projections to the next Finance Commission.

c) The State Government should take steps to identify innovative initiatives which could be entrusted to the Tribe Specific Councils for the benefit of the concerned tribes without affecting area development and local government concerns.

d) Suitable guidelines may be drafted for preparation of District and sub- District plans in the relevant areas through joint efforts of the Tribe Specific Councils and the Panchayati Raj Institutions.

Areas under Panchayati Raj Institutions formed under the provisions of the Seventy-Third Amendment

Out of 27 districts in the State, 6 have 'Sixth Schedule Councils'. The remaining 21 are covered under the Seventy-Third Amendment. As noted above, however, 12 districts in this group also play host to 6 tribe specific Inter-District Councils. The situation of rural local self governance, therefore, shows a degree of variety not encountered elsewhere in the country.

In pursuance of the Seventy-Third Amendment, the Assam Panchayat Raj Act-1994 has been enacted. The Act establishes a three tier Panchayati Raj structure viz (a) ten Member elected Gaon Panchayat (GP) with a directly elected President , (b) Block Level Anchalik Pnachayat consisting of an elected Member from each GP area and the GP Presidents (ex officio) with a directly elected President and (c) Zila Parishad with members directly elected (from four 'ZP' constituencies from each Assembly Constituency) and Presidents of Anchalik Panchayats (ex officio) with a directly elected President. Members of the House of the People and Legislative Assembly covering the jurisdiction of (b) and (c) are also ex officio members of these bodies.

With the inclusion of the Bodo areas in the Sixth Schedule very few areas of the State remain under the Fifth Schedule. For them a special legislation, the Panchayats (Extension of the Scheduled Areas) Act 1996 has been enacted which in essence provides that while the provisions of the Assam Panchayat Raj Act would apply to these areas, its application will be subject to local customs. In such areas the traditional tribal habitations rather than Revenue Villages constitute Gram Sabhas.

The recommendations made for effective functioning of Panchayati Raj Institutions in the Commission's report on "Local Governance" need to be implemented in letter and spirit for these areas of Assam.

Arunanchal Pradesh

Arunachal Pradesh embraces the erstwhile North Eastern Frontier Agency (NEFA) which before the commencement of the Constitution was loosely administered through a Political Officer by the Political Department of the Government of India. This was based on the arrangements made for administering the NWFP of British India which bordered Afghanistan. The Constitution treated the 'North Eastern frontier tracts' as a deemed Union Territory administered by the Governor of Assam in his discretion as the 'agent' of the President of India. Initially, the traditions of 'loose administration' were maintained. The 'frontier tracts' were kept in 'Part B' of the 6th Schedule i.e. areas which could be provided with autonomous District Councils only at a future date. While none of these 'tracts' were ever brought under 'Part A' of the Schedule, from the 1950s onwards, the area began receiving greater attention. In practice, the NEFA administration was carried out from Shillong- the capital of undivided Assam- by the Adviser to the Governor who enjoyed extensive powers over this territory. During the period 1953 to 1964 the Adviser worked closely with an Officer-on Special Duty (OSD) for Tribal Affair - a post held by the legendary anthropologist, Verrier Elwin.

A part of NEFA was transferred to the 'Naga Hills- Teunsang Administrative Area established in 1957- an area that was upgraded as the State of Nagaland in 1963. Affairs of this area were handled by the Union Government through the Ministry of External Affairs (MEA) - the post independence successor of the Political Department. After the Chinese aggression, the administration was brought more in line with that of other Union Territories. A nominated advisory body was established and the Ministry of Home Affairs replaced the Ministry of

External Affairs as the nodal Ministry for its administration in 1965. The post of Adviser was upgraded to that of Lieutenant Governor and the Governor of Assam was relieved of his special responsibilities. In 1972, NEFA was given the status of a Union Territory' with an elected legislative Assembly and was renamed, "Arunachal Pradesh". In 1986 a separate Act (the State of Arunachal Pradesh Act 1986) was enacted and the State of Arunachal Pradesh came into existence in the year 1987.

The State is multi-ethnic and multi-lingual being home to over 30 tribes, practicing a number of religions including Buddhism and various indigenous faiths native to the region. Given this diversity, it is not surprising that Hindi has emerged as the lingua franca of the region.

Status of Local Decentralization

Verrier Elwin, the celebrated anthropologist, and the author of Pandit Jawaharlal Nehru's tribal policy in the North East in his last work "Democracy in NEFA" has drawn attention to the traditions of 'indigenous democracy' through institutions like Kebang (Tribal Council) of the Adi tribe and brought home the crucial role of communal consensus in tribal life.

It is also noteworthy that an area which, at the commencement of the Constitution, was considered not ripe to have the benefit of decentralized governance under the Sixth Schedule is now within the purview of the 73rd amendment. (Article-243D which provides for reservation of seats for the Scheduled castes is not applicable here).

Under the Arunachal Panchayat Raj Act 1997 a three tier Panchayati structure has been brought into existence. While these bodies have been constituted, effective transfer of functions/ activities as envisaged under the Panchayat legislation has not yet taken placea single member (Otem Dai) Committee was constituted to work out the modalities of implementing the scheme of delegation. The State Government has agreed in principle that the Gaon Panchayat will be the exclusive agency for selecting beneficiaries under various schemes and programme. It has also been decided to place the Zila Parishad in charge of the DRDAs. The Comission has already made a large number of recommendations for effective functioning of Panchayati Raj Institutions created under provisions of the 73rd Consititutional amendement in its Report on 'Local Governance' (the sixth Report). All those recommendations need to be implemented in letter and spirit.

Other Issues

Although Arunachal Pradesh has not witnessed home-grown insurgency, some of its districts are presently affected by insurgency from neighbouring Nagaland as well as the demand for NAGALIM from some insurgent groups. This has disrupted the historical tranquility and development in these districts. The priority, therefore, needs to be on the restoration of peace, lest the virus spread.

The tribal societies in Arunachal Pradesh are egalitarian. However, during the last 50 years inequalities have emerged initially because of the uneven spread of education and unemployment. These inequalities were held in check by the system of community ownership of land. However, there are now signs of the weakening of this tradition particularly because community owned land is not bankable collateral. The Usha Thorat Committee constituted by the Reserve Bank of India on Financial Sector Plan for NER observed that, "for larger value of loans the banks are availing sufficient deposit receipt/grantee from the third party. The transfer of properties Act is not applicabvle in the State and as a result equitable mortgage can not be created. The banks are facing problem for financing high value proposals for want of security." This needs to be carefully handled in association with banks and all stake holders in the land.

The traditional system of dispute settlement both for civil and criminal cases known as the 'Kebang system' has weakened with the introduction of the Panchayati Raj System and the gradual expansion of the formal judicial system. Replacement of this system based on a negotiated system of disputes, focusing on satisfaction to the victims, by a system of adjudicated settlement of disputes is inevitable. However, the co- existence of the two systems during the period of transition requires careful consideration and decision. The Ministry of Home Affairs would need to examine Regulation 1 of 1945.

On its constitution, Arunachal Pradesh had five districts. It now has 15 districts. Reportedly some staff from Circle Offices in remote areas has been adjusted in the district headquarters consequently weakening the administrative set up in the Circle Offices. In view of Arunachal Pradesh's border with Tibet and a history of Chinese incursions, it is imperative that the focus on adequate administrative presence in remote border areas is not weakened.

Recommendations

a) The recommendations made in its Report on "Local Governance" for strengthening and empowering PRIs need to be implemented on priority.

b) Some districts of Arunachal Pradesh are presently affected by insurgency from neighboring States. Firm steps should be taken by both the Union and the State Government to restore peace in the affected areas.

c) Traditionally, land in Arunachal Pradesh is owned by the community. However, this system has gradually weakened primarily because community owned land is not a bankable collateral. This issue needs to be resolved in consultation with the Reserve Bank of India, banks and stake-holders in the land.

d) Because of the gradual expansion of the formal judicial system in place of the traditional 'Kebang system', it would be necessary for the Ministry of Home Affairs to examine the Assam Frontier (Administration of Justice)

Regulation Act 1945 in the State, to ensure a smooth transition to the formal judicial system.

Manipur

Manipur was a princely State that merged with the Indian Union in 1948 after some initial reluctance on the part of the then Maharaja. A peculiar feature of the State is that out of its total geographical area only 25% is in the valleys, which is home to around 70% of the total population (overwhelmingly non-tribal) while the hill areas are inhabited by various tribal communities belonging to Naga, Mizo and Kuki-Chin groups. The outbreak of insurgency in the Naga Hills in the 1950s affected Naga inhabited Northern, Eastern and Western Hills of the State too. Similarly, eruption of violence in Mizo Hills in the 1960s caused disturbances in the Southern hills dominated by kindred tribes. The Valley inhabited largely by the Meitei community, too, has been the scene of insurgency caused by local armed groups from the 1970s. "Integrity" of the State has been a major issue as there is a demand from certain Naga groups for merger of areas dominated by them in the Greater Nagaland. In short, the State has remained in the midst of conflict and violence for long.

Article 371C of the Constitution makes some special provisions for safeguarding the interests of tribal minorities of the State, which reads as under:

"(1) Notwithstanding anything in this Constitution, the President may, by order made with respect to the State of Manipur, provide for the constitution and functions of a committee of the Legislative Assembly of the State consisting of members of that Assembly elected from the Hill Areas of that State, for the modifications to be made in the rules of business of the Government and in the rules of procedure of the Legislative Assembly of the State and for any special responsibility of the Governor in order to secure the proper functioning of such committee".

In terms of Regulations framed under this provision, members of the State legislature elected from the hill areas have been given powers to deliberate on legislative proposals concerning matters affecting land, water, forests and tribal customs in such areassubjects which essentially form part of Paragraph 3 of the Sixth Schedule. Such legislations require approvals of the legislators as above. Budget and plan provisions for such areas also require clearance of this Committee.

Status of Local Decentralization

Manipur has had strong democratic traditions. When still a princely State in 1947, elections were held to the Legislative Assembly on the basis of universal adult suffrage for the first time anywhere on the Indian soil. The voter turn-out in successive elections has been one of the highest in the country. At the grass-roots level there are differential arrangements in the tribal dominated hills and the central valley.

Hill District Councils

Like Tripura, Manipur also has some areas which are covered under Part IX of the Constitution. They are the valley areas of the State. However, unlike Tripura, the hill areas of the State are not governed by the Sixth Schedule of the Constitution, but by a special State legislation, the Manipur Hill Areas District Councils Act, 1971.

This Act has provisions similar to those contained in the Sixth Schedule and has established six Autonomous Hill District Councils in Manipur, covering 5 districts. The activities of the Councils are confined to agriculture, horticulture, primary and adult education and tribal welfare.

No power to levy taxes is given to these bodies and they depend entirely on grants from the Government. The provisions of the Fifth Schedule are applicable to them. The details of these districts are as follows:

Hill District Councils of Manipur

Sl. No.	Name of the Hill District	Name of Autonomous District Council
1.	Senapati (Manipur North)	1. Senapati ADC 2. Sadar Hills ADC
2.	Churachandpur (Manipur South)	3. Churachandpur ADC
3.	Ukhrul (Manipur East)	4. Ukhrul ADC
4.	Tamenglong (Manipur West)	5. Tamenglong ADC
5.	Chandel (Manipur South East)	6. Chandel ADC

The responsibility of holding elections to these bodies vests with the State Government and not with the State Election Commission.

These Hill Councils have, however, remained defunct since 1990 when the term of the Councils elected in 1985 came to an end. The major impediment in holding elections to the Councils is the demand in the hill areas for bringing them under the Sixth Schedule. This demand is stoutly resisted by the majority of inhabitants of the Manipur valley who regard it as imperiling the 'territorial integrity' of the State and a prelude to the "dismemberment of Manipur". Attempts in the past to hold elections under the existing framework were resisted. The situation currently is one of a continuing impasse.

Villages in the Hill Areas do not have truly representative institutions. Much of village level governance is carried out by Village chiefs/headmen called Khulakpa and Gaon Burha. These functionaries hold hereditary positions in most of the non Naga communities while in Naga populated areas, they hold life-long elected positions based on a system of indirect election wherein the more powerful personality of the village is chosen by consensus. An old enactment - the Village Authority Act 1956 - gives the village headman the responsibility to control petty crime, assist in maintaining order and report on epidemics and sanitary conditions etc. In most of the Naga villages there is an informal system of electing one male representative from each clan; such elected representatives in turn form the Village Council which is headed by a Village chief. These bodies are now being used as Village Development Committees for overseeing development programmes.

PRIs in the Valley Areas

In the valley areas, Panchayati Raj institutions have been constituted as envisaged by the 73rd Constitutional amendments. Elections are being held regularly by the State Election Commission. PRIs have been involved in the implementation of poverty alleviation programmes. However, they have not been given control over the DRDAs.

Issues

1. **Constitution of Elected District Councils in the Hill areas;** As mentioned earlier, the Hill Councils constituted under the State enactment of 1971, are defunct since 1990. This is mainly on account of the conflict between the hill and the valley areas over the issue of inclusion of hill areas of Manipur in the Sixth Schedule and creation of Autonomous Councils thereunder. The non-existence of elected bodies at the local level is hampering the process of development and works against the interests of the tribal communities. The Expert Committee on 'Planning in Sixth Schedule Areas' observed that, "there is need to immediately constitute elected district councils, whatever the future course of action on the matter of inclusion of these areas under the Sixth Schedule might be. Since the elections to the district councils were stopped on the basis of a resolution of the Hill Areas Council, this matter ought to be reconsidered by them. Detailed discussions need to be held with the concerned groups to explain and drive home the adverse results of the status quo. There might be a fear that constituting of elected district councils

might dilute the demand for Sixth Schedule status. In this regard, the Committee emphasizes that the demand for Sixth Schedule Status can be examined independently of the priority to immediately constitute elected District Councils in terms of the existing State laws." So far the funds given to the local Councils have been meager and almost entirely consist of grants from the State Government. During 2006-07, the State Plan assistance to the Councils consisted of Rs.970.00 lakhs, inclusive of Rs.300 lakhs as Special Plan Assistance.

2. **Devolution of Subjects / Functions to the Councils:** The range of activities to be performed by the Hill Councils though a State enactment formed under the Fifth Schedule of the Constitution is limited as compared to that of the Autonomous Councils formed under the Sixth Schedule. Though there is plenty of scope for undertaking projects in sectors such as Health, Agriculture, Forests etc. in the absence of any participating mechanisms, the pace of development has suffered in these areas. Hence, steps need to be taken immediately to constitute the elected Hill Areas Development Councils. Thereafter, it will be imperative to devolve developmental activities along with the transfer of the concerned offices/departments and the parallel bodies to these Councils. These steps will need to be followed by adequate devolution of funds to them on a normative and transparent basis.

3. **Constitution of a representative body at the village level:** The majority of the non-Tribal population lives in the valley, which comprises of about 25% of the total land area of the State. They account for 70 percent of the population of the State. The valley shows a high degree of urbanization, with nearly 40 percent of the people living in urban areas. In contrast, the hill areas of the State, comprising nearly 75 percent of its area are entirely rural, scattered in groups of isolated communities. The tribal

population mainly consists of two Tribal ethnic groups, the Nagas and the Kukis, both of which have their distinctive traditional system of village governance.

Under the Manipur Hill Village Authority Act 1956 separate village councils have been established in the Hill Areas. This Act provides for the village councils to be democratically elected. It also provides reservations for women representatives, much in the manner of the Panchyati Raj legislation. However, there is strong opposition to these Councils more from the Kuki traditional chiefs, who perceive them to be competitors and rivals of the traditional Village Councils. Currently, limited financial powers have been assigned to these elected Village Councils. The State Government is considering to empower them on the model adopted in Nagaland.

The constitution of elected village level bodies is a must in order to accelerate the process of development. At the same time there is need to establish harmony between the traditional councils and the elected village level bodies. The local level conflicts in this regard need to be addressed by way of persuasive efforts for bringing a consensus between the divergent views. The Ramachandran Committee has suggested two ways in which these village level bodies could be established - first, to operationalise the provisions of the Hill Village Authority Act 1956, after discussions with the Traditional tribal chiefs and second, in case these discussions make no headway, to put in place an interim arrangement by adopting the village level planning and implementation mechanism for implementation of NREGA. The Committee also suggested that it may not be out of place to give the leadership of the village development bodies to the traditional leaders, to maintain continuity.

The Commission also considered the issue of District and Village level Councils in Manipur while examining modes of conflicts in the North East and observed that;

"In Manipur, the situation in the hill areas is a cause for concern. While the valley districts are covered under the

Seventy-third Amendment, hill areas are in the exempted category. Six statutory autonomous Hill District Councils consisting of elected members with a right of participation by the legislators from the district functioned till 1990 when the next elections were due. Elections since then have not been possible as there has been a demand from a significant section of tribal population for bringing these areas under the Sixth Schedule. The demand is strongly opposed by the valley areas on the ground that it would lead to dismemberment of the State. In the absence of these Councils, grassroots level services like primary education, veterinary care and local arts and crafts have been adversely affected and a forum for ventilating local problems has also been dispensed with. It appears that after hardening of attitudes on both sides, not much efforts have been made to break the stalemate. Manipur continues to be the only State where elected village councils have not so far been set up while the village authorities involved with regulation of village affairs are largely a body of traditional village principals. In the absence of representative grassroots level bodies, selection of beneficiaries and monitoring of poverty alleviation schemes and similar interventions has suffered considerably. While much greater efforts are required to build consensus on the issue of District Councils in the State, urgent action is needed to bring in suitable legislation to introduce elected village self-governance in the hill areas of the State".

The Commission recommended:-

"While continuous and vigorous measures are needed to bring about a consensus between various sections of society in Manipur about revival of the Hill Districts Councils, steps may be urgently taken to bring in suitable legislation to introduce elected village level bodies in the hill areas of that State."

The Commission once again reiterates this view. It believes the stalemate with regard to the non functional District Councils is clearly prejudicial to the development of hill districts of Manipur. While sincere, proactive measures are necessary to bring about a consensus among the various sections of society about the revival of these long defunct bodies, there is no reason why a beginning to introduce elements of accountable village level self governance should be delayed. Suitable incentives could be provided to the State for initiating legislative measures to usher in a system of village level democratization having regard to the local circumstances. Once the District Councils are revived, it will be imperative to devolve a major domain of developmental activities to them along with transfer of funds and functionaries. The local functionaries of the field offices of the State governments and the parallel bodies which are currently handling these activities at the district level will also need to be placed at the disposal of the District Councils.

As regards strengthening and empowering the PRIs, the Commission would like to reiterate its recommendations made in its Report on "Local Governance" (sixth Report).

Recommendations

a) Sincere, proactive measures should be taken to revive and activate the Hill District Councils in Manipur. It will be imperative to devolve a major domain of developmental activities to them. It will have to be done along with transfer of funds and functionaries. The local functionaries of the field offices/departments of the State Governments and the parallel bodies which are currently handing these activities at the district level will also need to be placed at the disposal of the District Councils.

b) All steps should be taken to put in place elected Village Councils in rural areas. Suitable incentives should be provided to the State for initiating proactive legislative measures in this direction having due regard to the local circumstances.

c) As regards the PRIs the Commission has already made a number of recommendations for their strengthening and empowerment in its Report on "Local Governance" (sixth Report) which needs to be implemented on priority.

Issues of Personnel Management in Manipur

The Commission during its visit to Manipur was apprised of the large scale demoralization prevailing among the government staff at all levels. It was because of threats of extortion and insurgency which had created an extremely troubled law and order situation throughout the State. As a result, staff posted in remote hill districts do not join their place of postings resulting in serious dislocation of public services. Schools were without teachers and health care centres without para-medical staff. This situation has also led to administrative aberrations like deployment of employees in urban centres far in excess of sanctioned posts. For example, in the Office of the Deputy Commissioner Imphal, there were 78 LDCs working against 15 sanctioned posts. Artificial shortages have often been cited as justification for adhoc/substitute recruitment. It has resulted in high incidence of irregular employment and payment of salary to "ghost" staff. In a bid to redress, the situation, Government of Manipur took a number of innovative steps. These included:-

(1) Computerisation of a Personnel Information Systems (CPIS) under which a data base was created of:

- All sanctioned posts in each office
- All regular government employees in each office

(2) It also generated a Unique Employee Identification Number (EIN) and it was ensured that salary would be paid to only those staff who had an EIN.

(3) The CPIS was regularly up-dated in respect of each promotion, transfer, retirement and recruitment.

The impact of this important measure included:-

i. Detection of 6311 ghost / fake employees (i.e. 10% of State's total man power)

ii. Rs 80 crores saved per year in salary payments

iii. It stopped back-door/unauthorized appointments

iv. Re-deployment of staff in outlying/remote hill offices

v. Clear information to each HOD about man power deployment

vi. Strong public appreciation

Another effective and noteworthy initiative on the part of the Manipur Government was the passing of the Manipur Public Servant Liability (MPSPL) Act in support of the CPIS and to check corruption. It provided "for personal liability of the public servants of Manipur for creation of unauthorized liability through irregular actions in form of appointment or engagement of persons, award of works, supply orders, payment of bills, signing and execution of contracts, providing grants, benefits, compensation, and such other acts in the name of Government or its agencies and recovery of such amounts from the personal incomes including salary and other entitlements of the Public Servants responsible for creation of such liabilities" .

A High Powered Committee under the Chief Secretary was set up to fix responsibility and order recoveries, through summary procedures.

The initial resistance to these initiatives was overcome because of extensive meetings and interactions at the Chief Secretary level with officers and explaining to them how these could be effectively used for improving governance and to check corruption. Prima-facie, as per reports, there has been perceptible improvements both in the presence of staff in remote locations as well as in governance in general because of these steps. But, the challenge is to ensure that they are sustained.

Recommendation

a) Initiatives of the Manipur Government in human resource management need to be sustained. Similar initiatives may also be considered by other States of the region.

Special powers to the Governor of Manipur under Article 371

Currently Manipur is the most severly affected State in the region in terms of increase in the number of cases of extortion and insurgency, etc. There have been instances when the elected governments failed to take decisive action at critical moments, often leading to complete breakdown of law and order and large scale disturbances in the State. Also, the process of political reconciliation to resolve complex situations has considerably weakened. Under these circumstances, there is need for the Union Government to consider giving special responsibilities to the Governor of Manipur to deal adequately and effectively with such situations. The Governors of Nagaland (Article 371A) and Arunahal Pradesh (Article 371H) have been given special responsibility under the Constitution for maintenance of law and order in these States because of the strategic location and the long history of insurgency and extremism in this region. In view of the problems of Manipur as stated above, the Commission is of the view that similar powers may also be given to the Governor of Manipur. Presently, under the provisions of Article 371C, the Governor of Manipur is entrusted only with the responsibility of submitting an annual report to the President on the administration of hill areas of the State. He should also be assigned special responsibility with regard to maintenance of law and order on the pattern of Article 371A and 371H. This could be done by appropriate redrafting of the existing Article 371C. The amended Article could read as follows:

> "The Governor of Manipur shall have special responsibilities with respect to law and order in the State of Manipur and in the discharge of his functions in relation thereto, the Governor shall after consulting the Council of Ministers, exercise his individual judgement as to the action to be taken:
>
> Provided that if any question arises whether any matter is or is not a matter as respects which the Governor is under

this clause required to act in the exercise of his individual judgement, the decision of the Governor in his discretion shall be final, and the validity of anything done by the Governor shall not be called in question on the ground that he ought or ought not to have acted in the exercise of his individual judgement.

Provided further that if the President on receipt of a report from the Governor or otherwise is satisfied that it is no longer necessary for the Governor to have special responsibility with respect to law and order in the State of Manipur, he may be order direct that the Governor shall cease to have such responsibility with effect from such date as may be specified in the order."

The Commission feels that by incorporating this provision in the Constitution, the Governor of Manipur will be in a position to play a more proactive role in case of breakdown of law and order and large scale disturbances in the State when there is reluctance or failure on the part of the elected government to take timely measures to deal with such situations.

Recommendation

In view of the circumstances prevailing in Manipur, the Governor of Manipur should be given special powers/responsibility with respect to law and order on the lines of the powers vested in the Governors of Nagaland and Arunachal Pradesh under Articles 371A and 371H of the Constitution respectively. This could be done by inserting a suitable paragraph in Article 371C.

Meghalaya

At the commencement of the Constitution, the present State of Meghalaya consisted of three Districts of Assam. Under the Sixth Schedule these Districts were provided two Councils – a joint or united Council for the Jaintia and Khasi Hills District, and a separate Council for the Garo Hills. In 1969 through the twenty-second amendment of the Constitution, a new provision,

Article-244A was added enabling the Parliament to form an 'autonomous State' within the Constitution. Pursuant to this amendment, Parliament established an 'autonomous State' called Meghalaya. Later under the North-Eastern Areas (Reorganisation) Act 1971, this autonomous State was given the status of a full fledged State in 1972.

With 7281 mm of annual rainfall, Meghalaya is not only the 'wettest' State in the country; it is among the regions with highest precipitation anywhere in the world. It is multi ethnic in character with three tribes, Khasi, Garo and Jaintiya accounting for more than 95% of the tribal population of the State. (the Schedule Tribes constitute 86% of the total population of the State).

Status of Local Decentralization

Meghalaya is the only State in the North-East Region where the Sixth Schedule provisions cover the entire territory except the so called "European Wards" of Shillong city.

Organisational arrangements in the Autonomous Councils:

The organisational arrangements in respect of the HADCs are largely similar. The Sixth Schedule lays down the details of their power and functions. Each Council consists of upto twenty six to thirty elected (and nominated) members which form the Legislature and which has powers to enact and frame Laws, Rules and Regulations on the subjects listed in the Sixth Schedule. From amongst them is elected the Chief Executive Member. Two Executive Members are appointed by the Governor. Each Executive Member is assigned a functional portfolio, much in the manner of a Minister of the State Government. The Executive is responsible for administration of the Council, realization of revenue, taxation on certain subjects, development works etc. The Judiciary consists of the village courts which try petty cases, subordinate and Districts Courts which have original and appellate jurisdiction. Appeals lie with the High Court.

These Councils appear to be miniature governments replicating all their paraphernalia.

The powers of the Hill Area Autonomous Councils cover the following areas:

1. Appointment/ succession of Chiefs/ Headmen
2. Construct/ manage primary schools (withdrawn by the State Government)
3. Management of land & forest
4. Control of money lending & trading by non-tribals
5. Marriage & Divorce
6. Inheritance of property
7. Ponds
8. Ferries
9. Road Transport & Waterways
10. Markets
11. Social Customs
12. Levy & Collection of Taxes

Considering the fact that the geographical jurisdiction of the Councils taken together and that of the State Government is co-terminus, it is not surprising that the additional powers conferred on the Autonomous Councils in other States under the Schedule have not been extended to the Councils in Meghalaya which exercise the 'pristine' powers of Paragraph 3 and 4 of the Schedule viz. jurisdiction over land, water and customs and administration of justice. There is growing discomfort between the State Government and the Councils in this regard, as these Councils are amongst the oldest in the Region and were recognized when the Constitution was framed.

Like other Sixth Schedule areas, there are no representative bodies at the village level in Meghalaya. The traditional system of village chiefs/headmen has been retained. They are:

1. Syiem, Sardar and Lyngdoh in Khasi Hills.
2. Dolloi, and Sardar in Jaintia Hills.
3. Nokma, and Lashkar in Garo Hills.

At present affairs of the village are managed by these traditional functionaries with support of male village elders. It is more or less the same as the system prevalent in Manipur.

Issues Concerning Autonomous District Councils

The Autonomous District Councils in Meghalaya have not been able to function effectively for many reasons. It has been a common finding of several Commissions and Committees which have examined the functioning of Autonomous Councils that there is considerable disaffection between the State Government and the Councils. While the Councils believe that they have a pre-eminent position in local governance, both on account of tradition and the fact that they draw their strength from the Sixth Schedule, the Meghalaya Government's attitude seems to be that these Councils should stick to their traditional role, which is to protect tribal culture, land and identity from being overwhelmed by the culture of the plains. The State Government feels the Councils do not have much of a role to play in developmental activities. At the district level, the only connection between the development administration and the District Council exists through the Chief Executive Member (CEM) who happens to be a member of the DRDA governing body. The Ramachandran Committee observed that "there is thus a crying need for reform on both sides, namely, for the State to understand that the District Councils could play an effective role in local development and for the District Councils to usefully use their autonomy to undertake reforms, in particular reorganize themselves to carry out effectively their statutory functions, and reorient themselves towards development. Moreover, within the district, the apparent contradiction between traditional institutions and a modern political system (as represented by the District Council) will have to be sorted out. This calls for a well structured and integrated system within the district from the District Council to village level institutions. In this regard, the Committee identified the following points of action that ought to be addressed on priority:

(i) Maximise participation of village people

(ii) Ensure gender sensitivity and empower women

(iii) Ensure transparency in its transaction

(iv) Ensure participation of the marginalized."

Other important observations of the Expert Committee are as under:-

(a) At the village level, the approach adopted in the IFAD project areas had indeed touched a responsive chord among the people, particularly women. Dovetailed into the NREGA planning process, this provided a powerful and well tested model for triggering local planning and execution of programmes at the village level. Therefore scaling up of this approach is required to cover all villages in Meghalaya.

(b) At the district level, the District Councils will have to reorient them towards development. There is need to strengthen and professionalise their activities. The first step in this regard would be to provide for women to be represented in the Hill Councils.

The Commission is of the view that as in the case of Panchayati Raj, there is a need for separation between the State Government and District Councils through a process of activity mapping. There should be clear demarcation of jurisdiction between the State Government and the District Councils. The links between the District Councils and the State Government should be effectively maintained. The State Government should hand over all subjects and departments that pertain to the domain of District Councils to them. The Union Government would also need to take similar action with regard to Centrally

Sponsored Schemes being implemented in these areas. As regards financial resources, from the interaction that the Commission had with the Councils of Meghalaya, it believes that the grants received from the State Government and their own revenues together are insufficient to do full justice to their financial needs. Therefore, the allocation of funds to the District Councils should be based on normative and transparent considerations. Also the fiscal transfer system operating between the State Government and the District Councils needs to be systematized. Funds for the District Councils should be budgeted for in detail and allocations should be handed over to the District Councils in two instalments. At the same time the Councils should take immediate action for improving their own revenues. It is equally important to improve internal administration and financial management capabilities of these Autonomous Councils in order to convert them into effective selfgovernance institutions.

Elected Village Councils

There is growing concern in the State about the need to involve rural communities in development programmes. A beginning has been made through 'pilot- testing' of an innovative approach in the National Rural Employment Guarantee Scheme in West and South Garo Hill Districts. This innovation is based on the model used for implementing the IFAD (International Fund for Agriculture and Development) sponsored project, "North Eastern Region Community Resource Management Project for Upland Areas (NERCORMP). This project seeks to improve the livelihood of vulnerable groups through improved management of the local resource base in selected areas. The project has a hierarchy of groups like the village level Natural Resource Management Groups (NaRMG) which function like the Gram Sabhas. A given number of such groups form a 'cluster'; the 'clusters' in a District constitute the Community Resource Management Society. The 'cluster' and 'community' level bodies consist of elected representatives of village level bodies, representatives of NGOs and Government officials.

The adaptations made by the State Government in the above model involve setting up a Village Employment Committee (VEC). The VEC has three members- two of them elected, one male and one female. The third member is the traditional village chief. The electorate consists of one adult male and female from each household. One of the elected member acts as the Secretary. The VEC is responsible for preparing schemes to be undertaken and monitors the implementation. Above the VEC there is Area Executive Committee (AEC). 'Area' comprises villages within a radius of 3.5 KMs. AEC consists of the village head and another member of the VEC subject to the condition that at least thirty percent members are to be females. The AEC issues Employment Cards under the NREGS. The AEC is to be headed by a local chief.

This experiment has the merit of bringing in an element of participation, including gender representation while retaining the traditional source of authority. The arrangement will, however, become meaningful only when the number of members of the VEC is raised (say to ten) and the AEC is provided a linkage with the Block and District level Committees. It will need some modification in its application to Khasi areas as the institution of "Darbar" in such areas may require some adjustment in the concept of VEC- "Darbars" do not necessarily coincide with village boundaries.

In its Seventh Report, it was recommended by the Commission that, "Government of Meghalaya may take steps for extension of the experiment of elected village committees in the Garo Hills for implementation of the National Employment Guarantee Act throughout the State for implementation of all rural development programmes".

The Commission reiterates the above recommendations. Further, in line with its thinking with regard to constitution of representative bodies at the village level in the Sixth Schedule Areas of Assam, and the hill areas of Manipur, the Commission is of the view that in the long run, directly elected village level representative bodies will need to be constituted and properly empowered in the Autonomous Hill Council areas of Meghalaya as well.

Recommendations

a) The fact of Autonomous District Councils should be accepted and the State should undertake comprehensive activity mapping with regard to all the matters mentioned in para 3 of the Sixth Schedule. This process should cover all aspects of the subjects viz planning, budgeting and provisioning of finances. This will necessitate full transfer of local functionaries of the field offices/departments and bodies relating to these activities at the district level to the control of the Councils. The State Government should set-up a task force to complete this work in a time bound manner.

b) Allocation of funds to the District Councils should be based on normative and transparent considerations. These allocations should be budgeted in detail and released in agreed instalments during the financial year.

c) The Union Government would also need to take similar action with regard to Centrally Sponsored Schemes being implemented in these areas.

d) Appropriate measures may be taken for capacity building in Autonomous Councils so that they are able to utilize the funds in a better way.

e) Government of Meghalaya may take steps for extension of the experiment of elected village committees in the Garo Hills for implementing the National Employment Guarantee Act and for implementation of other rural development programmes as well.

f) In the long run, directly elected village level representative bodies will need to be constituted and adequately empowered in autonomous Hill Councils areas of Meghalaya.

Mizoram

At the commencement of the Constitution, Mizoram was a District in Assam, known as Lushai Hills and was included in the Sixth Schedule. Renamed as Mizo Hills in 1954, the area experienced severe famines in the late 1950s and early 1960s which led to serious turmoil and insurgency spearheaded by the Mizo National Front (MNF). The District was separated from Assam and raised first to the status of a Union Territory in 1972 and then to full Statehood in 1987. Following an accord with the MNF in 1986 peace and tranquility has been restored in Mizoram. The State has made rapid strides and has emerged with the highest literacy in the country. Despite its small population and limited territory, it has considerable ethnic diversity. With the conferment of the status of Union Territory the Mizo Hill District Council was dissolved and now the State has three autonomous district councils catering to three non Mizo minority tribes- Mara, Lai and Chakma.

Status of Local Decentralization: Autonomous District Councils

In terms of Article 244(2) of the Constitution, the provisions of the Sixth Schedule apply to the administration of Tribal Areas in Mizoram. Three Autonomous District Councils have been accordingly constituted in accordance with Paragraph 20 of the Sixth schedule, namely, the Chakma Autonomous District Council (CADC), the Mara Autonomous District Council (MADC) and the Lai Autonomous District Council (LADC). These District Councils cover two administrative districts, namely, Lawngthlai and Saiha districts.

These Councils exercise legislative and executive powers over land, water, non reserved forests and tribal laws and customs along with limited judicial powers. The Chakma Council has in particular codified the relevant tribal laws. The Councils occupy parts of single districts and elections are conducted by the Deputy Commissioners concerned. Powers over development programmes have not been entrusted to these bodies; responsibilities in that behalf are with the State Government. DRDAs also function independent of the Councils.

Under paragraph 6(1) of the Sixth Schedule, District Councils have powers to establish, construct and manage primary schools, dispensaries, markets, cattle ponds, ferries, fisheries, roads, road transport and water ways. The Councils also have the power to assess, levy and collect revenue in respect of land and buildings, taxes on professions, trades callings and employments, animals, vehicles and boats, tolls on passengers and goods carried in ferries, and taxes on the maintenance of schools, dispensaries, or roads as listed in paragraph 8 of the Sixth Schedule.

The executive functions have been further clarified and elaborated through a detailed notification dated 22nd September, 1993, which modified the earlier notification dated 20-8-86.

Status of Village Councils

The State Government has constituted elected Village Councils all over the State i.e. over both the Council and other areas. These elected Councils have replaced the hereditary institutions of Chiefship and are involved in village governance, and development and in collecting local rates and taxes. Village Councils even cover urban areas including the State Capital Aizawl which is covered by several Village Councils. An examination of the relevant laws shows that Village Councils are quite representative, with one third of the members being elected and another one third being nominated. The powers of these Councils include mobilizing local funds and effort for community works. The Village Council (Chakma Autonomous Council) Act, 2002 contains detailed provisions regarding the scope of the powers of the Council. In a measure designed to curb infiltration from across the border, all Village Councils in Chakma areas are mandated to maintain Village Council population registers and immediately report any instances of infiltration from across the border to the Chakma District Council. The Lakher Autonomous

District Village Council Act, 1971 which continues to be in force in the Mara District Council District similarly contains detailed provisions regarding the Village Council. The powers of the Village Council include civil functions and also compelling people to undertake 'Tlarai' or 'Vatlarai', namely, work done collectively by villagers for the common good. Village councils are empowered to levy fines on individuals who refuse to undertake community works. Village Councils also implement several CSSs, as agents of the DRDAs. For example, IAY beneficiaries are selected by the Village Council. However, in doing so, they do not report to the District Councils and are not accountable to them.

Issues

Overlapping and competing jurisdiction of the State administration and the District Councils

A closer look at the present administrative arrangements in Mizoram reveals that there are two parallel administrative hierarchies functioning within the district, one headed by the Council, which has potentially wide executive and development functions and the other headed and coordinated by the Deputy Commissioner, who operates through separate agencies such as the DRDA and State level line department officers posted in the district. While Councils existed even prior to the Constitutional amendment, unlike Panchayats in other parts of the country, their position and status has weakened and their powers diffused over time. The Ramachandran Committee observed that

> "in Mizoram, these councils at first glance are over-structured, over-staffed and with patchy empowerment - while they have unbridled unaccountable freedom in one area, they have none in others. The problems of the Councils are also compounded by the fact that they covered very small populations of ethnic groups, thereby reducing the scope and scale of their operations."

The Committee also noted that–

"the problem was not only one of development but is also political. There are strong ethnic feelings, between tribal communities in the State, which undermines the spirit of collaboration and cooperation required between different levels of government for effective functioning. The Mizoram Assembly has passed resolutions for abolition of Councils and on the other hand the Councils have been demanding separate UT status and direct funding. There is a need for both the Government and the Councils to realize that to accelerate development; they will need to work as partners, as part of a seamless web and not as rivals. Many individuals within either system undertake good work and no institution can be condemned wholesale for the mistakes of some within it. The methods of working need to be so rearranged so that everybody can work together and achieve something."

In order to resolve the conflicts explained above, the following steps could be useful:-

i. Effective devolution of powers to the District Councils
ii. Internal reforms and capacity building within the District Councils
iii. Merger of DRDA with the District Council

The above issues have been considered by the Commission earlier in this Chapter as common issues relevant to all the Sixth Schedule States of the North East and separately in case of Assam and Meghalaya. As recommended therein, the State must undertake comprehensive activity mapping with regard to the matters which can be transferred to the autonomouc councils. This process should cover all aspects of the subjects viz planning, budgeting and provisioning of finances. This will necessitate full transfer of all departments and bodies relating to these activities to the control of the Councils and merger of parallel institutions [such as the District Rural Development Agency DRDA] related to these transferred matters and departments The State

Government should set-up a task force to complete this work within one year. The Union Government will also need to take similar action with regard to Centrally Sponsored Schemes being implemented in these areas.

The Commission would further like to suggest that a coordinating committee, either within the State Planning Board, or under the Chief Secretary, be constituted to monitor the reforms, and settle any issues that might arise in the process. The CEMs of all the three Councils and the Deputy Commissioners of the District concerned may be made members of this Coordination Committee. Representation may also be given to NGOs, associations of Women and the youth and selected Chairpersons of Village Councils, in the Committee.

Recommendations

a) The State should undertake comprehensive activity mapping with regard to all the matters mentioned in para 3 of the Sixth Schedule. This process should cover all aspects of the subjects viz planning, budgeting and provisioning of finances. This will necessitate full transfer of functionaries of the field offices/departments/bodies relating to these activities to the control of the Councils. The State Government should set-up a Task Force to complete this work in a time bound manner.

b) The Union Government will also need to take similar action with regard to Centrally Sponsored Schemes being implemented in these areas.

Nagaland

Nagas are a group of tribes with their own languages, social customs, folklore and territories who were clubbed together for administrative purposes by the ruling powers at different points of the history of the region. Many Naga areas were grouped in a single Naga Hills District in 1866 to bring these areas under direct British rule to safeguard tea plantations. The district did not, however, include many areas like the Northern and Eastern parts of Manipur and tracts, once known as "Naga tribal areas"- one of the 'agencies' of NEFA. The Sixth Schedule of the Constitution was initially conceived as an arrangement to meet the political aspirations of the people of this District – an arrangement that could not be implemented as it fel far short of the Naga demand for self rule. Violent insurgency had broken out in the early 1950s for an 'independent Nagaland' not only in the Naga Hills District but also in areas dominated by the Nagas in Manipur and NEFA. The District was initially upgraded as the "Naga-Tuensang Administrative Area" in 1957 with the merger of Tuensang frontier tract of NEFA and with an "Area Council"- a nominated body consisting of traditional opinion leaders of the constituent tribes. Disturbances, however, continued unabated even after the emergence of the State. It is now widely recognized that recourse to violence by various ethnic groups in the North East at different points of time was largely an 'inspiration' from Naga insurgency.

Hopes of lasting peace raised by the Shillong Accord with the Naga groups in 1975 proved short-lived as elements opposed to the Accord regrouped as the National Socialist Council of Nagaland (NSCN) and the cycle of violence continued. In the last few years, however, there has been an improvement in the situation with a 'cease fire' between major elements within the NSCN and the Union Government.

Status of Local Decentralization

The Sixth Schedule does not extend to Nagaland. It is interesting to recall that the founding fathers of the Constitution had envisaged the 'Sixth Schedule arrangement' for the tribal areas of Assam mainly to respond to the dissatisfaction among the Naga tribes about their status in the emerging Indian Union. The arrangements were, however, not acceptable to the Naga groups which continued to press for Independence for a long time and the dispensation devised primarily for the Nagas was applied to other tribal groups.

Naga society is essentially democratic with an element of election of headmen albeit within families traditionally 'supplying' such leaders. The State has, therefore, opted for a system of Village Councils and Village Development Boards as the key elements of local self governance. There is a Council for each village under the Village Councils Act- 1990. It combines traditional village functionaries and elected members who elect a chairman among themselves. The Councils are responsible for village administration to exercise general control over the activities of Village Development Boards (VADBs).

Village Councils in Nagaland

Under the Nagaland Village Councils Act 1990, every recognised village, established according to the usage and customary practices of the population of the area is required to have a Village Council (VC), with a five year term. This Council consists of members, chosen by villagers in accordance with the prevailing customary practices and usages as approved by the State Government. The Act provides that hereditary village chiefs shall be ex-officio members of such Councils, with voting rights. The Act also recognized that traditional village institutions such as the "Putu Menden" in Ao Areas, which is recognized as a village council, shall continue to function according to their custom and usage. The Village Council chooses a Member as Chairman and can select and appoint a Secretary who may or may not be a member of the Council. If the Secretary is not a member of the Council he does not have voting rights. The Village Council is required to meet at least once every three months. It is the job of the village council to formulate village development schemes, to supervise proper maintenance of water supply, roads, forest, education and other welfare activities to help Government agencies in carrying out development works in the village and to take up development works on its own initiative or on request by the Government. The Village Council also has the power to borrow money from various sources such as the Government, Banks or financial institutions, to apply for and receive grants-in-aid, donations, subsidies from the Government or any agencies and to raise funds for utility services within the village by passing a resolution subject to the approval by the State Government. However, all monetary transactions are required to be conducted through a scheduled bank or the Nagaland State Cooperative Bank. The Village Council also has the power to administer justice within the village limits in accordance with the customary law and usages and has full powers to deal with the internal administration of the village. The Village Council is subject to the central superintendence of the State Government/ Deputy Commissioner / Additional Deputy Commissioner or Sub-Divisional Officer (Civil) incharge of the Sub-Division, Extra Assistant Commissioner or Circle Officer.

The Village Development Board

The concept of the Village Development Board (VDB) began to take shape during the Seventh Plan period, when it was realized that there is a need to reconcile the traditional Tribal institution of the Village Council, which basically comprises of male members of each family in the village and is headed by a traditional Tribal Chief with the demands of modern inclusive development. The concept of having a separate Village Board, without displacing the traditional Village Council was first experimented and adopted in Phek District, in 1976. The initiative for the formation of VCFC and keeping of funds in banks came from the innovative initiatives of Shri A.M. Gokhale, the then Deputy Commissioner, Phek. This concept was taken further for the formation of VDBs in all existing 918 recognized villages in 1980-81.

In 1978, Nagaland enacted the Nagaland Village and Area Council Act, which enjoined that each Village Council should constitute a Village Development Board for the village concerned. These Village Development Boards are to exercise certain of the powers, functions and duties of the Village Councils, subject to the prior approval of the Chairman of the village council. The powers of these Village Councils were laid out in clauses 4,6,7,8,9 of Section 12 of the Act and included powers to formulate schemes, programmes of action for the development and progress of the village as a whole or groups of individuals or for individuals in the village, either using the village community or other funds. VDBs are responsible for preparation of Annual Plans, its implementation and proper utilization of funds. A unique power given to the VDB was to arrange for loans for community members and to even stand guarantee for these loans. Village Development Boards Model Rules 1980 were framed under the Village and Area Councils Act 1978 and these were revised in 1989. It is reported that so far, the cumulative expenditure since inception, through the VDBs has been Rs. 254 Crore, of which Rs. 63 Crore was spent on programmes for women and Rs. 50.83 Crore for the youth.

Composition of the Village Development Board

All permanent residents of the village are members of the Village Development Board and form the general body of the VDBs, with equal rights in all aspects of activity including the demanding of social audit. The Management Committee of VDBs is entrusted with the management of the Village Development Board and Funds of the VDBs. The members of the Management Committee are chosen by the Village Council for a tenure of 3 years unless decided otherwise by the VC by a resolution.. The members may include both members and non- members of the village council. The number of members of the Management Committee can vary from five to twenty five. One-fourth of the total number of members of the Management Committee must consist of women members. The members may include members of the VC or persons who are not members of the VC particularly those who are ineligible to be chosen as members of the VC by virtue of their age, or by virtue of tradition or custom. At least one woman shall be a member of the Management Committee. An innovation is that Government servants can be chosen as members of the Management Committee, with the permission of the government.

A member of the Management Committee may be replaced by a resolution of the VC, for reasons to be recorded in the Resolution. The Management Committee selects a Secretary from among themselves who gets a remuneration between Rs. 1000-3000/-. The Management Committee is expected to meet every month. The meetings are open to the public. Another unique feature of the Nagaland system is that the Deputy Commissioner or the Additional Deputy Commissioner of the District is to be the ex officio Chairman of each VDB in the District.

The Board is in the nature of Gram Sabha as its general body consists of the entire adult population of the village which elects an Executive Committee with at least 25% female members. The Village Council verifies the completion of development work by the Executive Committee and generally certifies completion of development work. The Board prepares and implements village development plans and for the purpose receives 'development grants' from the government at the rate of Rs 800 per households per year subject to a minimum of Rs 50000. For the State as a whole the grants are currently of the order of Rs 22 Crores. The Boards are also engaged in implementation of programmes like the SSGY, SGRY and the IAY etc.

There are also moves to create a corpus fund for each Council with participation of Union and State Government and NABARD against which loans can be raised by the Boards and individuals on the security of the Board.

The Communitization Experiment

In order to decentralize governance, the Nagaland Government has made innovative use of the "social capital" prevailing amongst its people. It has enacted the Nagaland Communitization of Public Services and Institutions Act 2002 commonly called the 'Communitization Act'. The intention is to improve the quality of various services being provided by the Government to the citizens by involving the community and by transferring control over the schemes/services to the actual beneficiaries. The legislation provides for the State Government to delegate its functions, including control over the personnel, involved with the 'delegated services' to such authorities.

Village Authorities can be invested with the functions of local authorities under the Act. This step has made a very positive impact on the functioning of many of the development programmes and brought an overall improvement in the quality and speed of services and even more important, in making the communities realize that they can make a positive contribution to their own development. An important result of the communitisation experiment is that the benefits of this initiative have spread to the urban areas where the traditional patterns of tribe specific community organization are not very significant. It may be noted that the model is analogous to the scheme envisaged in Article 243G (read with the Eleventh Schedule) of the Constitution which calls for a state legislation to transfer functions to the PRIs.

The Communitization Experiment has brought allround improvement in a large number of projects/schemens which deal with education, water supply, roads, forests, powers, health and sanitation and welfare schemes in the entire state. It has empowered people and increased efficacy and transparency in governance.

Recommendation

a) The Commission would like to reiterate the following recommendation in this regard made in its Seventh Report:-

   Nagaland has made commendable efforts to usher in a paradigm of decentralised village self-governance through effective use of "Social Capital". The State has communitised a large number of service delivery schemes. The Ministry of Rural Development should formally recognise this arrangement for implementation of various development and poverty alleviation initiatives in this State.

Sikkim

At the commencement of the Constitution, Sikkim was regarded as a princely state which, unlike similar other States was a 'protectorate'. Sikkim's governance as a protectorate was based on a treaty whereby a measure of internal autonomy under its Maharaja (Chogyal) subject to the overarching responsibility of the Government of India to safeguard the protectorate and conduct its foreign relations. Increasing public aspirations for a legal framework permitting peoples' participation in governance led to a popular uprising which culminated in introduction of a measure of democracy at the instance of the Government of India. The newly elected Assembly and the Chogyal could not come to a consensus on a popular government gave rise to further agitation demanding formal merger of the 'protectorate' as a State of the Indian Union. This resulted in the thirty-sixth Constitutional amendment in 1975 which introduced Article-371F in the Constitution. This Article, apart from declaring Sikkim as a part of the Indian Union makes some special provisions including vesting of discretionary powers on the Governor (subject to any orders of the President) to facilitate " peace and for an equitable arrangement for ensuring the social and economic advancement of different sections of the population". Since its merger with the Indian Union, Sikkim has made very strong progress on all fronts.

Through an amendment of the North Eastern Council Act 2002, Sikkim has become a member of the Council, though does not have a common boundary with any of the North Eastern States. As NEC is meant primarily as a regional planning and development body, a proviso was also added to section 4 of the Act authorizing the Council "to formulate specific projects and schemes" for Sikkim.

A recent development of potential long-term importance for the State is the initiation of Trans-border trade between India and the Tibetan autonomous region of Peoples' Republic of China after a gap of almost half a century. The volume of trade is currently very low with imports exceeding exports by a significant degree- unlike in the past when the Indo-Tibetan trade was heavily in favour of India.

Status of Local Decentralization

Sikkim has a long history of Panchayati Raj institutions. Even prior to its merger, a law was enacted by the Chogyal in 1965 to provide for elected, but non partisan, village Panchayats primarily for local disputes resolution. The seventy-third amendment applies to the State; soon after its coming into force, the Sikkim Panchayati Raj Act 1993 was enacted which provides for elected Gram Panchayats (GPs) and Zila Panchayats (ZPs). Gram Sabhas in the State are referred as Panchayat wards- six to eight wards constitute a GP. Sikkim is one of the first States to have transferred Primary and Secondary Education to Panchayati bodies. A number of steps have recently been initiated to further strengthen the role of Panchayats. Some of the more important of these are;

- Establishment of 'Gram Planning Forum' for each Panchayat to make the 'GP' the unit of local planning.
- Setting up District Technical Support Committee to assist Zila Panchayats in drawing up District Plans.
- Initiation of a system of specifically reflecting earmarking of funds for schemes to be taken up by Panchayats in the State budget.

The State does not have any Municipal body – a Municipal Corporation was established for the city of Gangtok in 1975, the legislation was, however, repealed in 1985 and urban governance is now directly looked after by the governments.

Personnel Position

Sikkim is the smallest State of the country with a population of 5,40,493 (2001 census) and an area of 7096 sq.km. The State has four districts with headquarters at Gangtok, Mangan, Namchi and Gyalshing.

A comparison of the cadre strengths of various services in this State with those in Uttarakhand, Nagaland, Manipur, Tripura is worthwhile.

Uttarakhand with a population of 84.89 Lakhs, area of 53484 sq.km and 13 districts has a cadre strength of 83 for IAS and 42 for IPS. Nagaland with a population of 19.88 Lakhs, area of 16579 Sq.Km. and 08 districts has a cadre strength of 52 for IAS and 42 for IPS, Manipur – Tripura with a combined population of 56.92 Lakhs, Area of 32818 Sq.Km. and 13 districts has a cadre strength of 165 for the IAS and 80 for the IPS.

Considering the population and area of Sikkim, its cadre strength for all the three All India Service officers seems to be on high. The Commission is of the view that there is need for its rationalization, in the interest of both good governance and the morale of the officers in accordance with actual requirements, including its operational requirements.

Recommendations

a) The Commission has made a number of recommendations for strengthening and empowering PRIs in its Report on "Local Governance" which needs to be implemented on priority.

b) There is need to rationalize the large cadre strength of various All India Services in the State, in accordance with actual requirements.

Tripura

Before Independence, Tripura was a princely State ruled by Maharajas of the Manikya dynasty. The Regent Maharani of Tripura signed an instrument of merger with the Indian Union on September 9, 1947. Tripura became a Union Territory without legislature with effect from November 1, 1956. However, a legislature was installed in July 1, 1963. Tripura attained Statehood on January 21, 1972.

Tripura, after Assam is the most populous State in the North East. While it accounts for barely 0.8% of the total area of the Region, it is home to more than 8% of its population with the highest population density in the region. Its adverse land-man ratio is aggravated by the fact that in the last 55 years the ethnic profile of the State has been drastically altered. Thus while currently the tribals, the indigenous inhabitants of the place, constitute around 31% of the population, this ratio was just the reverse in 1947 when geopolitical factors resulted in a massive influx from the adjoining Districts of the then East Bengal. The resultant socio-economic consequences caused much conflict and strife. In order to allay the apprehensions, areas with tribal concentration were brought under the Sixth Schedule in 1985.

A geographical factor of relevance to its development is the fact that the State has an international border of 839 Km with Bangladesh (surrounded by Sylhet in the North, Comilla in the West and Noakhali and Chittagong on the North East). Tripura's boundary with Assam and Mizoram is only 50 Kms. An idea of the imposed inaccessibility of the State can be formed by the fact that while the travel time to Kolkata via Bangladesh is hardly 12 hours, the same destination takes more than 48 hours through Assam and West Bengal.

The State has generally done well in areas like primary health care, poverty reduction and improvement of agricultural production. There are, however, indications that growth has been more pronounced outside tribal areas.

Status of Local Decentralization

Alienation of land belonging to tribals emerged as a major problem with independence and the merger of princely Tripura with the Indian Union. The Tripura Tribal Areas Autonomous District Council (TTAADC) was established as an independent council administering the tribal areas within the State through the TTAADC Act 1979 passed by the Indian parliament after a series of democratic movements launched by the tribal people of Tripura. The Council was set up on 18, January, 1982. Following the 49th amendment of the Constitution of India, the TTAADC was brought under the provisions of the Sixth Schedule of the Constitution with effect from 1 April, 1985. The principal objective of setting up the TTAADC is to empower the tribal people to govern themselves, bring all round development to them and protect and preserve their culture, customs and traditions.

The Autonomous Council operates in areas spread over 527 villages in all the four districts in identified pockets of tribal concentration. The Council has 30 members- 28 elected and 2 nominated. The powers of the Council are restricted to the original 'paragraph 3 subjects' viz land, water, non reserved forests and tribal customs and limited powers for administration of justice. Elections are expected to be conducted by the District Council in the manner it desires. The conduct of the last elections (2006) was entrusted by the Council to the State Election Commission.

Prior to the establishment of the District Council- initially by a State legislation under the Fifth Schedule- villages included in its jurisdiction had Panchayats like the rest of the State. Following the establishment of the Council, Tripura Panchayat Raj Act ceased to operate in that area and there was no village level body- elected or otherwise. In 2006, the State Government decided to hold elections to the Village Councils by treating them on par with village Panchayats in other parts of the State taking the view that nothing in Sixth Schedule precludes such a course of action. The Autonomous Council is, however, yet to transfer any functions to these newly established Councils. This step has important policy implications.

The rest of the State has a very robust three tier Panchayati structure as provided under the seventy-third amendment. Elections to these bodies are conducted by the State Election Commission. These bodies are responsible for implementation of development programmes.

Structure of TTAADC

The TTAADC is unique as its jurisdiction is not contiguous with Revenue district boundaries. It straddles four revenue districts. There are thirty five Rural Development Blocks in the State. Nineteen RD Blocks are within the Sixth Schedule area and eighteen mixed R. D. Blocks are within jurisdiction of both Sixth Schedule & PRI areas. The TTAADC area is divided into four Zones, each coterminous with the Sixth Schedule area of Revenue Districts. (Please see the TTAADC map placed below). Each Zone is further sub-divided into thirty two Sub-Zones, which are, except for a few, conterminous with the boundaries of R.D. Blocks.

The TTAADC has also constituted "TTAADC Blocks' in those Blocks that are fully within the TTAADC. Each TTAADC block has a Block Development Officer posted to it. Committees chaired by the MDCs/MLAs or chairpersons of the Village Committees (where there is no MDC / MLA in the area) have been constituted at the Block level. In those Development Blocks where only part of the area comes within the TTAADC jurisdiction, the District Council has constituted Sub-Zonal Development Committee, with the same composition of members as in Sixth Schedule Areas. In all 35 blocks that fall fully or partially within the TTAADC, the State Government has also constituted Block Advisory Committees (BAC) comprising of Chairpersons of all elected Village Committees in 35 RD Blocks for implementation of programmes of the State Government in Sixth Schedule Areas, chaired by MLAs or MDCs. The District Council has constituted 527 ADC Villages in the Sixth Schedule Area, co-terminus with Revenue villages.

Grassroots empowerment – TTAADC Village Committees

Elections to these Village Committees were conducted in February 2006 as per Tripura Tribal Areas Act 1994. There are 4165 elected members in all for 527 of Village Committees, of which one third are women members. Reservations are made for

Schedule Tribe and Schedule Castes in proportion to the percentage of their population. Chairpersons and Vice Chairpersons are elected by the Members of Village Committee.

Issues and Recommendations

1. **Decentralised Planning:** Tripura has an established system of decentralised planning in the form of the Gramodaya and Nagrodaya initiatives. The State plan is prepared through consolidation of the local plans prepared with the help of these initiatives. The district plan is formed by consolidating and amalgamating the village and block level plans pertaining to both the Sixth Schedule Areas and the areas covered under PRIs. However, the District Planning Committees (DPCs) have not been formed under the provisions of Article 243ZD of the Constitution. The Commission is of the view that there is need to constitute the DPCs with representation from both the TTADC and the District Administration as all the districts in Tripura comprise of both TTADC and Part IX areas. The TTADC should also be involved in the planning process at the State level.

2. **Role clarity between various levels of Governance:** As suggested in case of other States, there is need for unambiguous activity mapping in the State assigning functions to various levels operating within the system such as the District Council, Block level formations and Village Councils. The Expert Committee on Decentralised Planning in the Sixth Schedule Areas observed that "the system of dividing the TTAADC into Zones and sub-Zones, overlaps with the Blocks, Tehsils and the Block Advisory Committees. In fact, having the Block Advisory Commttees chaired by MLAs and the Zone and sub-Zone advisory bodies headed by elected representatives of the TTAADC is a recipe for conflict and lack of role clarity.

While endorsing the observation of the Expert Committee, the Commission is of the view that in order to avoid conflict and overlapping jurisdictions, it may be ensured that there is only one intermediate structure between the village and the district bodies of the TTAADC. In the meantime, the State Government should try to evolve a mechanism for coordination between the block level committees and zones/sub-zones.

Recommendations

a) DPCs may be constituted in all the districts of Tripura with representation from both the TTADC and the District Administration as all the districts in Tripura comprise of both TTADC and part IX areas. The TTADC should also be involved in the planning process at the State level.

b) Immediate steps should be taken to ensure that there is only one intermediate structure between the village and the district bodies of the TTAADC.

c) The State Government should take steps to evolve a mechanism which could coordinate block level committees chaired by MLAs and zones and sub-zones which are headed by elected representatives of TTAADC.

d) The State may also undertake comprehensive activity mapping exercise to delineate functions among various levels operating within the system such as the District Council, the Block committee and the Village Council.

6

Managing State Finances

An effective financial management system is the cornerstone of good public administration. In our federal system, where the Constitution empowers the States to collect revenue and spend on public programmes, a prudent and effective financial management system in the States is a matter of vital concern for the country's polity and economy. The extent to which the overall economic development of the nation is dependent on the management of state finances is further borne out from the fact that on an average, the States combined together get about 62-64% of the combined revenue receipts of the Union and States. The following table gives the year-wise position of State Finances since the VIIth Finance Commission (1980 onward). In terms of combined revenue expenditures, the figure stands in the range of 56 to 58%.

Apart from implementing the programmes and schemes undertaken through its own budget, a State plays a key role in implementing various Centrally Sponsored and Central Sector Schemes.

Appropriate selection of programmes and projects, prudent financial planning, normative expenditure methodology and concurrent and post expenditure scrutiny are the vital processes which decide how the finances of the Government are being utilized and managed.

Table No.: 6.1 : Share of States in Combined Revenue Receipts and Expenditures

Average*	Revenue Receipts Before and After Transfers		Revenue Expenditures**
	Before	After	
VIIth FC	35.3	61.4	58.0
VIIIth FC	34.6	62.0	55.7
IXth FC	37.5	64.7	56.9
Xth FC	38.6	63.0	56.8
2000-01	38.6	63.9	56.0
2001-02	39.3	63.9	58.0
XIth FC (Avg. 2 years)	39.0	63.9	57.1

Source (Basic Data): Indian Public Finance Statistics.
*Average for years under recommendation period.
** Net of inter-governmental transfers.

The core principles that should form the foundation of a sound Public Finance Management System such as adopting prudent economic assumptions, aligning annual budgets with the medium term plan, relaxing central input controls, adoption of topdown budgeting principles, focusing on value for money and introducing transparency and simplicity in various procedures have already been referred to in Chapter 1 of this Report.

Within these broad outlines, the following issues are of importance in sustainable financial administration of the State Governments.

1. Financial Delegation and Operational Flexibility
2. Avoiding Fiscal Profligacy
3. Expenditure Management
    (a) need to review relevance and utility of continuing programmes and schemes
    (b) ensuring expenditure uniformity over the year

4. Prudent Budget formulation
    - Realistic estimates and assumptions for budget preparation
    - Avoiding inaccurate and incomplete disclosure of financial situation
    - Public consultation in budget formulation
    - Issue of supplementary demands
    - Off budget and contingent liabilities
    - Multi-year budgeting
5. Revenue forecast and need for a tax research unit
6. Mechanism for internal control
7. External audit

Financial Delegation and Operational Flexibility – the IFA system

The organization of the Finance Department (FD) in terms of the number of Secretaries, divisions/ sections, etc. has evolved depending upon each individual State's history and circumstances. Although there is a lot that is common, details and numbers vary from State to State. In Maharashtra the "Administrative Reforms Committee (2002)" comprehensively reviewed the organization of the State Finance Department along with the rest of the State machinery. The point that emerged was that it was not so much the organization as the role and responsibilities of the Finance Department that were a matter of major concern. In most States there is concentration of powers in the Finance Department particularly those relating to expenditure control which greatly constrains the line departments in meeting the programme objectives in a time bound frame.

In order to ensure, financial delegation and operational flexibility in the functioning of various Ministries/Departments, the Union Government introduced the scheme of posting senior officers as Integrated Financial Advisers in Ministries/Departments in 1975. In consultation with the Secretary of the concerned department, the IFA is empowered to take budgetary and financial decisions of considerable financial value. The system has been of considerable use to the Union Ministries/Departments in planning, programming and budgeting. The scheme has worked well in the Government of India. The Commission is of the view that the experience of the Union Government with regard to IFA should motivate the States to introduce/strengthen a similar system of the IFA in the State administration.

Recommendation

Based on the experience of the Union Government with regard to the IFA, States should take steps to introduce/ strengthen the IFA system in the State administration.

Avoiding Fiscal Profligacy

Selection of programmes and projects is an important component of the State planning. It has to be a considered exercise based on both the medium term planning commitment as well as the State's annual budget.

In spite of detailed instructions and guidelines in budget manuals, projects and schemes continue being announced on an ad-hoc basis, often before elections or during visits of high-level functionaries. Such announcements involving huge funds seriously distort plan allocations and disturb the faithful implementation of schemes already approved under the budget. Often such announcements are not followed by formal approvals thereby resulting in discontent among people and financial indiscipline. On the other hand, there have been cases where schemes were framed without due diligence and got funded. Such ab-initio unsustainable schemes have led to waste of public money.

The Commission is of the view that the selection of programmes and projects should be solely on considerations of objectivity and sustainability. The State Governments need to take steps to ensure that projects are included in the budget only after well considered deliberations and processes. The practice of announcing projects and schemes on an ad-hoc basis needs to be abandoned.

Recommendation

a) The State Governments need to take steps to ensure that projects and programmes are included in the budget only after well considered deliberations and processes. The practice of announcing projects and schemes on an ad-hoc basis needs to be done away with.

Expenditure Management

In most of the States, the expenditure pattern is highly skewed. Though the plan / budgetary indications for a particular financial year are indicated to the departments of the State Government in the preceding year, the process of getting actual sanction, in practice, is time consuming. The first two quarters of the financial year are mostly spent in preparing detailed project reports and in getting sanctions. The result is that the bulk of expenditure takes place in the later part of the year, particularly in the last quarter. There is considerable rush in the month of March to draw money and to park it somewhere or to spend it hastily. The Government of India has tried to overcome this problem by introducing the Monthly Expenditure Plan (MEP). Some of the States too have taken similar steps. The Commission is of the view that all the States should take positive measures to improve their expenditure profile; (a) Detailed project reports of schemes should be finalized in the preceding year and (b) the financial sanctions should be given to the departments during the first two months of the current financial year. This would ensure that the actual execution of the project/scheme starts latest by the beginning of the third quarter.

Need to review relevance and utility of continuing programmes/schemes

Often, the Government programmes and schemes once taken up, seem to continue forever. Some schemes, though conceived appropriately may lose value as a result of natural changes or due to change of technology. In the Government, there is practically little attempt to review their utility and relevance and take appropriate mid-term corrective steps.

The Commission is of the view that there is need for a zero-based review of programmes and schemes which are more than five years old and which involve large sums of public money. (Say over 50 crores)

Recommendations

(a) The States should take priority steps to improve their expenditure profile by (a) finalizing the detailed project reports of schemes in the preceding year and (b) ensuring that the financial sanctions are given to the departments in the first two months of the current financial year.

(b) The States should conduct a zero-base review of programmes and schemes which are more than five years old and which involve large sums of public money. (Say over 50 crores)

Prudent Budget formulation

Realistic estimates and assumptions for budget preparation

Budget making is the most vital component of any financial management system. Having realistic estimates and proper assumptions are the two most important requirements for it.

There is need to have economic assumptions which are prudent and realistic in order to formulate budget estimates which are accurate and not overly optimistic. At the end of every financial year, the gap between the estimates and the actuals should be analysed so that the underlying economic assumptions could be suitably calibrated for the future.

Public Consultation

Till some years ago, Budget making was a secret process. In the absence of appropriate feed back, the budget makers often worked in isolation. Though the Union Government initiated a system of having pre-budget consultations with industry associations and stakeholders think tanks etc. some years ago, most of the State Governments have not yet taken steps to open up on this issue. Andhra Pradesh was the first State to take initiative in this direction. It released the annual fiscal framework 2002-03 about four weeks ahead of the budget presentation date. It organised workshops and discussions at both State and the district levels and obtained suggestions from different sources. The Commission is of the view that such interactive processes between the State Government and the people would lift the veil of secrecy from "Budget Making". It will be a major step towards transparency and objectivity in budget formulation. It also needs to be emphasized that such consultations would be effective and meaningful only when (a) citizens have access to information and (b) effective steps are taken to educate citizens and leaders of society on budget making and its implications.

Multi-year Budgeting

As per the prevailing budget norms in the State Governments, all unspent allocations lapse at the end of the financial year (even if the allotment of money was made in the last quarter of the financial year). It leads to (a) hasty expenditure and/or (b) attempt to draw the money and park it in commercial banks/ other financial institutions for subsequent use. Both these actions are against financial norms and interests of the Government. This problem could be partially solved if the implementing agencies are allowed to use the current allocation in the next financial year with certain conditionalities.

The Commission is of the view that the State Governments should shift to multiyear budgeting and give the estimates of revenue and expenditure for a period of four years in addition to the year which the budget pertains. This should be done on a roll-on basis. This will enable better estimation of the fund requirements of on-going schemes, programmes and projects. It will also ensure realistic budgeting.

Medium Term Fiscal Plan

In this context, preparation of a Medium Term Fiscal Plan (MTFP) will be of relevance. MTFP is a statement of the government's, medium-term fiscal objectives which provides projection of key financial variables for the current fiscal together with a block of next three to four years. Each MTFP also reports performance against targets. The MTFP serves two purposes. First, it helps to put annual budget formulation within the mediumterm context. Second, it serves as a communication channel to the people, of government's fiscal intentions and strategy. The Commission believes that the States should follow the practice of preparation and implementation of the MTFP.

Off-Budget and Contingent liabilities

The budget and the financial statements of the State Government often do not reflect the complete picture. For example, government's contingent liabilities owing to the guarantees furnished by it against the borrowings by various parastatals are not captured in the budget or the financial statements. In many States till some years ago, the government executed capital works programmes through Special Purpose Vehicles (SPV) which were financed through bonds guaranteed unconditionally and irrevocably by the government. Since the SPVs did not have a tangible revenue stream of their own, the implicit arrangement was that the repayments were committed to be made out of the budget. These effectively become borrowings of the government.

Since payment of such liabilities devolve on the State Government much later, in the annual financial statements of subsequent years, in a way taking recourse to these offbudget guarantees goes against the spirit and intent of article 202 of the Constitution. This practice hurts the State's credibility and adversely influences its credit rating. A cap on such guarantees would improve the confidence of investors in the States.

The Commission agrees with the above view that offbudget borrowings are bound to have an adverse impact on State finances in the long run. Every State Government must set a limit up to which it can expose itself to the guarantees. The Commission realizes that in some situations, such guarantees may be inevitable. But, the State Governments need to adopt caution and diligence with regard to viability of such projects. They need to be assessed and evaluated comprehensively.

Maintenance of Assets

The studies conducted by the Commission on this subject in various States led to two important conclusions:

a) there is excessive emphasis/importance given to plan schemes in creation of new capital assets; maintenance of assets created in the past (also called non-plan expenditure) gets neglected,

b) even in the plans, there is a tendency to include new projects instead of according priority to complete the on-going ones, particularly in the irrigation sector.

Very often, not only do projects remain incomplete due to lack of funds, even when they are completed, their maintenance and utilization suffers due to poor provisioning of funds. It would be stating the obvious to say that whole idea of creating an asset is to use it productively. This often, does not happen in practice because of either lack of maintenance or some associated facility such as an operator or place has not been provided. This is due to the belief that non-plan expenditure is essentially unproductive. While funds are generally available for a plan scheme any non-plan expenditure is viewed with suspicion. It is felt that one way of overcoming this inbuilt prejudice against non-plan expenditure is to provide for maintenance of the asset in the capital value of the asset and ensure its maintenance at least for five years after it is acquired. For example, the government can sign an annual maintenance contract (AMC) with the vendor at the time of purchase itself so as to avoid seeking funds for its maintenance in subsequent years under non-plan expenditure.

This action needs to go hand in hand with recovery of adequate user charges.

Recommendations

a) There should be prudent and realistic economic assumptions in formulation of budget estimates. At the end of every financial year, the gap between the estimates and the actuals should be analysed so that the underlying economic assumptions could be suitably calibrated for the future.

b) There should be interaction between the State Government and stakeholders including industry associations, think tanks etc. in budget formulation. In order to make such consultations effective and meaningful, steps should be taken to (a) provide information-access to citizens and (b) educate citizens and leaders of society on budget making and its implications.

c) State Governments should shift to multi-year budgeting and give the estimates of revenue and expenditure for a period of four years in addition to the year which the budget pertains. This should be done on a roll-on basis.

d) The States should follow the practice of preparation and implementation of the MTFP.

e) In order to remove prejudice against non-plan expenditure, the State should take steps to provide for maintenance of the asset in the project cost itself and ensure its maintenance for at least five years after it is acquired. This action should go hand in hand with recovery of adequate user charges.

Revenue Forecast and Need for a Tax Research Unit

Estimates of revenue in the budget are based more on optimism and hope (and sometimes as balancing entries to reduce the gap in resources) than on any systematic attempt at assessing the likely revenue. There are two issue involved when it comes to estimating revenues -

a) whether the tax potential of revenue is being fully exploited and

b) if the revenues are not of the expected level whether there are any leakages.

Moreover, a wide variance between the estimated and actual revenue adversely affects expenditure management. From all counts it is important that revenue forecasting is taken up seriously. Some States (for instance, Karnataka) have a research cell assisting the Finance Department in revenue forecast, while most States resort to marking up previous year's revenue collection on *ad hoc* basis. Therefore, the Commission is of the view that there should be a dedicated cell within the Finance Department in every State to provide input on the revenue forecast with the reasons thereof. This would add value to budget formulation exercise.

Recommendation

a) The State Governments should initiate steps to set up dedicated cell within its Finance Department to provide input on the revenue forecast with the reasons thereof.

Mechanism for Internal Control

It is necessary to develop a strategic view of internal audit to move beyond the financial regularity and compliance audit to exert a wider role. In the light of this strategic view, the scope and role of internal audit needs to be redefined. Their should be proper staffing and capacity building of internal audit units. The Commission has suggested constitution of audit committees in respect of Government of India. The same could be considered by the State Governments too.

Recommendation

The State Governments should take steps to set up internal audit committees in each of its departments.

External Audit

The Public Accounts Committees in some States have a practice of examining all paragraphs and performance audit reports included in the CAG's Audit Reports, while others have adopted the selective approach. In the former case, due to the volume of work involved, the Reports of the CAG are sometimes not discussed for years together, often up to 10-15 years and the arrears keep mounting.

To overcome the situation, the Legislative Committees may consider adopting a time frame within which they would complete examination of audit reports and submit their reports to the Legislature. The State Governments may, therefore, specify a time frame for the Departments for necessary follow up action on the recommendations of Audit and forwarding of the ATN after incorporating such action to Audit for vetting before their final submission to the State PAC/ COPU. It is also necessary to ensure that all Departments adhere to the prescribed time limits.

Recommendation

The State Governments should specify a time frame for the Departments for necessary follow up action on the recommendations of Audit and forwarding of the ATN after incorporating such action to Audit for vetting before their final submission to the State PAC/ COPU. All Departments should adhere to the prescribed time limits.

Projectisation and Appraisal

A common practice in the State Governments is to understate the magnitude of a project so as to get it somehow included in the plan basket. Then, as the years go by, the true financial implications emerge. As a result projects are not able to get fully funded, implementation slips and there are both cost and time overruns. In some cases, it may also be because of poor project formulation and appraisal capacity of the concerned department. Comprehensive project configuration, costing and realistic financial commitment are necessary for proper planning of capital outlays.

The Commission believes that in many cases, it is possible for the Government to deploy public funds as a sound business proposition, with inbuilt financial closure. Various departments of the States need to develop/enhance their project formulation and appraisal capacity.

Recommendation

In order to deploy public funds prudentially, with inbuilt financial closure, the States should take steps to strengthen their project formulation and appraisal capacity.

In addition to the above, there are important policy and functional issues such as; Transfer of Resources from the Union Government, Revenue Expenditure, Sectoral Emphasis in Plan Funding, Special Area Programmes, Utilization of External Aid, issue of subsidy etc. which significantly impact the Financial Administration in the States. Since, many of these issues are being examined separately by the 13th Finance Commission, they are not being covered in this Report.

7 Administrative Divisions of India

The Administrative divisions of India are Indian subnational administrative units; they compose a nested hierarchy of country subdivisions. Indian states and territories frequently use different local titles for the same level of subdivision (e.g., the mandals of Andhra Pradesh correspond to tehsils of Uttar Pradesh and other Hindi-speaking states and taluka of Gujarat, Maharashtra, Karnataka, Kerala and Tamil Nadu).

The smaller subdivisions (villages and blocks) exist only in rural areas. In urban areas Urban Local Bodies exist instead of these rural subdivisions.

In the context of the Indian Constitution, local government bodies are the subject of the State List and are thereby governed by State Statutes, or in the case of Union Territories, by the Union Parliament. Federal recognition of local government was substantively expressed in the 74th Constitution Amendment Act of 1992.

Zones

The States have been grouped into six zones having an Advisory Council 'to develop the habit of cooperative working" among these States. Six Zonal Councils were set up vide Part-III of the States Reorganisation Act, 1956. The present composition of each of these Zonal Councils is as under:

The Northern Zonal Council, comprising the States of Haryana, Himachal Pradesh, Jammu & Kashmir, Punjab, Rajasthan and Union Territory of Chandigarh;

The North Central Zonal Council, comprising the States of Uttarakhand, Uttar Pradesh, Bihar, National Capital Territory of Delhi and Madhya Pradesh;

The North-Eastern Council, comprising Assam Valley, Arunachal Pradesh, Manipur, Tripura, Mizoram, Meghalaya and Nagaland;

The Eastern Zonal Council, comprising the States of Chhattisgarh, Jharkhand, Odisha, Sikkim and West Bengal, (it is headquartered at West Bengal's capital Kolkatta);

The Western Zonal Council, comprising the States of Goa, Gujarat, Maharashtra and the Union Territories of Daman and Diu and Dadra and Nagar Haveli; and

The Southern Zonal Council, comprising the States of Andhra Pradesh, Karnataka, Kerala, Tamil Nadu and the Union Territory of Puducherry.

States and Union Territories

India is composed of 28 states and 7 union territories (including a national capital territory).[2] The union territories are governed by administrators, appointed by the President of India. Two of the territories (Delhi and Puducherry) have been given partial statehood, with elected legislatures and executive councils of ministers, but limited powers.

States

No.	State	Code	Capital
1	Andhra Pradesh	AP	Hyderabad
2	Arunachal Pradesh	AR	Itanagar
3	Assam	AS	Dispur
4	Bihar	BR	Patna
5	Chhattisgarh	CG	Raipur

(*contd.*)

No.	State	Code	Capital
6	Goa	GA	Panaji
7	Gujarat	GJ	Gandhinagar
8	Haryana	HR	Chandigarh
9	Himachal Pradesh	HP	Shimla
10	Jammu and Kashmir	JK	Srinagar/Jammu
11	Jharkhand	JH	Ranchi
12	Karnataka	KA	Bengalooru
13	Kerala	KL	Thiruvananthapuram
14	Madhya Pradesh	MP	Bhopal
15	Maharashtra	MH	Mumbai
16	Manipur	MN	Imphal
17	Meghalaya	ML	Shillong
18	Mizoram	MZ	Aizawl
19	Nagaland	NL	Kohima
20	Odisha	OD	Bhubaneswar
21	Punjab	PB	Chandigarh
22	Rajasthan	RJ	Jaipur
23	Sikkim	SK	Gangtok
24	Tamil Nadu	TN	Chennai
25	Tripura	TR	Agartala
26	Uttar Pradesh	UP	Lucknow
27	Uttarakhand	UK	Dehradun
28	West Bengal	WB	Kolkata

Union Territories

No.	Union territory	Code	Capital
1.	Andaman and Nicobar Islands	AN	Port Blair
2.	Chandigarh	CH	Chandigarh
3.	Dadra and Nagar Haveli	DN	Silvassa
4.	Daman and Diu	DD	Daman
5.	Lakshadweep	LD	Kavaratti
6.	National Capital Territory	ND	New Delhi
7.	Puducherry	PY	Pondicherry

Regions

Some of the states of India are divided into regions. The Regions of India are not official administrative divisions. They have no official administrative governmental status. They are purely geographic regions; some correspond to historic countries, states or provinces. A region may comprise one or more divisions, averaging about three divisions per region. However, the boundaries of the regions and the boundaries of the divisions do not always coincide exactly. So far there has been no movement to give the regions official administrative status. If this was to be done, it would presumably require that the boundaries of the regions be slightly modified so that they correspond exactly with their constituent districts.

- Regions of Assam
- Regions of Gujarat
- Regions of Kerala
- Regions of Maharashtra
- Regions of Uttar Pradesh

Divisions

Some of the Indian states are subdivided into divisions, each comprising several districts:

- Divisions of Assam
- Divisions of Bihar
- Divisions of Haryana
- Divisions of Jharkhand
- Divisions of Karnataka
- Divisions of Madhya Pradesh
- Divisions of Maharashtra
- Divisions of Rajasthan
- Divisions of Uttar Pradesh

- Divisions of Uttarakhand
- Divisions of West Bengal

Districts

States and territories (or divisions) are further subdivided into Districts (zilla), of which there are 655.

Sub-districts

Tehsils, talukas, blocks or mandals (sub-districts but can also refer to division), headed by a *Tehsildar* or *Talukdar*, comprise several villages or village clusters. The governmental bodies at the Tehsil level are called the panchayat samiti.

States use varying names for their sub-districts. Detailed information is as follows:

State or U.T.	Name for sub-district	No. of sub-districts
Jammu and Kashmir	Tahsil	59
Himachal Pradesh	Tahsil/Sub-Tahsil	109
Punjab	Tahsil	72
Chandigarh	Tahsil	1
Uttarakhand	Tahsil	49
Haryana	Tahsil	67
Delhi	Tahsil	27
Rajasthan	Tahsil	241
Uttar Pradesh	Tahsil	305
Bihar	C.D.Block	533
Sikkim	Sub-Division	9
Arunachal Pradesh	Circle	149
Nagaland	Circle	93
Manipur	Sub-Division	38
Mizoram	R.D.Block	22
Tripura	C.D.Block	38
Meghalaya	C.D.Block	39

(*contd.*)

State or U.T.	Name for sub-district	No. of sub-districts
A and N Islands	Tahsil	7
Andhra Pradesh	Mandal	1125
Assam	Circle	155
Chhattisgarh	Tahsil	97
Dadra and Nagar Haveli	Taluk	1
Daman and Diu	Taluk	2
Goa	Taluka	12
Gujarat	Taluk	226
Jharkhand	C.D.Block	210
Karnataka	Taluk	175
Kerala	Taluk	63
Lakshadweep	Sub-Division	4
Madhya Pradesh	Tahsil	259
Maharashtra	Taluka	353
Odisha	Police Station	485
Puducherry	Commune Panchayat	10
Tamil Nadu	Taluk	201
West Bengal	C.D.Block	341

Local Level

Blocks

The block is often the next level of administrative division after the tehsil.

Hoblis

A *hobli* is a subdivision of a taluka which groups adjoining villages in the state of Karnataka. They may have been made for administrative purposes by the revenue department of the state.

Villages

Villages are often the lowest level of subdivisions in India. The governmental bodies at the village level are called Gram

Panchayat, of which there were an estimated 256,000 in 2002. Each Gram Panchayat covers a large village or a cluster of smaller villages with a combined population exceeding 500 (Gram Group). Clusters of villages are also sometimes called *Hobli* or *Patti.*

Habitations

Certain governmental functions and activities - including clean water availability, rural development, and education - are tracked at a sub-village level. These hamlets are termed "habitations". India is composed of approximately 1.6 million habitations. In some states, most villages have a single habitation; in others (notably Kerala and Tripura) there is a high ratio of habitations to villages.

Municipalities

Municipalities of India are governed by Municipal Corporations *(Mahanagar Paalika)* for large urban areas, Municipal Council *(Nagar Paalika)* for smaller urban areas, and Town Councils *(Nagar Panchayats)* for suburban areas. Municipalities can be as large as a district or smaller than a Tehsil.

Responsibilities and authorities

The Constitution of India distributes the sovereign powers exercisable with respect to the territory of any State between the Union and that State. "Article 73 broadly stated, provides that the executive power of the Union shall extend to the matters with respect to which Parliament has power to make laws. Article 162 similarly provides that the executive power of a State shall extend to the matters with respect to which the Legislature of a State has power to make laws. The Supreme Court has reiterated this position when it ruled in the Ramanaiah case that the executive power of the Union or of the State broadly speaking, is coextensive and coterminous with its respective legislative power.

8 District Administration since Independence

District as a basic unit of field administration has been in existence through the ages. It is surprising to know that it has not changed substantially since the times of Manu in his description of a district in Manusmrithi where 1000 villages were grouped together to form a district and placed under the charge of an officer. However, the territorial structure of administration of India can be traced to the Mauryan era where revenue villages were called 'gramas', a group of revenue villages called 'stana' (visaya or taluk), several 'stanas' called 'aharas' or the District, a group of Districts called 'Pradesh' or the region/ state and several 'pradeshas' called the 'Janapada' or a province/ country.

The head of the District Administration had both revenue as well as police functions and is comparable to the present day District Collector. The District Collector's office succeeded the office of Kirori/Faujdar in the Mughal period.

Under the British rule and their experiments with the field of administration, in 1781 the district again became the unit of administration under the District Collector as the District head.

Thus, the present day District Administration has historical roots. However, this was non transparent and was laid out for loyalty to the British rule and establish its hegemony through the length and breadth of the country through a strong, disciplined and supervised office of the District Collector for regular collection of revenue.

Independence, and adoption of welfare state necessitated a complete reorientation of the concept of District Administration. The main stress has been on Development Administration and the introduction of the Panchayati Raj Institutions was a radical change in the field of district administration as it called for strengthening of the local units vs the office of District Collector and reducing the latter's role to that of a supervising and coordinating authority only in many states (Andhra Pradesh & Rajasthan)whereas in some states the Zilla Parishad or District level bodies still retain a stronghold (Maharashtra and Gujarat).

DISTRICT ADMINISTRATION SINCE INDEPENDENCE

The District in India is the cutting edge of administration. The District administration is headed by the District Collector/ Dcputy Commissioner, drawn from IAS and he is responsible among others for the general control and direction of the police which is headed by the Superintendent of Police.

The District is split up into a number of sub divisions called 'Talukas' for the purpose of Administrative convenience. And to have a better supervision of the many Taluks, there has been a grouping of the taluks, each group of taluks under a Division which is headed by an official called 'Tehsildar'. These Tehsildars are state level officers and are called subdivisional or revenue divisional officers. Right at the bottom of Dsitrict>Divisions> Taluks there are the basic units which are the villages. in some states the Blocks and Taluks are coterminous in District Administration. The District Collector through the ZIila Parishads, Blocks (Panchayat Samithis)/Taluks and Gram Panchayat administer development programmes and supervises them. However, massive non-transparency due to illiteracy among people these officials are often found involved in wrong doings and erratic behaviour as well as functioning as agents of the ruling state party or Union/centre's leading to revolts and outbursts from time to time. This hinders growth and development majorly.

CHANGING ROLE OF THE DISTRICT COLLECTOR

We have already discussed the evolution and role of the District Collector before Independence, now we shall look into its growth and status post independence.

District Collector (DC) is also known as the Deputy Commissioner in States such as Karnataka and Punjab.

Ever since the creation of this office in 1772, the District Collector's office continues to be the administrative head of District Administration. Basically, the DC has three major functions namely revenue, magisterial and developmental. Apart from these major functions, a large number of miscellaneous functions are also entrusted to him by state and Central governments like conduct of elections, dealing with calamities, supervising local govt. institutions, etc..

Collector was mainly entrusted with revenue administration, however, since Independence with the considerable change in the nature of the state from police rule to development and welfare his role to has shown a shift in the direction of development as he implements all the development programmes. The collector has overall control of the police administration of a state and this he is assisted by the Superintendent of the Police who is in charge of the whole district police force. The Collector advises the government on various aspects of law and order.

Since he is a Generalist, he coordinates the activities of overall departments under Specialists like Engineers, doctors, etc. by holding meetings among them at periodic intervals.

He is also to be the Friend, Philosopher and Guide of the Panchayati Raj Institutions.

FUNCTIONS OF THE DISTRICT COLLECTOR

i) Maintenance of Land records, collection of Land revenue and allied matters.

ii) Land acquisition.

iii) Control over extraction of Minor Minerals and collection of royalty for minor minerals.

iv) Local Self Govt.

v) Resettlement of Project Affected Persons during Disaster management and during riots/external aggression.

vi) Town Planning

vii) Elections

viii) Entertainment

ix) Civil Supplies

x) Land reforms

xi) Poverty alleviation

xii) Law and Order, supervision of police and jails, supervision of subordinate executive magistracy, hearing cases under the preventive section of the Criminal Procedure Code, certification to execute capital punishments.

This is the changing role of the Collector from the ancient times and British times to the contemporary times since Independence.

Even though the District Collector's office has undergone many changes since its inception, he still holds major importance in Centre-State relations and development at the local levels.

UNION-STATE LOCAL RELATIONS

When the British left India, Sardar Patel pressed for, and got the approval for retaining the ongoing civil services machinery, however, with a more welfare and people oriented approach in order to maintain the highest possible standard of efficiency and giving the civil service an experience at the Centre; leading to efficiency and administrative experience of the District, and of it serving as a liasion between the states and the Union/Central govt, and of introducing both in the states and at the Centre a progressive and wide outlook and freshness and vigour of administration. Thus, was born the All India Administrative Services.

Though the local government comes under the subjects of the state list, still, the overall policy framework, funding and Planning in India is centrally controlled. So, since functioning and day to day affairs of the state local government offices and officials come under the state list therefore, the Centre provides for policy making and Planning functions as well as funding and the implementation part is passed on to the states for efficiency and successful implementation of the schemes purposes. And this is reviewed by the Union/Centre from time to time as discussed in the Planning Commission article earlier in this blog.

Therefore, welfare policies/schemes and programmes are of three types:

i) Centrally-sponsored - Where the Centre takes responsibility of the all or 2/3rd of funding.

ii) Centre-State-sponsored - Where the funding is shared equally between the two governments.

iii) State-sponsored schemes - Where funding is totally from the state side.

One must take note that the District Collector is a Union/ Central officer as he is appointed by the state government from the Indian Administrative Services. All his career progression and service related issues and grievances are handled by the Central Government.

It has been systemised in such a manner so that the DC functions in a neutral and unbiased manner, without any fear, regarding his/her duties and responsibilities, and implementation of welfare/development activities of both the Centre and the state in the respective district he/she has been assigned to.

Even though the DC's career and service matters are dealt with the Centre and he will eventually proceed from the states to the centre in his career graph, he has to first prove his mettle at the state level, and at this level he works under the supervision of the state government and reports to them regarding discharge of his functions.

Secondly, coordination between centre-states is important for proper supervision of implementation of these schemes and programmes to achieve the welfare policies.

IMPERATIVES OF DEVELOPMENT MANAGEMENT AND LAW AND ORDER ADMINISTRATION

Development management deals with the coordination and management processes of international development programs and projects. The dominant paradigm in development management is the intervention in the form of a transfer of aid by an external agency/donor and the oversight of the related project cycle, i.e. project identification, planning (formulation and appraisal), implementation and monitoring, and evaluation.

The term development management is used in the sense of achievement and objectives with optimum use of limited resources in manpower, finance, material, time and also active contribution to the clarification and reformation of policies and objectives.

The urgency/imperativeness of this is seen in light of the LPG era and immense pressure being put on developing nations to achieve goals and policies being set by the International organisations and the obligation to fulfill these to remain updated and in the race. However, one must note that not every country can compete as the other, however, India specifically needs to shift its focus from development administration to a more efficient development management perspective and practice in order to remain in the league. For this many courses as well as programmes are being rolled out bu the country's education system as well as sponsored by the international organisations. Also, there should be a lot more emphasis on re-training of administrators in service to develop these management skills and become more efficient to achieve these goals and objectives.

Law and order (judiciary, Police, etc.) administration is one of the most important function performed by the Government. Infact, the survival of administration depends upon maintenance of law and order in a country. The functioning of law and order administration comes under the state list with the Union/Central government having advisory and coordinating role (discussed in last post on this blog). Unfortunately, in view of the prevailing atmosphere of violence in the country, attention to law and order is called for, but, the sad part is that this is being neglected in favour of development administration.

Therefore, it is imperative that law and order is given adequate attention and it is built up both on the infrastructural as well as intelligence and implementation level and its grievances and issues sorted out if we want a sound welfare state where development and law and order go hand in hand otherwise development will be stalled.

DISTRICT ADMINISTRATION AND DEMOCRATIC DECENTRALISATION

Democratic decentralisation here is used in reference to the 73rd and 74th amendment acts of 1992 that set up rural and urban local government bodies, viz. Panchayati raj institutions (PRIs) and Municipalities respectively.

The PRIs were set up to move decision making centres closer to the people by transferring the powers of decision making from higher authorities to them, all development schemes and its funds to be channelised through them, inculcating leadership qualities among the rural masses, encouraging people's participation in planning and policy making, etc.

However the ground relaities are:

i) Bureaucratic resistance to delegation of power to PRIs

ii) Vested interests of higher officials and middlemen take over in between.

iii) Elitist behaviour and biasedness among the bureaucrats and government officials.

iv) No incentive to the DC in development activities.

However, there has been constant debate as to whether the District Collector who represents the Centre and states be a part of this or he should simply supervise as the minds of the rural people are constantly suspicious towards them. This causes a lot of problems in effective administration and implementation of programmes.

Another aspect to this debate is that with so much of responsibility, the DC will be distracted from his other major functions like law and order, etc.

9 Issues Concerning e-Governance

e-Governance in India has steadily evolved from computerization of Government Departments to initiatives that encapsulate the finer points of Governance, such as citizen centricity, service orientation and transparency. The National e-Governance Plan (NeGP), takes a holistic view of e-Governance initiatives across the country, integrating them into a collective vision and a shared cause. In this section we are highlighting the initiatives of the Central and State governments to bring public services closer to the citizens.

STATE MISSION MODE PROJECTS (MMPS)

Crime and Criminal Tracking Network & Systems

The Crime and Criminal Tracking Network &amp Systems (CCTNS) Scheme has been approved by Cabinet Committee on Economic Affairs (CCEA) in June, 2009 with a provision of Rs 2000 Crores as a 100% Centrally sponsored Scheme to be implemented during the remaining part of the 11th five year plan period (2009-2012).

Crime and Criminal Tracking Network & Systems (CCTNS) MMP aims at creating a comprehensive and integrated system for enhancing the efficiency and effective policing at all levels and especially at the Police Station level through adoption of principles of e-Governance, and creation of a nationwide networked infrastructure for evolution of IT-enabled state-of-the-art tracking system.

Agriculture

There have been several initiatives by State and Central Governments to meet the various challenges facing the agriculture sector in the country. The Agriculture MMP has been included in NeGP in an effort to consolidate the various learnings from the past, integrate all the diverse and disparate efforts currently underway, and upscale them to cover the entire country.

The MMP is to be operationalised by Department of Agriculture and Cooperation (DAC), and aims to provide services, such as:

- Information to farmers on seeds, fertilizers, pesticides
- Information to farmers on Govt. Schemes
- Information to farmers on Soil recommendations
- Information on crop management
- Information on weather and marketing of agriculture produce

Public Distribution System

The Apex Committee for the National e-Governance Plan (NeGP) chaired by Cabinet Secretary has approved the inclusion of Public Distribution System (PDS) as a Mission Mode Project (MMP) under the NeGP.

Computerisation of the PDS is envisaged as an end-to-end project covering key functional areas such as supply chain management including allocation and utilisation reporting, storage and movement of food grains, grievance redressal and transparency portal, digitisation of beneficiary database, Fair Price Shop automation, etc.

Education

Education is a Concurrent Subject under Constitution of India and involves an ecosystem that comprises many activities of other Ministries and Departments both at the Centre and in the States. Administration of mid-day meals, administration of hostels, disbursement of scholarships, etc are a few examples of activities that require coordination with other agencies of the government. Several flagship schemes of the GoI – Sarva Shiksha Abhiyan, Mid-Day Meal, Rashtriya Madhayamik Shiksha Abhiyan, etc require ICT for their implementation and monitoring.

MHRD is working on a National Policy on ICT in School Education to provide guidelines to assist the States in optimising the use of ICT in school education.

Department of School Education and Literacy of the Ministry of Human Resource Development (MHRD) has been made the nodal Department for the design and implementation of this MMP.

Keeping in view the federal nature of its implementation, the MMP would be designed on the principle of centralised planning and decentralised implementation.

The Mission Mode Project (MMP) in School Education needs to cover a multitude of stakeholders in the ecosystem and arrive at a set of end user-centric services that have an impact over an agreed project time frame. Currently, a preliminary study to identify the services and possible ICT interventions is being undertaken.

Health

The Apex Committee for the National e-Governance Plan (NeGP) chaired by Cabinet Secretary has approved the inclusion of Health as a Mission Mode Project (MMP) under the NeGP.

ICT for programme management has been undertaken by the Ministry of Health & Family Welfare in the Mother and Child Tracking System (MCTS) programme and the Ministry envisages a more comprehensive use of ICT including for Hospital Information Systems, supply chain management for drugs and vaccines, providing ICT tools to ASHA and ANM workers, programme management of National Rural Health Mission (NRHM), etc through this MMP.

Employment Exchange

Ministry of Labour & Employment is in the process of conceptualising this MMP. It is expected that the MMP will help match the requirements of employers against employee database. It is also expected that the MMP will have mechanisms to provide valuable guidance and career counseling to the unemployed, and facilitate online registration of vacancies by employers.

e-panchayat

The Panchayati Raj Institutions (PRIs) are saddled with the problems of inadequate physical and financial resources, technical capabilities and extremely limited computerization. As a result, the potential of PRIs as the preferred delivery channel for the schemes of State and Centre as well as for citizen services has not been fully realised. While some computerization efforts for PRIs have been made by NIC over the years, the e-Governance revolution sweeping the country has not touched the PRIs yet in significant measure. The Ministry of Panchayati Raj, Government of India has therefore decided to take up the computerization of PRIs on a mission mode basis.

Municipalities

e-Governance in Municiplaities is a unique initiative of the Government of India conceptualized under the umbrella of the overall National e-Governance Plan (NeGP) and the Jawaharlal Nehru National Urban Renewal Mission (Jnnurm) aimed at improving operational efficiencies within Urban Local Bodies (ULBs).

This initiative envisages covering Urban Local Bodies (ULBs) in 35 mission cities identified, from 15 states (~ 80 ULBs), having more than 1 million population as per 2001 census to improve the efficiency and effectiveness of delivery of municipal services to citizens. A minimum of Eight services (citizen centric and ULB centric) have been identified as a part of the program that will be deployed at state level as a centralized application and will subsequently be used by the ULBs of respective states.

Treasuries

The State Treasuries are the structural and financial unit of the Government Financial System and are responsible for handling the day-to-day transactions of receipt and payment of Government.

The computerisation of treasuries started in various states in a disjoint manner and by 2009 most States were already working on treasury computerization, each State having adopted its own strategy and pace.

Consequently various States were at different levels of computerization. However, a need was felt to have an integrated approach in order to achieve the objectives of a 'single source of truth', access to dependable data to support decision making, easier budgeting exercises and improvement in service levels. Minimization of reconciliation based on a single source of truth was expected to lead to efficiency and timeliness in decision-making. It was realised that the above objectives could be achieved by capturing transaction level and by using appropriate software to present data in different ways to support different decision-making processes. Other activities that were felt necessary included connecting DDOs, treasuries and various offices, creating and applying bridging software where required and business process reengineering to ensure that paper-less transactions and information sharing becomes possible. Considering that the basic work on treasury functions emanates from the level of DDOs it was felt that the States must decide the level at which DDOs are to be connected with the system, and also how the connectivity is to be phased. It was also felt necessary that for the scheme to be successful, or even possible, standardization of treasury formats and re-engineering of business processes needs to be undertaken. While common Head of Account numbers were available upto minor head level in all States, however, codes below the minor head are within the States' discretion. Therefore standardization of codes below the minor head level was required to facilitate collation and use of data.

Vision

Increasing efficiency of treasury functions, transparency in financial administrative systems, better cash flow management, better accounting of receipts and payments, improved regulatory mechanism, better control on State Finances, stronger MIS, accuracy and speed in accounts and budget preparation, among others.

Mission

Computerize treasuries and link treasury systems with other relevant systems across the nation in order to capture data on all transactions to facilitate transparency in decision making.

Commercial Taxes

The administration of the commercial taxes like VAT, CST etc. involves handling of a large number of dealers, who act on behalf of the State Departments to collect tax from consumers and deposit it in the State treasury. The Commercial Taxes Department of every State registers the dealers and issues registration certificates. The department fixes the periodicity of the returns to be filed by the dealers of the State. The department adds to the revenue of the State by collecting tax through challans and Net Payments. The Department is responsible for assessments, Tax Refunds, Form Issuance (eg. C form), Tax accounting, Recovery and Appeals. Commercial Taxes MMP will support the States and UTs Governments to computerize their Commercial Tax administering departments and enable States and UTs to quickly install requisite hardware and application software system in networked environment on a wide-area basis.

This MMP envisions creation of a modern indirect tax administration environment across the States, supported by a suitably enabling Information Technology (IT) infrastructure that is conducive to investment, economic growth and free flow of goods and services within a common market of India. The Scheme aims at building up the capacities across States harmoniously with flexibility to accommodate locally felt needs while subsuming the already ongoing initiatives. It intends to transform key processes leading to improved service delivery and build capacities among all the stakeholders to enable people delivering the services to perform better and while doing so it adopts a service oriented approach to the process re-engineering.

e-District

e-District is one of the 31 Mission Mode Projects under National e Governance Plan (NeGP) with the DIT, GoI being the nodal ministry. This project aims at providing support to the basic administrative unit i.e. District Administration• by undertaking backend computerization to enable electronic delivery of high volume citizen centric government services which would optimally leverage and utilize the three infrastructure pillars of State Wide Area Networks (SWAN), State Data Centers (SDC) and Common Service Centers (CSCs) to deliver services to the citizen at his doorsteps. e-District pilot projects have been initiated in 41 districts across 16 States with the objective of delivering high volume services at the District level, which are currently not covered by any MMP under the NeGP, and undertake backend computerization, up to the sub-district/ tehsil level, to e-enable the delivery of these services through Common Services Centers (CSCs) in a sustainable manner, within a specific time frame. It is now proposed to rollout the e-District MMP to cover all the districts in the country.

Road Transport

The Ministry of Road Transport & Highways has been facilitating the process of computerization of approximately 1000 Road Transport Offices (RTOs) across the country for the last 5 years. Almost 90% of the RTOs have been computerized and connectivity has been provided to 80% of the RTOs. Since the documents generated by the RTOs (Registration Certificate-RC

& Driving License-DL) are valid across the country it was imperative to define the same standards for these documents on a pan-India level to ensure interoperability and correctness and timely availability of information. The SCOSTA committee was setup for this purpose and in addition to defining the Smart Card standards, had recommended uniform standardized software across the country, which has been designed and developed by NIC. The software namely VAHAN and SARATHI are being implemented across the country.

In order to reap full benefit of information technology, it is necessary to establish centralized database (State Register & National Register).

National Land Records Modernization Programme (NLRMP)

A Project for Computerisation of Land Records (CLR)was launched in 1988-89 with the intention to remove the inherent flaws in the manual system of maintenance and updation of Land Records. In 1997-98, the scheme was extended to tehsils to start distribution of Records of Rights to landowners on demand. The focus of the entire operation has always been to employ state of the art information technology (IT) to galvanize and transform the existing land records system of the country.

The second important scheme, viz.,Strengthening of Revenue Administration and Updating of Land Records (SRA&ULR)was launched in 1988-89 to help States and UTs in updating and maintaining the land records, setting up and strengthening of survey and settlement organisations and the survey training infrastructure, modernization of the survey and settlement operations and strengthening of the revenue machinery.

However, the activities included in the schemes of CLR and SRA&ULR were basically meant for strengthening of revenue administration although they also included activities that contribute to conclusive titling. The choice of activities was left to the States/UTs most of whom chose activities that strengthen revenue administration but not necessarily helped in moving towards conclusive titling. A hamper-of-activities™ was followed which led to eddying; and each activity became a goal in itself rather than a step in the systematic, ladder-like approach towards reaching the stage of conclusive titling. Moreover, the way the schemes were framed no timeframe for achieving the goal of conclusive titling could be set and technology options for survey were not indicated and the work remained neglected in most of the States. Further, both the schemes excluded interconnectivity, geographic information system (GIS) mapping, connectivity with banks and treasuries and Registration-the last of which is a vital link in updating the land records.

Hence, the National Land Records Modernization Programme (NLRMP) was formulated by merging two Centrally-sponsored schemes CLR and SRA&ULR to usher in the system of conclusive titles as per the 'Torrens System' with title guarantee in the country.

Land Records

Maintenance of land records and the availability of easily accessible land information is one of the most important issues facing governance today. "Land Records" itself is a generic expression and can include records such as, the register of lands, Records of Rights (RoRs), tenancy and crop inspection register, mutation register, disputed cases register, etc. It can also include geological information regarding the shape, size, soil-type of the land; and economic information related to irrigation and crops.

The Land Records MMP, being implemented by Ministry of Rural Development (MoRD), seeks to accomplish the following across States:

* Completion of all data entry related to digitisation of land records
* Provision of legal sanctity to computerised Records-of-Rights (RoRs)
* Stopping further issue of manual RORs

* Setting up computer centers at Tehsils
* Enabling Web access

The main objectives of the MMP are:

* To facilitate easy maintenance and updates in land databases
* To provide for comprehensive scrutiny to make land records tamper-proof (in an effort to reduce the menace of litigation and social conflicts associated with land disputes)
* To provide the required support for implementation of development programmes for which data about distribution of land holdings is vital
* To facilitate detailed planning for infrastructural as well as environment development
* To facilitate preparation of an annual set of records in the mechanised process, thereby producing accurate documents for recording details such as collection of land revenue, cropping pattern, etc.
* To facilitate a variety of standard and ad-hoc queries on land data
* To provide database for agricultural census

Core Services offered under the Land Records MMP are:

* Issue of copies of RoRs
* Crop, irrigation and soil details
* Filing and tracking of status of mutation cases
* Availability and submission of forms

Police

This MMP has been included in NeGP in light of the ever-increasing threats of terror attacks and of continually ascending crime graphs. It includes aspects such as creation of- and sharing of- crime-related databases across departments, effective personal management, and efficient inventory control.

Given the large variations in these functions across States, the MMP professes a phased approach towards implementation. The first phase broadly targets those functions that are common across States and which are driven by the Criminal Procedure Code (CrPC).

The National e-Governance Plan (NeGP)

The National e-Governance Plan (NeGP) has been formulated by the Department of Electronics and Information Technology (DEITY) and Department of Administrative Reforms and Public Grievances (DARPG). The Union Government approved the NeGP, comprising of 27 Mission Mode Projects (MMPs) and 10 components on May 18, 2006.

The NeGP aims at improving delivery of Government services to citizens and businesses with the following vision:

> "Make all Government services accessible to the common man in his locality, through common service delivery outlets and ensure efficiency, transparency & reliability of such services at affordable costs to realise the basic needs of the common man."

Implementation Strategy, Approach and Methodology of NeGP

Implementation of e-Governance is a highly complex process requiring provisioning of hardware & software, networking, process re-engineering and change management. Based on lessons learnt from the past and the experience from successful e-Governance applications, the approach and methodology adopted for NeGP contains the following elements:

i. Common Support Infrastructure: NeGP implementation involves setting up of common and support IT infrastructure such as: State Wide Area Networks (SWANs), State Data Centres (SDCs), Common Services Centres (CSCs) and Electronic Service Delivery Gateways.

ii. Governance: Suitable arrangements for monitoring and coordinating the implementation of NeGP under the direction of the competent authorities have also been substantially put in place. The programme also involves evolving/ laying down standards and policy guidelines, providing technical support, undertaking capacity building, R&D, etc. DEITY is required to adequately strengthen itself and various institutions like NIC, STQC, CDAC, NISG, etc. to play these roles effectively.

iii. Centralised Initiative, Decentralised Implementation: e-Governance is being promoted through a centralised initiative to the extent necessary to ensure citizen-centric orientation, to realise the objective of inter-operability of various e-Governance applications and to ensure optimal utilisation of ICT infrastructure and resources while allowing for a decentralised implementation model. It also aims at identifying successful projects and replicating them with required customisation wherever needed.

iv. Public-Private Partnerships (PPP): PPP model is to be adopted wherever feasible to enlarge the resource pool without compromising on the security aspects.

v. Integrative Elements: Adoption of unique identification codes for citizens, businesses and property is to be promoted to facilitate integration and avoid ambiguity.

vi. Programme Approach at the National and State levels: For implementation of the NeGP, various Union Ministries/ Departments and State Governments are involved. Considering the multiplicity of agencies involved and the need for overall aggregation and integration at the national level, NeGP is being implemented as a programme, with well-defined roles and responsibilities of each agency involved. For facilitating this, appropriate programme management structures have also been put in place.

vii. Facilitator role of DEITY: DEITY is the facilitator and catalyst for the implementation of NeGP by various Ministries and State Governments and also provides technical assistance. It serves as a secretariat to the Apex Committee and assists it in managing the programme. In addition, DEITY is also implementing pilot/ infrastructure/ technical/ special projects and support components. DARPG's responsibility is towards Government Process Re-engineering and Change Management, which are desired to be realised across all government departments. Planning Commission and Ministry of Finance allocate funds for NeGP through Plan and Non-plan budgetary provisions and lay down appropriate procedures in this regard.

viii. Ownership of Ministries: Under the NeGP, various MMPs are owned and spearheaded by the concerned line Ministries. In case there are any ongoing projects which fall in the MMP category, they would be suitably enhanced to align them with the objectives of NeGP. For major projects like Bharat Nirman, Rural Employment Guarantee Schemes, etc. the line ministries concerned are advised to make use of e-Governance as also automation techniques from the inception stage. States have been given the flexibility to identify a few additional state-specific projects, which are relevant for the economic development of the State.

10

Powers and Functions of Governor, Chief Minister, Secretariat, Chief Secretary, Directorates and District Collector

INTRODUCTION

The Constitution of India provides for a federal Government, having separate systems of administration for the Union and the States. The Constitution contains provisions for the governance of both. It lays down a uniform structure for the State Government in Part VI of the Constitution, which is applicable to all the States, except the State of Jammu and Kashmir (which has a separate Constitution for the State.)

The pattern of Government in the States is the same as that for the Union. The executive head (the Governor) being a Constitutional ruler, who has to act according to the advice of Ministers responsible to the State Legislature, except in matters where the Governor is Constitutionally authorised to act in his discretion (Article 163).

THE GOVERNOR

Just as the President stands at the head of the Union executive, the Governor heads the State executive. The executive power of the State is vested in the Governor and all executive action of the State is taken in the name of the Governor. Normally, there is one Governor for each State, but it is possible to appoint the same person as the Governor of two or more States (Article 153).

Appointment, Qualifications, Tenure and Emoluments

The Governor of a State is appointed by the President and holds his office at the pleasure of the President. In order to be appointed as Governor a person must be a citizen of India, over 35 years of age. He must not hold any other office of profit, nor be a member of the Legislature of the Union or of any State. If a member of a Legislature is appointed as Governor, he ceases to be a member immediately upon such appointment.

The normal term of office of Governor is five years. But it may be terminated earlier by (i) Dismissal by the President, at whose 'pleasure' he holds office, or (ii) Resignation. He can be reappointed. There is no bar to a person being appointed Governor more than once. The Governor receives a monthly salary besides rent-free official residence and prescribed travelling, sumptuary and other allowances for discharging the duties of his office with convenience and dignity.

Powers of the Governor

The Governor has no diplomatic or military powers like the President, but he possesses executive, legislative and judicial powers analogous to those of the President.

Executive Powers

The Governor is the executive head of the State and all executive powers are vested in him. His powers extend to the administration of all matters included in the State List. In case of matters specified in the Concurrent List, the powers of the Governor are subject to the exercise of the powers of the President.

The Governor has the power to appoint the Chief Minister, the Council of Ministers, the Advocate-General and the Members of the State Public Service Commission. The Ministers and the

Advocate-General hold office during the pleasure of the Governor. But the Members of the State Public Service Commission can be removed only by the President on the report of the Supreme Court and not by the Governor.

The Governor has the power to nominate one member of the Anglo-Indian community to the Legislative Assembly of the State, if he is of the opinion that the community is not adequately represented in the Assembly. If the State concerned has a bicameral legislature, the Governor can nominate persons having special knowledge or practical experience in respect of matters such as literature, science, art, co-operative movement and social service to the Legislative Council.

Legislative Powers

The Governor is a part of the State Legislature just as the President is a part of Parliament. He has a right to address and to send messages, to summon, prorogue and dissolve the State Legislature. He causes to be laid before the State Legislature, the annual financial statement and the Money Bills. The Bills passed by the Legislature are sent to the Governor for his assent. He may give his assent or may withhold assent. He may even reserve the Bill for the consideration of the President. The Bills may be sent back by the Governor for reconsideration but if they are again passed with or without amendments he has to give assent to them.

Financial Powers

Money Bills can be introduced in the Assembly on the recommendation of the Governor. The Finance Minister submits to the Legislature the annual financial statement or budget showing estimated receipts and expenditure for the next financial year in the name of the Governor. No demand' for grants may be made except on the recommendation of the Governor. The Legislature may reduce the grants sought by the Governor but cannot increase them. The Governor is the custodian of the

Contingency Fund of the State and has the power to make payments in emergency without prior sanction of the State Legislature.

Judicial Powers

The Governor has no power to appoint Judges of the State High Court but he is entitled to be consulted by the President in the matter. He determines the question of appointments, postings and promotions of District Judges and other judicial officers in the State.

The Governor has the power to pardon, commute or suspend sentence of any person convicted of any offence against any law relating to matters to which the executive power of the State extends. He can exercise this power either before the trial or during or even after the trial.

Emergency Powers

Under Article 356 of the Constitution, the Governor has the power to make a report to the President whenever he is satisfied that a situation has arisen in which Government of the State cannot be carried on in accordance with the provisions of the Constitution. The Governor, however, has no emergency powers to meet the situation arising from external or internal aggression as the President has.

Discretionary Powers

Though in the exercise of all his powers the Governor is aided and advised by the Council of Ministers, in the exercise of his discretionary powers the Governor is not required to act according to the advice of his Ministers or even to seek such advice. If any question arises as to whether a matter is or is not a matter for which the Governor is not required by the Constitution to act in his discretion, the decision of the Governor is final.

Following are the functions which are specially required by the Constitution to be exercised by the Governor in his discretion:

— Article 239(2) authorises the President to appoint the Governor of a State as the administrator of an adjoining Union Territory and where he is so appointed, he exercises his functions as administrator 'independently of his Council of Ministers'.

— Article 371(2) provides that "the President may by order made with respect to the State of Maharashtra or Gujarat, provide for any special responsibility of the Governor for

  (a) the establishment of separate development boards for Vidarbha, Marathwada Saurashtra, Kutch and the rest of Gujarat;

  (b) the equitable allocation of funds for developmental expenditure over the said areas, subject to the requirement of the State as a whole; and

  (c) an equitable arrangement providing adequate facilities for technical education and vocational training, and adequate opportunities for employment in services under the control of the Slate Government, in respect of all the said areas. subject to the requirements of the State as a whole."

— Article 371 A(l)(b) states that "the Governor of Nagaland shall have special responsibility with respect to law and order in the State of Nagaland for so long as in his opinion internal disturbances occurring in the Naga Hills-Tuensang area immediately before the formation of the State continue therein or in any part thereof and in the discharge of his functions in relation thereto the Governor shall, after consulting the Council of Ministers, exercise his individual judgement as to the action to be taken."

— Similarly, Article 371C(1) empowers the President to direct that the Governor of Manipur shall have special responsibility to secure the proper functioning of the Committee of the Legislative Assembly of the State consisting of the members elected from the Hill areas of the State.

— Article 371F(g) imposes on the Governor of Sikkim, a "special responsibility for peace and for an equitable arrangement for ensuring the social and economic advancement of different sections of the population of Sikkim" and further states that "in the discharge of his special responsibility under this clause, the Governor of Sikkim shall, subject to such directions as the President may, from time to time deem fit to issue, act in his discretion."

The report to the President under Article 356 that a situation has arisen in which the Government of State cannot be carried on in accordance with the provisions of the Constitution is made by the Governor in his own discretion. The Governor is also the medium through which the Union keeps itself informed as to "whether the State is complying with the Directives issued by the Union from time to time.

Further, after a President's rule is imposed in the State, the Governor acts as the agent of the President as regards those functions of the State Government which have been assumed by the President under the proclamation of emergency.

In some other matters, such as the reservation of a Bill for consideration of the President, the Governor may not always be in agreement with his Council of Ministers, particularly when the Governor happens to belong to party other than that of the Ministry. In such cases, the Governor may be justified in acting without Ministerial advice, if he considers that the Bill in question would affect the powers of the Union or contravene any of the provisions of the Constitution even though his Ministry may be of a different opinion.

Miscellaneous Powers

The Governor receives the annual report of the State Public Service Commission, submits the same to the Council of Ministers and after its consideration to the State Legislature for discussion.

He also receives the report of the Auditor-General regarding income and expenditure made by different departments under the State Government.

Position of the Governor

The position of Governor of the State is the same as that of the President of the Union. Theoretically, he is the chief administrator. But in practice, it is not so. The Constitution provides that the Governor shall function with the aid and advice of the Council of Ministers, headed by a Chief Minister.

Even in the exercise of his discretionary powers, the Governor is not free in the sense that he has to act under instructions from the President of India or in accordance with some set conventions.

For instance, it is a set convention that the Governor invites only the leader of the majority party in the Assembly to be the Chief Minister since only such a leader is capable of forming a stable Government. If no party has a clear majority, the Governor invites the leader of the largest single party to form the Government. Thus, it is only in the latter instance that he uses his discretion.

In summoning, proroguing or dissolving the House, the Governor has to seek the advice of the Ministers. There is no denying the fact that the Governor plays a dual role. On the one hand, he is the Constitutional head of the State, acting on the advice of Council of Ministers and advising the State Ministry on various important political and administrative issues, on the other hand, he serves as an agent of the Central Government and keeps the Centre informed of the working of the State Government.

The Governor is an essential part of our federal system. The success of this system depends on the personality of the Governor, his knowledge and ability to solve the problems in an impartial manner.

THE CHIEF MINISTER

The position of the Chief Minister of the State corresponds to the position of the Prime Minister at the Centre. The Chief Minister, who is appointed by the Governor is the head of the State Council of Ministers. He is the leader of the majority party in the State Legislative Assembly.

Functions of the Chief Minister are:

1. To communicate to the Governor all the decisions of the Council of Ministers relating to the administration of the affairs of the State and proposals for legislation.
2. To furnish such information relating to the administration of the affairs of the State and proposals for legislation as the Governor may call for.
3. If the Governor so requires, then the Chief Minister submits for the consideration of the Council of Ministers any matter on which decision has been taken by a Minister but which has not been considered by the Cabinet.

Evaluation of the Role of the Chief Minister

The Chief Minister is the sole link of communication between the Cabinet and the Governor and plays an important role as the chief of the Cabinet. Though the Constitution has given a very important position to the Chief Minister, our Chief Ministers, for various reasons, have not always come up to the expectation. The foremost reason is that in most of the States, the same party is in power as in the Centre. They work in accordance with the wishes of the party High Command. Often, Chief Ministers are sent from the Centre, who, for obvious reasons, are unable to take an independent and an unbiased stand. However, the Chief Ministers of States like West Bengal, Tamil Nadu, Jammu and Kashmir, Andhra Pradesh have proved their worth as they are independent of the control of the Central Government.

The position of State Cabinet largely depends upon the personality of the Chief Minister, strength of the ruling party in the State Assembly, and the relationship between the Chief Minister and the central party organisation and leadership. In ordinary circumstances, the Council of Ministers in the State enjoys all effective powers. It has control over all policy decisions, appointments, transfers and removals.

President's Control over the State Executive

As regards matters on which the Governor is empowered to act in his discretion or on his 'special responsibility", the Governor is under the complete control of the President. But in other matters, though the President has the power of appointing and removing the Governor from office, the President is not entitled to any effective control over the Stale Government against the wishes of a Chief Minister who enjoys the confidence of the State Legislature. The President, nevertheless, has the right to keep himself informed of the affairs of the State through the reports of the Governor, which may even lead to the removal of the Ministry.

Dismissal of Chief Minister

There is a sharp controversy as to whether a Governor has the power to dismiss a Council of Ministers, headed by the Chief Minister, on the assumption that the Chief Minister and his Cabinet have lost their majority in the popular House of the Legislature. The Governor has the power to dismiss an individual Minister at any time. He can dismiss a Council of Ministers or the Chief Minister (whose dismissal means a fall of the Council of Ministers), only when the Legislative Assembly has passed a no-confidence motion against the Council of Ministers. The Governor cannot dismiss the Chief Minister at his pleasure, on his subjective estimate of the strength of the Chief Minister in the Assembly at any point of time. It is for the Legislative Assembly to enforce the collective responsibility of the Council of Ministers to itself.

THE SECRETARIAT

The word Secretariat refers to the complex of departments whose heads administratively are Secretaries and politically are Ministers. The Secretary is the Secretary to the Government as a whole, not to the individual Minister. The Secretary is normally a generalist civil servant. But in the case of the Public Works Department, the Chief Engineer is usually the Secretary.

Normally, more than one department is entrusted to one Secretary. Hence, the number of Secretariat departments is greater than the number of Secretaries. Like his Central counterpart, the Secretary is

(a) the principal adviser to the Minister,

(b) head of the department(s) under his charge,

(c) responsible for carrying out the policies and decisions made by the political chief, and

(d) representative of his deparlment(s) before the legislative committees.

Organisation of a Department

A department consists of officers among whom arc included, besides the Secretary, the Deputy Secretary, Under Secretary and/or Assistant Secretary. The larger departments may also have Additional and Joint Secretaries. Secretaries, Additional Secretaries, Joint Secretaries, Deputy Secretaries and Under Secretaries are all, except those belonging to the Secretariat Civil Service, subject to the Tenure System. They are, thus, appointed to the Secretariat for a fixed term. However, the Chief Secretary is not subject to the Tenure System.

Let us now briefly discuss the functions of the officers of the departments:

1. **Secretary:** The Secretary is the overall incharge of the department. He is the chief advisor to the Minister regarding matters pertaining to his department. He allocates work among the various officers of his department

and represents his department before the committees of the Legislature.

2. **Special/Additional Secretary:** When the work in a particular department becomes too heavy, some-posts of Special/Additional Secretaries may be created to relieve the Secretary of some of the workload. These officers can directly perform some of the functions of the Secretary and may submit files directly to the Minister in respect of the delegated functions performed by them.

3. **Deputy/Joint Secretary:** The Secretary is assisted by the Deputy Secretary. In some States the posts of Joint Secretaries have been created in order to distinguish between the officers of different seniorities. Sometimes the officers coming from the State civil service are designated as Deputy Secretaries while those coming from the IAS are designated as Joint Secretaries. However, they perform the same functions. The Deputy/Joint Secretaries are placed in charge of a definite wing of the Department and supervise the work of the Under Secretaries.

   Some powers, to dispose of certain routine cases, are also delegated to the Deputy Secretary. He sends important cases to the Additional Secretary or the Secretary, depending upon the scheme of delegation of work. The Deputy Secretaries are supposed to have a thorough knowledge of the wing controlled by them. They are supposed to analyse the various policy alternatives before sending the files upwards.

4. **Under Secretary:** Under Secretaries are the lowest level officers who perform the vital function of providing a link between the office and the officers. They are placed in charge of a number of sections each headed by a Section Officer. Section is the lowest unit of work. In some States, the Section is headed by an Assistant Secretary whereas in others it is headed by a Section Officer. The Section Officer is responsible for the distribution of work among

the various functionaries of the section. He supervises the work of the Assistants and Upper Division Clerks working in his section, makes them present the cases suitably docketed and referenced and thus ensures the timely submission of files to the officers. Precedents of similar cases have also to be cited while presenting the files.

Besides the officers, the department also consists of the office. The office comprises the Superintendent (or Section Officer), Assistants, Upper Division and Lower Division Clerks, Steno-typists, and Typists. Unlike officers, the office constitutes the permanent element in the Secretariat system.

While the officers analyse the case and suggest alternative courses of action, the function of the office is to present the cases in the proper form before the officers. Whereas the Lower Division Clerks/Typists do the usual work of typing, referencing, dispatching, etc., the Upper Division Clerks/Assistants connect the incoming papers with the previous files and present them along with the precedents. The latter also point out various laws, rules, regulations, practices, etc., connected with the case in question. Their main task is the timely presentation of cases. They are not usually supposed to analyse the cases or suggest alternatives. The work of Assistant Secretary/Section Officer is to ensure that every one is doing his work properly.

Secretariat Personnel

Senior officers (Secretary, Special Secretaries, Additional, Joint and Deputy Secretaries) of the Secretariat come on deputation from the IAS. In some States, the position of Deputy Secretaries is also manned by State civil service officers on deputation. The Tenure System of placing officers in the Secretariat also applies in the States as in the Central Secretariat. However, the operation of the tenure rule in the States is much more flexible. In the States, Government officers are frequently transferred without any reference to any fixed tenure.

In the Secretariat, most of the positions are manned by the officers from the civil services but some officers are brought to the Secretariat from technical services also, e.g., posts of Deputy/ Joint/special Secretaries in technical departments like Public Works Department, Irrigation, etc. In a large number of States even the post of Secretaries in the technical departments arc being occupied by technical services personnel.

The officers of the IAS, the State civil service and other services come on deputation to the Secretariat and go back to the field on completion of their tenure. But unlike the officers, the functionaries in the Secretariat office are not deputationists. Most of them belong to the services recruited for the Secretariat. There are Subordinate Service Commissions in many States to conduct the examinations for their recruitments. Their recruitment, promotion and service conditions, etc., are governed by the relevant rules. These services are managed by the General Administrative Department of the State Government which functions directly under the Chief Secretary.

Number of Secretariat Departments

The number of Secretariat departments varies from State to State, ranging between 11 and 34. Most States, however, have the following Secretariat departments:

(1) General Administration
(2) Home
(3) Revenue
(4) Food and Agriculture
(5) Planning
(6) Panchayati Raj
(7) Finance
(8) Law
(9) Public Works
(10) Irrigation and Power

(11) Education
(12) Industries
(13) Co-operation
(14) Transport
(15) Local Government
(16) Jails
(17) Labour and Employment
(18) Excise and Taxation.

Distinction between Secretariat and Executive Departments

In the words of the Simon Commission, the executive department:

> 'is an administrative unit, separate from the Secretariat, which reaches its apex, usually, in a single officer like the Inspector-General of Police, or the Chief Conservator of Forests, outside the Secretariat altogether. Such a head of department will usually be concerned principally with a single Secretary to Government and a single Minister, for his orders and the funds which he has to spend.'

Not all departments, however, have executive departments attached to them. Some of the Secretariat departments are engaged in advisory and controlling functions and do not, therefore, have executive departments reporting to them, e.g., the departments of Finance and Law

Functions of the Secretariat

1. It assists and advises the Minister in the formulation of Government policies and programmes.
2. It collects the necessary data from different sources and analyses it with a view to suggest various courses of action necessary for policy formulation.
3. It gives general direction and guidance to the Directorates and other field agencies for the efficient implementation of Government policies and decisions.

4. It monitors the implementation of various programmes and evaluates the performance of different field agencies.
5. It also suggests corrective action.
6. It acts as the spokesman of the Government and maintains contact with the Central Government and other State Governments and outside agencies.

Critical Evaluation

The Secretariat is being criticised for becoming expansionist in its attitude and behaviour and for arrogating to itself powers and functions which do not come under its purview. A number of factors explain this phenomena but the most important factor happens to be parliamentary democracy itself. The Minister who is responsible to the Legislature for efficient functioning of his department, has to answer questions relating to his department.

The Minister, therefore, intends to closely supervise the department. This also explains the centralisation of functions in the Secretariat and its expansion. Besides, there are human and psychological factors as well. The Secretariat's tendency to concentrate powers in its hands has led to inefficiency in the working of the Government. Thus, attempts are being made to contain this expansion of the Secretariat by preparing a list of the functions which are to be looked after by it.

It is also alleged that the functioning of the Secretariat is very slow like the examination of proposals, etc. This slow and tardy processing of the cases in the Secretariat impairs the efficiency of the field agencies.

There is a general tendency, among the officers, to make efforts to stay on in the Secretariat as it offers attractive salary, remuneration, educational and medical facilities, etc. Apart from all this, by working at the Secretariat, in close contact with the 'heads' the officers aggregate much power and influence. This tendency on the part of the officers is a great hindrance to the Tenure system. By staying for too long at the Secretariat the officers lose touch with the field problems.

THE CHIEF SECRETARY

Genesis of the Office

The office of the Chief Secretary, dates back to 1799 when Lord Wellesley, the then Governor-General of India, appointed G.H. Barlow as the Chief Secretary for the first time. It may be noted that the office of the Chief Secretary, which started functioning in the Central Government, disappeared in course of time from the Central Government. At present, there is no office in the Government of India which is equivalent to that of the Chief Secretary in the State.

Role of Chief Secretary

In every State, the Chief Secretary is the head of the General Administration Department. He is the kingpin of the Secretariat and his control extends to all the departments of the Secretariat. He is head of the civil services in the State, their mirror and conscience-keeper. He provides leadership to the administrative system of the State and is the chief public relations officer of the Government and the main channel of communication between the Government and the Central and other State Governments.

Functions of the Chief Secretary

1. He is the principal adviser to the Chief Minister in all administrative matters including appointments to senior positions.
2. He is the Secretary to the Cabinet and prepares the agenda for its meetings and maintains records of the proceedings.
3. He exercises general supervision and control over the entire Secretariat and its field administration.
4. He is the head of the civil service and has the authority to make postings, transfers, etc., of Government personnel. An empirical study conducted by a State Government reveals that two out of every three cases dealt with by the Chief Secretary relate to personnel matters.

5. By rotation, he becomes the Secretary of the Zonal Council of which his State is a member.
6. He exercises administrative control over the Secretariat buildings, including allocation of rooms in them.
7. He exercises control over the staff attached to the Ministers.
8. He has control over the central record branch. the Secretariat library, and the conservancy and watch and ward-staff who serve all the departments of the Secretariat.
9. He performs all the residuary functions, i.e., matters not falling within the responsibilities of other Secretaries.
10. As chief of all Secretaries, he presides over a large number of committees and is appointed a member of many other committees, concerned with high level policy.
11. He plays an important role in times of crisis. Until 1973, the Chief Secretary was not necessarily the senior most official in all the States. In 1973, the post of Chief Secretary was equated with that of the Secretary to the Government of India, giving him the emoluments admissible to the latter.

Chief Secretaries' Conference

The Chief Secretaries' Conference is convened at the instance of, and presided over by the Cabinet Secretary of the Central Government. It is meant for discussing problems of mutual interest. It, thus, acts as an administrative bridge between the Centre and the States.

Evaluation

The office of the Chief Secretary has a pivotal importance and, so, must be filled up very carefully. Allowance to political considerations in his appointment are bound to prove fatal to the health of the administration. With increasing political interference in State administration, doubts have been expressed as to whether the Chief Secretary would continue to be appointed on purely administrative grounds, and also if he would be allowed to function with objectivity, independence and fearlessness. Thus, suggestions have been made to prepare a national roster of senior officers who alone could be appointed as Chief Secretaries of the Stales.

It has also been suggested that his tenure of office should be sufficiently long so as to enable him to function effectively and to make his impact felt on the administration of his State.

ARC's Recommendations

The Administrative Reforms Commission (ARC) has recommended that in order to improve the functioning of the Chief Secretary's office:

> "The Secretarial organisation needs co-ordination and discipline. This can be done by strengthening the position of the Chief Secretary who is to function as the chief coordinator under the Chief Minister Being the captain of the team of Secretaries to the Government, the Chief Secretary should be a senior person of outstanding ability. He should not only command respect and confidence of all the Services in the Stale but also enjoy good reputation at the Centre so that he can deal with the Secretaries to the Union Government on equal terms."

The ARC further recommended that:

> "The selection of the Chief Secretary should be made with great care. He should usually be the senior most fit person who by virtue of his ability, experience, integrity and impartiality commands the respect and confidence of all officers. He should be the senior most person due regard being paid to merit. He should have a minimum tenure of three to four years. He should be relieved of routine and non-essential work and, where necessary, given proportionate staff assistance to enable him to ensure quick implementation of the Cabinet decisions and effective co-ordination in the policies and programmes of the State Government."

DIRECTORATES

Each State has a number of Directorates which function more or less as specialised agencies of the departments. For instance, the Education Department has a Directorate of Education headed by a Director who is assisted by Assistant Directors for the districts.

District Collector : Changing Role

District has been placed under the charge of a district officer, called either Deputy Commissioner or District Collector. The Collector acts as the eyes, ears and arms of the State Government. The district also serves as a unit of administration for various departments of the State Government.

Thus, many State functionaries like the Superintendent of Police, Assistant Registrar of Cooperative Societies, District Agriculture Officer, District Medical Officer, etc., are located at the district headquarters and their jurisdiction extends to the district. However, the unit of administration of the department of irrigation is not coterminous with the district. The unit follows channels of irrigation quite often transcending district boundaries. Agencies operating in the district come under the co-ordinating discipline of the District Collector.

The office of the District Collector can be traced to the Mughal era. The District Collector succeeded the Karori-Faujdar of the Mughal Government. However, with the decline of the Mughal empire the institution suffered a decay and eventually disappeared. The present office is the creation of the British in India and dates back to the year 1772. The District Collector belongs to the General Administration Department of the State Government, while the officials over whom he exercises control and supervision belong to a variety of departments, in the district hierarchy of which he may or may not have a formal assignment. The position of the District Collector can best be illustrated with the help of the following diagram :

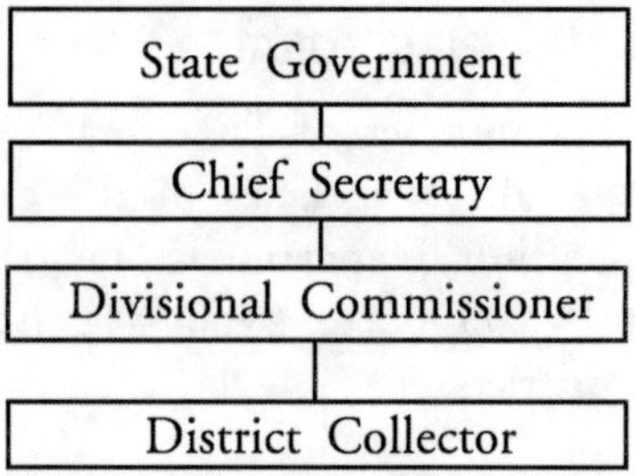

As head of the district, the District Collector is involved in a network of inter-relationships with other district level functionaries such as –

(a) with officers whose head at the district level is the Collector in all matters, and who represent departments having no district heads of their own, e.g., the Tehsildar.

(b) with officers whose head at the district level is the Collector for only administrative and certain disciplinary matters but who, in technical matters, are under the control of their own district level officers, e.g., District Agricultural Officer, District Excise Officers, etc.

(c) with officers who are themselves heads, at the district level, of their field staff but are made subordinate to the Collector only in certain specified matters. Besides, they are also under the control of their respective regional officers, e.g., the Superintendent of Police, the Civil Surgeon, the Assistant Registrar of Co-operative Societies, the Executive Engineer of the Public Works Department, etc.

(d) with officers, the control over whom does not at all vest in the Collector, e.g., Labour Officer, Sales Tax Officer, etc.

Recruitment of District Collector

The District Collector is usually a member of the Indian Administrative Service. As the IAS consists of both direct recruits and of promotees from State civil services, these two sub-groups constitute the two natural sources from which District Collectors are drawn. Direct recruits to the office, that is, those who join the IAS through a competitive examination, are young men, usually in their thirties. The office is also occupied by officers who were originally recruited to the State civil services and who have since been, promoted to the IAS. This category belongs to a higher age group. There may also be some District Collectors who are not members of the IAS. Such officers belong to the State civil service, to be soon promoted to the IAS. They are on the verge of retirement, and so, are afforded the satisfaction of functioning, and then retiring as District Collector.

Role of District Collector in Revenue Administration

Historically, prompt and fair collection of land revenue and other taxes has been his first charge as the title "Collector' signifies. As the head of the revenue department of the district, the District Collector performs the following functions:

1. Collection of land revenue, canal dues and other Government dues.
2. Distribution and recovery of taqavi loans.
3. Assessment of losses to crops, etc. during natural calamities and to make recommendations for relief work.
4. Distribution of distress taqavi.
5. Relief of fire sufferers.
6. Control over land records and land records establishment.
7. Collecting and furnishing multifarious agrarian statistics regarding rainfall, crops, etc.
8. Land acquisition work.
9. Supervision of treasury and sub-treasuries.
10. Sanctioning land revenue assignment.
11. Payment of Zamindari Abolition compensation and Rehabilitation Grant.
12. Assessment and realisation of agricultural income-tax.

13. As ex-officio Deputy Director of Consolidation of Holdings, hearing appeal against the orders of the lower authorities.
14. Taking relief measures in case of scarcity conditions caused by natural calamities like fire, drought, flood, water-clogging, etc.
15. Enforcement of the Stamp Act.
16. Management of Government estates.

To discharge his revenue functions the Collector has a territorial set up as shown below:

Officer	Jurisdiction
Collector	District
Sub-Divisional Officer	A group of Tehsils
Tehsildar	Tehsil
Naib Tehsildar	Parts of a Tehsil
Kanungo or Revenue Inspector in Chennai	A group of Patwari Circles
Patwari	A group of Villages

The revenue functions can be broadly divided into two branches, viz. :

(a) Revenue branch

(b) Land Records branch

At the lowest level Kanungos and the Patwaris are the common functionaries of the revenue branch as well as land records branch. Though their administrative control vests in the revenue officers, they perform the work of land records also. The main function of the land records branch is to help the Collector and the Revenue officers in the maintenance of land records.

The officers of the Land Records Department - the Superintendent and Assistant Superintendent (Land Records) - also tour the different areas. The discrepancies noticed by them are notified to the revenue officers who get them rectified. Informally, they may be allotted different areas for the purpose of tours and inspections, but usually they do not form part of the territorial set up like the revenue branch.

The functions and powers of the revenue branch may be discussed as follows:

1. At the sub-division level the charge is in the hands of a Sub-Divisional Officer (SDO), who is known by different names in different States. He exercises supervision over Tehsildar, Naib Tehsildar and other functionaries in his sub-division and is incharge of many of the functions of the Collector in a sub-division. The SDO hears appeals against the revenue cases decided by the Tehsildars and Naib Tehsildars. He has to make extensive tours and has to keep a check on the land records as well as the revenue work of the functionaries in his subdivision. In this way he serves as a valuable aid to the District Collector.

2. The sub-division comprises of one or two tehsils. A tehsil is called taluk in Tamil Nadu and taluka in Maharashtra. It is the basic unit for purposes of general administration, treasury, land revenue, land records and other items of work. It has the most intimate contact with the rural population. The Tehsildar, incharge of a tehsil, belongs to the State civil service and is the principal official in the district administration responsible for actual revenue collection. In times of distress it is the Tehsildar who recommends remissions or other concessions to the District Collector.

   The Tehsildar is assisted by a Naib or Deputy Tehsildar, Kanungos and Patwaris. The administration at the tehsil level is the farthest unit of administration for revenue and land questions. The distribution of staff below the district level follows departmental needs, and, so, all departments are not necessarily re-presented at this level.

3. The next lower unit in revenue administration is known as Pargana in U.P., Circle in Maharashtra, and Firka in Tamil

Nadu and their heads are respectively known as Supervisor Kanungo, Circle Inspector and Revenue Inspector. He is incharge of revenue administration and land records of every village within his area and is the first line supervisor in the chain of revenue administration in the States.

4. The lowest unit for all administrative and fiscal purposes in all the States in India is the village. The village is administered by an establishment comprising of Lekhpal and Chowkidar in U.P., Patel and Talati in Maharashtra, and Village Headman and Karnam in Tamil Nadu is the most powerful Governmental functionary at the village level, combining as he does both police and revenue functions. He is the custodian of all Government property in the village and represents the Government in the village. Patel in Maharashtra is equal to the Village Headman of Tamil Nadu, as he also performs police, revenue and administrative functions. U.P. has no functionary corresponding to the 'Village Headman' in Tamil Nadu and the Patel in Maharashtra.

The bottom level functionty is Lekhpal in U.P., Talati in Maharashtra and Karnam in Tamil Nadu. The Patwari is responsible for all the work connected with land problems. He is the busybody of the Government, performing a multitude of functions including collection of village statistics.

Role of District Collector in the Maintenance of Law and Order

Sound law and order situation is the basis of orderly and civilised life and so it is by far the most important function of the District Collector. He performs this function as the District Magistrate with the assistance of the district police and other agencies. His law and order functions include :

(a) Supervision over the investigation of crimes etc.

(b) Prevention of breach of peace and maintenance of law and order.

With the separation of the executive and the judiciary, the supervision of investigation of crimes, etc., is now mainly performed by the Judicial Magistrates. However, the responsibility for maintaining peace, law and order still rests with the District Collector.

In his capacity as District Magistrate the District Collector performs the following functions:

- He controls and supervises the subordinate magistracy and orders magisterial postings during festivals.
- He promulgates orders whenever there is any danger or breach of public peace and tranquility.
- He disposes of all the petitions and miscellaneous general complaints received from Government and others.
- He makes jail inspections and expedites disposal of cases of under-trial prisoners.
- He grants superior classes to prisoners or releases them prematurely or on parole.
- He deals with mercy petitions from prisoners.
- He controls and directs the action of the police.
- He submits an annual criminal report to Government.
- He appoints and punishes village chowkidars.
- He inspects police stations once a year.
- He sanctions expunction of a crime from the crime register.
- He recovers repatriation charges.
- He performs functions relating to accidents, payments under the Workmen's Compensation Act, labour problems, strikes, etc.
- He prosecutes persons guilty of infringing Sugar Factories Control Act and the Trade Mark Act.
- He is also responsible for sanction of temporary electric connections including, enquiries regarding breaches, for granting and cancelling of many kinds of licences.

- He exercises supervision over supply office and rent control and eviction officer under Rent Control Act and in supply matters.
- He also exercises supervision and control over local bodies, municipal board, notified areas and town areas.
- Recommends issue of passports and visas, and also schemes for the development of forests.
- He is the issuing authority for certificates of domicile, scheduled and backward classes, etc.

Under normal circumstances, the law and order is maintained by the District Magistrate with the help of normal district police. However, if the law and order situation deteriorates, the District Magistrate can seek the assistance of Central reserve Police Force, Rapid Action Force or Border Security Force battalions may be made available by the Government of India through the State Government. The Central Government may also arrange for the reinforcement of the District and State Police by requesting the other State Governments to send their armed forces. And if the civil police is not able to control the law and order situation, the District Magistrate can seek the assistance of the Army'.

Maintenance of law and order requires a sound intelligence system which is organised by the Special Branch of the State Government. The Special Branch of the State Government has a small unit in the district which supplies information to the State as well as keeps the Superintendent of Police and District Magistrate informed of the developments having a bearing on the law and order situation. However, the latter do not depend solely on the information gathered thus but also have independent sources to check and cross-check the information gathered by official units. An eye is kept on the sensitive areas in the district and the people who are known as 'mischief mongers'.

Role of District Collector in Development

With the dawn of independence India has embarked upon a new era of welfare state and community life. The Collector is the most appropriate person to look after developmental activities in the district.

The Balwant Rai Mehta team which made a study of Community Projects and National Extension Services recommended that At the district level, the Collector or the Deputy Commissioner should be the captain of the team of officers of all development departments and should be made fully responsible for securing the necessary co-ordination and co-operation in the preparation and execution of the district plans for community development.'

The District Collector's developmental duties comprise of:

(a) dispelling of ignorance,

(b) eradication of superstition,

(c) spread of co-operative institutions and Panchayats,

(d) increase of community projects and national extension schemes,

(e) rehabilitation of refugees,

(f) encouragement of awareness about rights and duties, etc.

The performance of these duties gives the Collector ample opportunities to come in contact with the people and to prove his worth as a public servant in the true sense.

The Ministry of Food and Agriculture set up in 1963, a Working Group of Inter-departmental and Institutional Co-ordination for Agricultural Production under the chairmanship of Ram Subhag Singh to report on ways of ensuring speedy execution of agricultural production programmes and for effective co-ordination between the activities of agriculture, co-operation and other allied departments in the Slates and of the community development and Panchayati Raj institutions. The Group assigned a crucial role to the Collector.

It made some very significant recommendations which are as follows:

1. The District Collector should be the Chairman of the Agricultural Production Committee of the Zila Parishad. If there is no Zila Parishad, such a committee should be formed with the district officers of the departments concerned with agricultural production and representatives of nonofficial organisations, as members, with the Collector as Chairman. The Committee should be responsible for co-ordination of the activities of all departments concerned with agricultural production. In particular, the committee should consider and approve a co-ordinated agricultural production plan for the district, assign specific tasks and responsibilities to the officers and institutions concerned, receive and review progress reports from them and remove any bottlenecks or difficulties.
2. The District Agricultural Production Officer should assist the Collector in coordinating the efforts of all the departments concerned with agricultural production at that level and should function under the overall direction of the Agricultural Committee. State heads of departments should continue to deal directly with their district officers as at present, but in matters relating to the work of the Agricultural Production Committee, they should communicate through the District Collector.
3. The District Collector should be effectively involved in assessing the work of district level functionaries. The Deputy Directors at the regional level should initiate the annual entries in the character roll of all district officers under their control and route them through the District Collector to the heads of department concerned.

Changing role of the District Collector

The importance of the district administration can be realised from the fact that there is hardly any activity of the people which is in some way or the other not affected by the district administration. During the British period, people looked the district administration as their father and mother. The District

Collector is the head of the revenue organisation. He exercises general supervision over the law and order machinery.

Though the position and prestige of the District Collector have changed and undergone several modifications, he is still the responsible head of general administration in the district and representative of the Government. He is the only officer in the district who can correspond directly with the Government.

Bibliography

Arora, Ramesh K. & Rajni Goyal, *Indian Administration.*

Avasti & Avasti, *Administrative Theory.*

Avasti & Maheswari, *Public Administration.*

Bagchi, K. (2005). Factors contributing to global digital divide: Some empirical results. *Journal of Global Information Technology Management*, 8(3), 47-65

Basu, Rumki, *Public Administration Theory and Concepts.*

Bharat Maheshwari, Vinod Kumar, Uma Kuma and Vedmani Sharan. E-Government Portal Effectiveness: Managerial Considerations for Design and Development.

Bhattacharya, Mohit, *New Horizons of Public Administration.*

Bingham, Lisa Blomgren (2006), "The New Urban Governance: Process for Engaging Citizens and Stakeholders", *Review of Policy Research*, Vol. 23, No.4, pp. 815-826.

Chadwick A. (2009), "Web 2.0: New Challenges for the study of E-Democracy in an Era of Informational Exuberance", I/S: *A Journal of Law and Policy for the Information Society*, Vol. 5, No. 1, pp 9-42.

Dey, Bata K. (2000), "E-governance in India: Problems, Challenges and Opportunities - A Futures Vision", *Indian Journal of Public Administration*, Vol. XLVI, No. 3.

Diwedi, S.K., Bharti A.K. "E-governance In India - Problems And Acceptability, *Journal of Theoretical and Applied Information Technology.*

Dr B.Ramadoss and Dr.Ram Palanisamy Issues and Challenges in Electronic Governance Planning International Conference building effective e-Governance 2002

Driscoll, J. W. (1978). Trust and participation in organizational decision making as predictors of satisfaction. *Academy of Management Journal*, 21(1), 44 - 57.

E-Readiness rankings 2009 The usage imperative A report from Economist intelligence unit.

Fahnbulleh, N. (2005). The future of electronic government. *Futurics*, 29(1-2), 7-12.

Fang, Z. (2002), "E-Government in Digital Era: Concept, Practice and Development", *International Journal of the Computer, the Internet and Management*, Vol. 10, No.2, pp. 1-22.

Freeman, C. (1993). Technical change and future trends in the world economy. *Futures*, 25(6),621-635.

Gilbert, D., Balestrini, P., & Littleboy, D. (2004). Barriers and benefits in the adoption of e-government. *The International Journal of Public Sector Management*, 17(4/5), 286-301.

Jack A. Nickerson , Barton H. Hamilton , Tetsuo Wada •\Market Position, Resource Profile, and Governance: Linking Porter and Williamson in the Context of International Courier and Small Package Services in Japan,. , *Strategic Management Journal*, 22, 3 (2001): 251-273.

Kochhar, S., G. Dhanjal (2004). "From governance to e-governance: An initial assessment of some of India's best projects", Technical Report, New Delhi: Skoch Consultancy Services.

Maheswari, S.R., *Administrative Thinkers.*

Maheswari, S.R., *Indian Administration.*

Maheswari, S.R., *Local Government.*

Ministry of Communication and Information Technology, "National e-Governance Plan", Government of India.

Prabhu, C S R. "Cost Effective Solution for Effective e-Governance/ e-Panchayat (Example of Exemplary Leadership and ICT Achievement of the year)".

Prasad, R. and Prasad, *Administrative Thinkers.*

Report of the Working Group on Information Technology Sector Twelfth Five Year Plan (2012-17).

Rhoda C Joseph and David P. Kitlan. *Key issues in E-Government and Public Administration.*

Rogers, E. M. (1995). *Diffusion of innovations* (4th ed.). New York: The Free Press.

Sadan and Sharma, *Public Administration.*

Servon, L. (2002). Bridging the digital divide: Technology, community and public policy. Malden, MA: Blackwell Publishing.

Sharon, Dawes, (e)Governance: a research framework for an uncertain future LOG-IN Africa June 2008

Singh, S K. (2008). *Panchayati Raj and Good Governance*, Centre for World Solidarity, Hyderabad.

Vakul Sharma, Law and E-Governance in International Conference building effective e-Governance 2002.

Verma, R.K., Kumari A. (2010) "E-Governance at Grassroots Level in South Asia: A Study of Citizen-centric e-Panchayats in India". *Asia-Pacific Journal of Rural Development* Vol. XX, No. 1

Wong, K. F., Tam, M. K. W., & Cheng, C. H.(2006). E-government . A Web Services framework. *Journal of Information Privacy & Security,* 2(2), 30-50.

Index

V

Z

❑❑❑